AA003905

SMART 2017

The Sixth International Conference on Smart Systems, Devices and Technologies

SMART INTERFACES 2017

The Symposium for Empowering and Smart Interfaces in Engineering

June 25 - 29, 2017

Venice, Italy

SMART 2017 Editors

Lasse Berntzen, University College of Southeast, Norway
Nadine Couture, ESTIA, France
Georg Aumayr, Johanniter Österreich Ausbildung und Forschung gemeinnützige GmbH, Austria

Printed from e-media with permission by:

Curran Associates, Inc.
57 Morehouse Lane
Red Hook, NY 12571

Some format issues inherent in the e-media version may also appear in this print version.

Printed by Curran Associates, Inc. (2017)

International Academy, Research, and Industry Association (IARIA)
412 Derby Way
Wilmington, DE 19810

Phone: (408) 893-6407
Fax: (408) 527-6351

petre@iaria.org

Additional copies of this publication are available from:

Curran Associates, Inc.
57 Morehouse Lane
Red Hook, NY 12571 USA
Phone: 845-758-0400
Fax: 845-758-2633
Email: curran@proceedings.com
Web: www.proceedings.com

TABLE OF CONTENTS

SMART 6 / SMART INTERFACES III: EMPOWERING AND SMART INTERFACES IN ENGINEERING III

SMART 2017

Forward

The Sixth International Conference on Smart Cities, Systems, Devices and Technologies (SMART 2017), held between June 25-29, 2017 in Venice, Italy, constituted the inaugural event covering tendencies towards future smart cities, specialized technologies and devices, environmental sensing, energy optimization, pollution control and socio-cultural aspects.

Digital societies take rapid developments toward smart environments. More and more social services are digitally available to the citizens. The concept of 'smart cities' including all devices, services, technologies and applications associated with the concept sees a large adoption. Ubiquity and mobility added new dimensions to smart environments. Adoption of smartphones and digital finder maps, and increasing budgets for technical support of services to citizens settled a new behavioral paradigm of city inhabitants.

The conference had the following tracks:

- Internet of things in smart environments
- AHA&MHealth
- Smart information processing
- Smart interfaces

The conference included the following symposiums:

- **URBAN COMPUTING 2017**, The International Symposium on Emerging Frontiers of Urban Computing and Smart Cities
- **SMART INTERFACES 2017,** The Symposium for Empowering and Smart Interfaces in Engineering

We take here the opportunity to warmly thank all the members of the SMART 2017 technical program committee, as well as all the reviewers. The creation of such a high quality conference program would not have been possible without their involvement. We also kindly thank all the authors that dedicated much of their time and effort to contribute to SMART 2017. We truly believe that, thanks to all these efforts, the final conference program consisted of top quality contributions.

We also gratefully thank the members of the SMART 2017 organizing committee for their help in handling the logistics and for their work that made this professional meeting a success.

We hope that SMART 2017 was a successful international forum for the exchange of ideas and results between academia and industry and to promote further progress in the area of smart cities, systems, devices and technologies. We also hope that Venice, Italy provided a pleasant environment during the conference and everyone found some time to enjoy the unique charm of the city.

SMART 2017 Chairs

SMART Steering Committee
Wolfgang Leister, Norsk Regnesentral, Norway
Christine Perakslis, Johnson & Wales University, USA
Brendan O'Flynn, Tyndall National Institute | University College Cork, Ireland
Sanja Lazarova-Molnar, University of Southern Denmark, Denmark
Lasse Berntzen, University College of Southeast, Norway
Markus Taumberger, VTT Technical Research Center of Finland Ltd., Finland
Jianguo Ding, University of Skövde, Sweden

SMART Industry/Research Advisory Committee
Steffen Fries, Siemens AG, Germany
Andrea Vinci, CNR - National Research Council of Italy | Institute for High Performance Computing and Networking (ICAR), Italy
Marko Jaakola, VTT Technical Research Centre of Finland, Finland

URBAN COMPUTING 2017

URBAN COMPUTING Advisory Committee
Salvatore Distefano, Kazan Federal University, Russia / Università di Messina, Italy
Carla Merkle Westphall, UFSC, Brazil
Caixia Wang, University of Alaska Anchorage, USA
Vladimir Bataev, Zaz Ventures, UK

SMART INTERFACES 2017

SMART INTERFACES Chairs
Nadine Couture, ESTIA, France
Brygg Ullmer, Louisiana State University, USA

SMART INTERFACES Advisory Committee
Nadine Couture, ESTIA, France
Jeremy Legardeur, ESTIA, France
Xavier Fischer, ESTIA, France
Christophe Merlo, ESTIA, France

SMART 2017
Committee

SMART Steering Committee

Wolfgang Leister, Norsk Regnesentral, Norway
Christine Perakslis, Johnson & Wales University, USA
Brendan O'Flynn, Tyndall National Institute | University College Cork, Ireland
Sanja Lazarova-Molnar, University of Southern Denmark, Denmark
Lasse Berntzen, University College of Southeast, Norway
Markus Taumberger, VTT Technical Research Center of Finland Ltd., Finland
Jianguo Ding, University of Skövde, Sweden

SMART Industry/Research Advisory Committee

Steffen Fries, Siemens AG, Germany
Andrea Vinci, CNR - National Research Council of Italy | Institute for High Performance Computing and Networking (ICAR), Italy
Marko Jaakola, VTT Technical Research Centre of Finland, Finland

SMART 2017 Technical Program Committee

Sukaina Al-Nasrawi, Beirut Arab University, Lebanon
Cristina Alcaraz, University of Malaga, Spain
Ryosuke Ando, TTRI (Toyota Transportation Research Institute), Japan
Georg Aumayr, Johanniter, Austria
Petko Bakalov, Environmental Systems Research Institute (ESRI), USA
Jie Bao, Microsoft Research, China
Karolina Baras, Madeira Interactive Technologies Institute (M-ITI) - University of Madeira, Portugal
Kashinath Basu, Oxford Brookes University, UK
Lasse Berntzen, University College of Southeast, Norway
Ramon F. Brena, Tecnologico de Monterrey, Mexico
David Brosset, Naval Academy Research Institute, France
Nélio Cacho, Federal University of Rio Grande do Norte, Brazil
Juan-Carlos Cano, Universitat Politecnica de Valencia, Spain
Rosa Cervera, Universidad de Alcalá, Spain
Dimitris Chatzopoulos, The Hong Kong University of Science and Technology, Hong Kong
DeJiu Chen, KTH Royal Institute of Technology, Sweden
Yao-Yi Chiang, University of Southern California, USA
Jacek Chmielewski, Poznan University of Economics and Business, Poland
Francesco Ciari, ETH Zürich | IVT - Institute for Transport Planning and Systems, Switzerland
Patrizio Dazzi, ISTI-CNR,

María del Mar Gómez Zamora, Universidad Rey Juan Carlos, Spain
Jianguo Ding, University of Skövde, Sweden
Mariagrazia Dotoli, Politecnico di Bari, Italy
Abdelali El Bouchti, Bournemouth University, Poole, UK / Hassan 2nd University, Casablanca, Morocco
Markus Endler, PUC-Rio, Brazil
Ava Fatah gen Schieck, The Bartlett School of Architecture - University College London, UK
Adrian Florea, 'Lucian Blaga' University of Sibiu, Romania
Steffen Fries, Siemens AG, Germany
Ivan Ganchev, University of Limerick, Ireland / Plovdiv University "Paisii Hilendarski", Bulgaria
Yann Glouche, INRIA, Caen, France, France
Katie Goeman, KU Leuven - University of Leuven, Belgium
Jorge J. Gomez-Sanz, Universidad Complutense de Madrid, Spain
Carlos Guerrero, University of Balearic Islands, Spain
Carlos Henggeler Antunes, University of Coimbra, Portugal
Gerold Hoelzl, University of Passau, Germany
Tzung-Pei Hong, National University of Kaohsiung, Taiwan
Maysoun Ibrahim, Beirut Arab University, Lebanon
Sergio Ilarri, University of Zaragoza, Spain
Marko Jaakola, VTT Technical Research Centre of Finland, Finland
Ravi Jhawar, University of Luxembourg, Luxembourg
Abdelmajid Khelil, Bosch Software Innovations / Baden-Wuerttemberg Cooperative State University, Germany
Pinar Kirci, Istanbul University, Turkey
Francine Krief, Bordeaux INP, France
Kirill Krinkin, Saint-Petersburg Electrotechnical University, Russia
Sanja Lazarova-Molnar, University of Southern Denmark, Denmark
Wolfgang Leister, Norsk Regnesentral, Norway
Dan Lin, Missouri University of Science and Technology, USA
Giovanni Livraga, Università degli Studi di Milano, Italy
Tatiana K. Madsen, Aalborg University, Denmark
Francisco Martins, University of Lisbon, Portugal
Manuel Mastrofini, LAST Horizon / University of Rome Tor Vergata, Italy
Natarajan Meghanathan, Jackson State University, USA
Zahéra Mekkioui, University of Tlemcen, Algeria
John-Jules Charles Meyer, Utrecht University, Netherlands
Jolanta Mizera-Pietraszko, Institute of Mathematics and Informatics | Opole University, Poland
Young Moon, Syracuse University, USA
Matteo Mordacchini, IIT-CNR,
Helena Nadais, CESAM - Centre for Environmental and Marine Studies | University of Aveiro, Portugal
Dmitry Namiot, Lomonosov Moscow State University, Russia
Ulrich Norbisrath, University of Applied Sciences Upper Austria (FH UA) Linz, Austria / George Mason University, USA

Carlo Alberto Nucci, University of Bologna, Italy
Brendan O'Flynn, Tyndall National Institute | University College Cork, Ireland
Maurizio Palesi, Kore University of Enna, Italy
Edoardo Patti, Politecnico di Torino, Italy
Luis Paulo Reis, University of Minho, Portugal
Jun Peng, University of Texas - Rio Grande Valley, USA
Wilma Penzo, DISI - University of Bologna, Italy
Cathryn Peoples, The Open University, UK
Christine Perakslis, Johnson & Wales University, USA
Nuno Pereira, School of Engineering of the Polytechnic of Porto, Portugal
Heng Qi, Dalian University of Technology, China
Sherif Rashad, Florida Polytechnic University, USA
Jose M. Reyes Alamo, CUNY - New York City College of Technology, USA
Enrique Romero-Cadaval, University of Extremadura, Spain
Alessandra Russo, Imperial College London, UK
Demetrios Sampson, Curtin University, Australia
Farhan Siddiqui, Walden University, USA
Steffen Späthe, Friedrich Schiller University Jena, Germany
Young-Joo Suh, POSTECH, Korea
Markus Taumberger, VTT Technical Research Center of Finland Ltd., Finland
Michele Risi, University of Salerno, Italy
Andrea Vinci, CNR - National Research Council of Italy | Institute for High Performance Computing and Networking (ICAR), Italy
Ouri Wolfson, University of Illinois, USA
Mudasser F. Wyne, National University, USA
Chia-Hung Yeh, National Sun Yat-sen University, Taiwan
Wuyi Yue, Konan University, Kobe, Japan
Sherali Zeadally, University of Kentucky, USA
Petros Zerfos, IBM T.J. Watson Research Center, USA
Sotirios Ziavras, New Jersey Institute of Technology, USA

URBAN COMPUTING 2017

URBAN COMPUTING Advisory Committee

Salvatore Distefano, Kazan Federal University, Russia / Università di Messina, Italy
Carla Merkle Westphall, UFSC, Brazil
Caixia Wang, University of Alaska Anchorage, USA
Vladimir Bataev, Zaz Ventures, UK

URBAN COMPUTING 2017 Technical Program Committee

Amin Anjomshoaa, Massachusetts Institute of Technology (MIT), USA
Vladimir Bataev, Zaz Ventures, UK

Amitava Chatterjee, Jadavpur University, Kolkata, India
Salvatore Distefano, Kazan Federal University, Russia / Università di Messina, Italy
Ava Fatah gen Schieck, The Bartlett School of Architecture | University College London, UK
John Favaro, Intecs SpA, Pisa, Italy
Sergio Ilarri, University of Zaragoza, Spain
Vana Kalogeraki, Athens University of Economics and Business, Greece
Carla Merkle Westphall, UFSC, Brazil
Luis Moreira-Matias, NEC Europe Ltd., Germany
Daniela Nicklas, University of Bamberg, Germany
Ulrich Norbisrath, University of Applied Sciences Upper Austria (FH UA) Linz, Austria / George Mason University, USA
Christine Perakslis, College of Management | Johnson & Wales University, USA
Jean-Claude Thill, University of North Carolina at Charlotte, USA
Ferdinand von Tüllenburg, Advanced Networking Center | Salzburg Research, Austria
Peter Wagner, German Aerospace Center, Berlin, Germany
Caixia Wang, University of Alaska Anchorage, USA

SMART INTERFACES 2017

SMART INTERFACES Chairs

Nadine Couture, ESTIA, France
Brygg Ullmer, Louisiana State University, USA

SMART INTERFACES Advisory Committee

Nadine Couture, ESTIA, France
Jeremy Legardeur, ESTIA, France
Xavier Fischer, ESTIA, France
Christophe Merlo, ESTIA, France

SMART INTERFACES 2017 Technical Program Committee

Nadine Couture, ESTIA, France
Jeremy Legardeur, ESTIA, France
Xavier Fischer, ESTIA, France
Christophe Merlo, ESTIA, France
Laurence Nigay, Université Grenoble Alpes, France
Eric Papon, Université de Bordeaux, France
Thierry Ferreira, Thales Avionique, France
Seddik Bacha, Université Grenoble Alpes, France
François Pellerin, Région Nouvelle-Aquitaine, France
Jean-Yves Choley, SUPMECA, France
Gilles Rouquet, Orange, France

Eric Barquissau, ESTIA, France
Clement Marquet, Télécom ParisTech, France
Jacques Péré-Laperne, LaBRI-CNRS and ESTIA, France
Brygg Ullmer, Louisiana State University, USA

Copyright Information

From Crowdsourcing to Crowdsharing: The Smart Environmental Sensing Web of EPA

Shuenn-Chin Chang
Environmental Protection Administration
Taipei City. Taiwan (R.O.C.)
scchang@epa.gov.tw

Yeuh-Bin Wang
Environmental Protection Administration
Taipei City. Taiwan (R.O.C.)
ybwang@epa.gov.tw

His-Chi Lin
Environmental Protection Administration
Taipei City. Taiwan (R.O.C.)
hsclin@epa.gov.tw

Chun-Ming Huang
Environmental Protection Administration
Taipei City. Taiwan (R.O.C.)
chmihuang@epa.gov.tw

Yu-Ling Liang
Environmental Protection Administration
Taipei City. Taiwan (R.O.C.)
ylliang@epa.gov.tw

Yu-Chieh Huang
Environmental Management Consultant Technologies
Inc. Taipei City. Taiwan(R.O.C.)
sophia@emct.com.tw

I-Ting Tseng
Environmental Management Consultant Technologies
Inc. Taipei City. Taiwan(R.O.C.)
tiffany@emct.com.tw

***Abstract*—This article describes how the Environmental Protection Administration (EPA) under the Executive Yuan of Taiwan (R.O.C.) leverages its Smart Environmental Sensing Web comprising crowdsourcing and crowdsharing built on its existing Internet of Things (IoT) based environmental monitoring system to make the public care more about the quality of their living environment, and create positive feedback loops of information flows. Furthermore, we use data visualization technology and location-based services to design graphical dashboards and interactive maps to enable users to access real-time local environmental sensing information at any time. Taiwan EPA will also continue to maintain the concept of open, transparent and innovative applications to serve society with public, diversified, and convenient information services.**

Keywords- Citizen as Sensor; Crowdsourcing; Internet of Things; Location-Based Service; Social Networks; $PM_{2.5}$.

I. INTRODUCTION

This article describes how Taiwan EPA leverages its Smart Environmental Sensing Web comprising crowdsourcing and crowdsharing [1] built on its existing IoT-based environmental monitoring system. This Smart Environmental Sensing Web includes continually expanding Micro Environmental Sensors, an environmental quality sensor networking platform, an Environmental Info Push application for smart phones, and an i-Environment website. Combining environmental sensing data from different sources through common transmission protocols and Open Geospatial Consortium (OGC) Standards, we used data visualization technology and location-based services to design graphical dashboards and interactive maps enabling users to access real-time local environmental information at any time, while also adding a convenient notification function that sends alerts when needed.

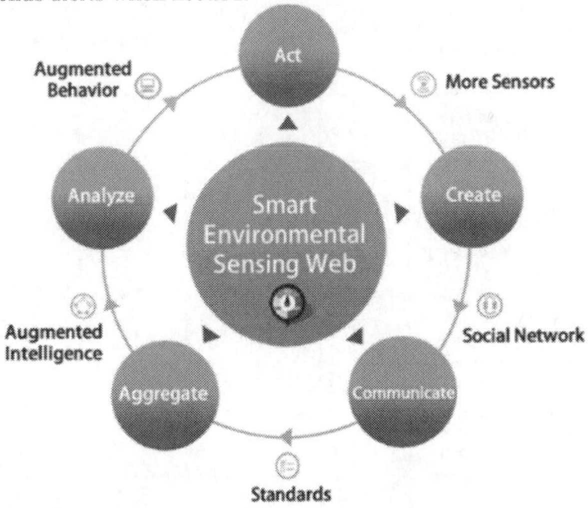

Figure 1. The Conceptual Cycle of Smart Environmental Sensing Web

We also encourage the deployment of sensors, Open Data and crowdsharing to maximize the benefits of the Smart Environmental Sensing Web. Users can not only freely use these Open Data on environmental quality to design their own innovative value-added services and explore environmental issues, but also they can make use of the existing platform to share their personal feelings regarding the environment and publish these on the community website. Users may also use community links to stimulate other people's concern about the quality of living environment to create positive feedback cycle of data flows (in Figure 1).

II. METHODS

A. *Data enrichment— Crowdsourcing*

In addition to collecting and disseminating the various types of environmental monitoring information generated by Taiwan EPA, the Smart Environmental Sensing Network will also incorporate data from Micro Environmental Sensors operated by local governments, educational institutions, enterprises, and individuals. These Micro Environmental Sensors (list in TABLE I.), inspired by the Maker Movement, are designed to operate as a network of sensors managed by the public and experts. The sensors will continuously monitor air pollutants ($PM_{2.5}$), temperature, and humidity, and upload their real-time sensing data via wifi to an open or self-built IoT platforms. The platform provides Application Programming Interfaces (APIs) for Open Data to aid the development of display interfaces and application services for these types of environmental information. Currently, the number of micro-sensors has reached 2,100 units, which are mainly distributed in Taiwan's densely populated metropolitan areas, as well as at public primary schools in several counties and cities.

TABLE I. DIFFERENT SOURCES OF ENVIRONMENTAL SENSING NETWORK

Deployment	Number of Devices	Sensors	Trans-mission	Device Provider
Airbox Taipei City	155	$PM_{2.5}$, Temperature, Humidity	Wifi	Edimax
Airbox New Taipei City	298			
Airbox Taichung City	232			
Airbox Tainan City	214			
Airbox Kaohsiung City	242			
AirBox (other)	621			
LASS	97	$PM_{2.5}$, Temperature, Humidity	Wifi	Open Community
MAPS	83	$PM_{2.5}$, Temperature, Humidity	Wifi or LoRa	IIS-NRL of Academia SInica
EPA Monitoring Site	76	O_3, $PM_{2.5}$, PM_{10}, CO, SO_2, NO_2	ADSL	EPA or Local Goverment
EPA Industrial Parks	33	O_3, $PM_{2.5}$, PM_{10}, CO, SO_2, NO, NO_2, NO_X, THC	ADSL	
Local Government Monitoring Site	26	O_3, $PM_{2.5}$, PM_{10}, CO, SO_2, NO_2	ADSL	
EPA Large-scale Enterprises	70	O_3, $PM_{2.5}$, PM_{10}, SO_2, NO_2	ADSL	
EPA Mobile	20	$PM_{2.5}$, Temperature, Humidity	Bluetooth	
EPA Fix	200	$PM_{2.5}$, PM_1, O_3, NO_2, CO, Temperature, Humidity, Noise	Wifi	

Data from pm25.lass-net.org [2] and EPA

In order to increase the density of the environmental sensing network, Taiwan EPA encourages citizens to join the network by installing personal air sensors in their living environment, such as AirBox and Location Aware Sensing System (LASS), which monitors air quality that people actually breathe. Since 2016, Taiwan EPA has also continued to develop new sensors that can transmit real-time data to the Smart Environmental Sensing Web via other modes of transmission, such as Bluetooth, Wifi, or Long range (LoRa) [3]. Since LoRa technology has advantages of low power consumption and long range capability, Taiwan EPA has begun deploying these sensors in a certain industrial park.

The Environmental Info Push App provides the public with environmental information that is updated every minute. Internet access is all it takes for people to know the air quality near their home or the place they plan to visit, so they may take appropriate measures to protect their health.

B. *Technique of implementation*

Through the Open Platform for Environmental Resources [4], Taiwan EPA compiles real-time monitoring information to create i-Environment [5], a thematic interactive map browsing platform, and the Environmental Info Push app to serve the people's demand for this type of information.

Figure 2. i-Environment Webpage (2016)

Based on governmental open data, "i-Environment" is the first government website designed for the Hybrid Web. It is developed using data visualization technology, which helps present reports, statistics, quantitative figures, and other information in a visual manner. An interface with dashboards and interactive maps provides location-based services that allow users to easily browse and search the environmental information they need (see Figure 2). In addition to these convenient information services, the sensor network also provides air quality alerts to the public, along with suggestions for appropriate activities under the various circumstances reminding users of immediately responding to discomfort and risks from environmental pollution, and to maintain their best health.

III. CURRENT PRACTICES—CROWDSHARING

To raise the public's environmental awareness and call attention for sources of air pollution in people's immediate living environment, Taiwan EPA has monitored the Mazu Goddess Tour, a month-long procession of a sea goddess touring Taiwan, greeted by the way by of celebrations involving massive fireworks that push up $PM_{2.5}$ values into the hundreds or even above 1,000 since 2016.

Firstly, in the spirit of crowdsourcing, EPA launched AirPhoto, a function of Environmental Info Push app through which people can share a photo stamping real-time air quality data on it, and share the photo on the map as well as on one's own Facebook Wall. Thus, through crowdsourcing and crowdsharing, the public is engaged as "citizen sensors" and made more aware of environmental issues.

Secondly, in response to the development era of Internet of Things, Taiwan EPA has developed Bluetooth transmission modules that can be deployed around temples and those places where celebrations were held to monitor the environmental conditions on the ground. After the dynamic data was measured and uploaded, it can be immediately seen on mobile phones with the app and also uploaded to the IoT cloud platform of Taiwan EPA (see Figure 3.).

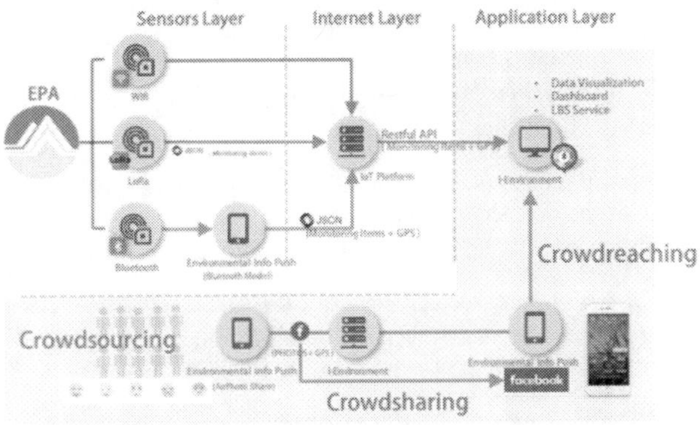

Figure 3. New Structure of Environmental Sensing Web of EPA (2017)

During events, people can view real-time information on the i-Environment website, including real-time air quality monitoring values, photos shared through the AirPhoto, as well as statistical charts and data. In addition, the public can use trend maps that compute spatial changes in combination with real-time sensor information and interactive features of maps on the i-Environment website (see Figure 4).

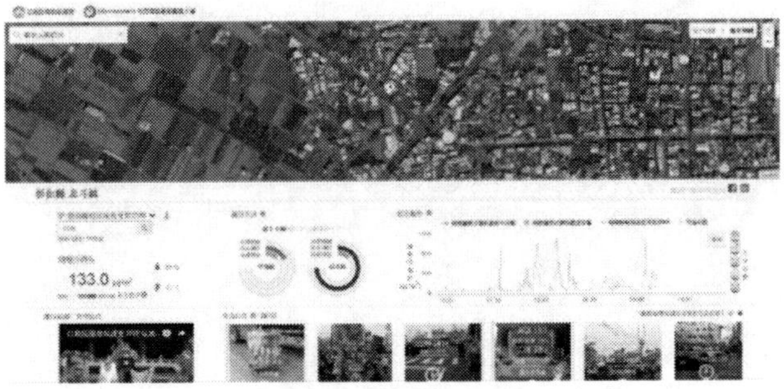

Figure 4. New Web design of Environmental Sensing Web of EPA (2017)

IV. CONCLUSION

In light of the worldwide positive acclaim of Open Data, Taiwan EPA will continue to maintain the concept of open, transparent and innovative applications [6] to serve society with public, diversified, and convenient information services to facilitate people's decision-making that involves environmental aspects. Taiwan EPA furthermore hopes that the Smart Environmental Sensing Web along with the relative apps will encourage crowdsourcing and crowdsharing to make the public more concerned about the quality of their living environment, and create positive feedback loops of information flows.

REFERENCES

[1] M. N. Kamel Boulos et al., "Crowdsourcing, citizen sensing and sensor web technologies for public and environmental health surveillance and crisis management: trends, OGC standards and application examples,"

International Journal of Health Geographics, vol. 10, no. 1, p. 67, 2011, http://dx.doi.org/10.1186/1476-072X-10-67

[2] IIS-NRL, PM2.5 Open Data Portal. [Online]. Available from:https://pm25.lass-net.org/zh_tw/ 2017.03.22.

[3] LoRa Alliance, LoRaWAN What is it. Technical Marketing Workgroup 1.0, Nov., 2015. Available from: https://www.loraalliance. org/portals/0/documents/whitepapers/ LoRaWAN101.pdf 2017.06.16

[4] Environmental Protection Administration. *Environmental resource database.* [Online]. Available from:http://erdb.epa.gov.tw/ 2017.03.22.

[5] Environmental Protection Administration. *i-Environment.* [Online]. Available from: https://ienv.epa.gov.tw/ 2017.03.22.

[6[Environmental Protection Administration. *Opendata.epa*, http://opendata.epa.gov.tw/ 2017.03.22.

Low Cost Mobile Embedded System for Air Quality Monitoring

Air quality real-time monitoring in order to preserve citizens' health

Adrian Florea
Computer Science and Electrical Engineering Department
'Lucian Blaga' University of Sibiu
Sibiu, Romania
email: adrian.florea@ulbsibiu.ro

Lasse Berntzen, Marius Rohde Johannessen
Department of Business, History and Social Sciences
University College of Southeast Norway
Kongsberg, Norway
email: {lasse.berntzen, marius.johannessen}@usn.no

Daniela Stoica, Ionel Stelian Naicu
National Environmental Protection Agency
Sibiu, Romania
email: danastoica68@yahoo.com, office@apmsb.anpm.ro

Vlad Cazan
Civic Alert
Bucharest, Romania
email: vlad.cazan@civicalert.ro

Abstract - **This paper reports on a case study using a mobile platform for air-quality monitoring. This case study was done in Sibiu, Romania, and includes a description of related work, a survey, a summary of existing results regarding air quality, a description of the mobile air quality monitoring platform, and the results of trials done in February 2017. The aim of the case study is to pave the road for further studies of using mobile low-cost units for air quality monitoring.**

Keywords-air quality monitoring; environmental monitoring; sensor platform; traffic optimization; crowdsensing.

I. Introduction

This paper reports on a case study using a mobile platform for air-quality monitoring as part of a research project jointly conducted by the "Lucian Blaga" University of Sibiu, Romania and University College of Southeast Norway. The case study was done in Sibiu, Romania. Sibiu experience air quality problems caused by traffic. The design and development of the platform has been described in an earlier paper [1], and will only be briefly described here. The aim is to show how the platform is used, and to compare with other studies. The case study includes a survey among university students and employees to investigate their concerns about air quality.

A. Background

Europe and the rest of the world face severe societal challenges, especially related to energy consumption, environment and security. Air quality has become an important issue in most industrialized and urban areas. The use of fuels for cars, ships and production of energy, heavy traffic and inefficient modes of transport, waste burning, and industrial activities degrade air quality [2][3]. Information and communication technologies contribute around 2% of the global CO_2 emissions and approximately 8% of the European Union´s use of electricity [4]. Contamination of the air is both a global and a local problem. On a global level the emissions of CO_2 and NO_X influences climate and global warming. On local level air pollution (detectable particles from smoke, ash, dust, spore, pollen and mildew) has an important impact on human health, causing health issues like asthma, allergies and bronchitis. According to World Health Organization (WHO) report from September 2016, 3 million deaths a year are linked with exposure to outdoor air pollution [5]. Air pollution may also reduce the value of properties in exposed areas.

Many cities, including London, Madrid and Paris, experience severe problems with air quality, especially during the winter season. Air pollution on cold days affects many citizens, and forces them to make quick decisions to avoid exposure, either to stay inside or choose an alternative route.

Even Norwegian cities such as Oslo and Bergen suffer due to climatic conditions, as the polluted air doesn't get warm enough to escape the cities surrounded by hills or mountains. When pollution levels are high, the cities of Bergen and Paris restrict the use of cars based on the last digit of the number plates. In January 2017, Oslo was closed for diesel cars for a short period. The city council considers raising traffic tolls on days with high pollution levels. Air pollution is a top priority for citizens especially in megacities from all around the globe [6]. More than that, each flight Paris-New York is melting 3 cube meter of icecap. If the trend continues, the Arctic ice cap will disappear in 30 years [7].

According to information presented by Dr. L. Roman from Autohaus Huber SRL (Sibiu), in a workshop[1] organized as part of the project, the pollution levels caused by automobiles change (to the worse) depending on several factors such as:

- Road traffic contributing to particle pollution both because of car tires wearing down the asphalt surface, and due to incomplete combustion.
- Quality of the fuels and lubricants.
- State of wear of the mechanical components of the engine and its auxiliary installations.

---

1 http://www.ulbsibiu.ro/myaccount/src/file.php?file=file1&news=true&id=2816

- State of wear of electrical and electronic components.
- Running distance on which the vehicle is used daily.
- Quality of car maintenance.
- Driving quality (skill) of the vehicle users.
- Political decisions of reducing taxes on importing second hand cars.

In most cases, it is no quick fix for air pollution. Shutting down power stations or industries polluting the air are normally long-term projects. The use of filters and catalyzers may reduce the output of pollution. However, small projects may help reduce local pollution. One example is to provide passages for pedestrians under or above heavily trafficked roads [8], and building viaducts over railroads. This can increase the flow of vehicles and reduce the pollution caused by still-standing cars.

To combat air pollution, it is necessary to have objective air-quality measurements. Today, most of the air quality monitoring is done by a relatively small number of expensive stationary units. This causes a problem with granularity. A stationary unit collects data from a single geographical point and the data may not be representative for a larger area.

One strategy to improve air quality is to reduce traffic, and optimize the remaining traffic. This can be done in a multitude of ways: increasing traffic tolls, improving public transport, introducing smart parking systems that direct the driver to an available parking spot, and by disallowing certain types of cars to be used. In Oslo, cars need to pay a special tax if the car uses winter tires with spikes, to encourage car owners to choose more environmentally-friendly tires. (The spikes wear down the asphalt and create dust particles.)

The cities may implement different regulatory measures to reduce the emission of pollutants. For example, the mayors of Paris, Madrid, Athens and Mexico City have announced that trucks will not be allowed to enter their city centers from 2025. Also, diesel cars will be banned and the city councils are considering raising tolls on days with high pollution levels [9]. Walking and cycling will be encouraged and citizens will be provided incentives for the use of electric or hybrid vehicles [10].

The aim of this paper is to present a project to measure air quality by using a mobile platform for monitoring. This platform can provide more accurate information on air quality issues. Such monitoring can help raise awareness of air quality problems, their causes, and their impact, and thereby contribute to better decision making.

The project goals are:

- Give citizens a real image of the air quality in cities by making the mobile monitoring platform collect information from sensors, and send the data to a server for further analysis and visualization.
- Improve the quality of environmental monitoring by designing and developing a low cost "proof of concept" prototype for use in cars.
- Cars host the mobile environmental monitoring platform. Whenever the car is parked, the platform will start monitoring the environment around itself, and forward this information to the server. (The platform can also be used when the car is moving).
- The platform may perform some preprocessing of data to reduce the data traffic generated. Instead of sending data at fixed intervals, the platform can send alerts when changes happen. This can improve the scalability of the solution.

The rest of the paper is organized into four sections, where Section II briefly reviews some state of the art papers related to this study. Section III presents the Sibiu case study, including the survey, some existing studies from the Romanian National Network of Air Quality Monitoring, and information from traffic and roads administration. Section IV describes the research design - the mobile platform for environmental monitoring - both from hardware and software point of view, including some obtained results. Finally, in Section V, we provide implications and conclusions.

II. Related Work

Air quality monitoring has been around for many years, but has mostly been done by public authorities responsible for environmental monitoring. In most cases, the monitoring is done by expensive monitoring platforms in fixed locations. The aim of our project was to investigate alternative ways of obtaining measurement results to improve the granularity of measurements.

A. Hand-held units connected to smartphones

One approach is to use hand-held units to be carried around by citizens. Such units normally connect to a smart phone, and use the smartphone to obtain access to the internet.

Leonardi, Cappellotto, Caraviello, Lepri and Antonelli [11] developed an air quality monitoring unit to be carried around by citizens. An important reason for developing the mobile unit was: "*Official authorities use to monitor and publish air quality data collected by networks of static measurement stations. However, this approach is often costly, hard to maintain and not scalable in the long term*". They also argue that fixed station provides "*a lack of accuracy in the intra-urban air pollution maps*". The authors collected data from 80 persons in Trento, Italy. The unit, called "*SecondNose*", measures temperature, light, humidity, altitude, pressure and two air pollution parameters: carbon-monoxide (CO) and nitrogen-dioxide (NO_2). The unit communicates with an app installed in an Android smartphone through Bluetooth. The unit weighs only 28 grams, and has a battery capacity of five days.

Dutta, Chowdhury, Roy, Middya and Gazi [12] developed "AirSense", a monitoring platform based on Arduino Nano equipped with two sensors, one for air quality (MQ135) and one for carbon-monoxide (MQ7). The platform connects to an Android smartphone through Bluetooth, and weighs around 60 grams. The authors cited inadequate number of fixed monitoring stations as the reason for developing "AirSense".

CITI-SENSE, an EU-funded project, developed a hand-held sensory unit to be carried around [13]. The "*Little Environmental Observatory*" (LEO) is a portable sensor pack. It measures NO, NO_2 and O_3 using electrochemical sensors. It also provides information about the current temperature and relative humidity. LEO connects to an Android smartphone through Bluetooth. CITI-SENSE also developed an app to let citizens report their own perception of air quality. CITI-SENSE ran from 2012 to 2016.

AIRALERT [14] is a service recently launched by the Romanian NGO CivicAlert. The service obtains data from a handheld sensor platform "*AirBeam*" with Bluetooth connection to an Android smartphone. Their idea is to collect data by issuing units to volunteer bicyclists. AIRALERT is using an existing visualization package to display results.

Z. Pan, H. Yu, C. Miao and C. Leung [15] used a somewhat different approach, by using smartphone cameras to detect air pollution through artificial intelligence techniques to determine particle pollution. This solution requires humans to actively do measurements.

B. Units equiped with GSM communication

Another approach is to equip the monitoring platform with built-in Global System for Mobile Communications (GSM) communication capabilities.

C. Migliore [16] developed a platform mounted on a bike, "*SwarmBike*", to measure air pollution. The unit has a Global Positioning System (GPS) receiver, a GSM module to handle communication, and sensors for barometric pressure, temperature, humidity and a CO sensor. His thesis describes other types of sensors for measuring air quality.

The projects OpenSense and OpenSense II [17] installed air quality measurement units on trams in Zurich and buses in Lausanne, Switzerland. The sensor platform measures ozone (O_3), nitrogen-dioxide (NO_2), carbon-monoxide (CO) and ultra-fine particles (UFP). The platform has a GPS-receiver, and transmits data to a server using GSM. A sensor was also installed in a Citroen C-Zero.

C. Related work compared to our platform

The problem with hand-held units is that someone must carry them around. Several solutions require Android smartphones. This excludes the large number of Apple iPhone users. Users may also be reluctant to provide access through their own phones. It seems that most of the projects described above lasted for a limited period.

Leonardi, Cappellotto, Caraviello, Lepri and Antonelli [11] reported that usage of "*SecondNose*" declined over time. Users said they were curious in the beginning, but soon learnt the characteristics of the places they measured. This may partially explain the non-sustainability of the projects using hand-held sensors.

Our unit is autonomous. No human is needed to carry it or turn it on or off. It uses a GSM module, and does not need smart phone for communication. It also has a built-in GPS. Insert a SIM-card and connect to car battery, and it is operating (plug-and-play).

The hand-held units described above seem to be more expensive. The sensor used by Leonardi, Cappellotto, Caraviello, Lepri and Antonelli [11] (SensorDrone) costs around USD 200. It only contains sensors and Bluetooth.

The components for our unit cost around 130 Euro, including sensors and GSM/GPS-module.

The OpenSense platform [17] closely resembles our platform, but collects data from trams and buses on the move. This brings some uncertainty caused by trucks being close to the measurement platform.

Our novel approach is to use parked cars. Parked cars provide the possibility to measure from one location over time. It is not dependent on human intervention to make the measurements. A city always owns cars used to provide services. But it is also possible to call on volunteers to host the platform in their cars.

D. Shared characteristics of monitoring platforms

Environmental monitoring platforms might be used by the municipality to create another layer in the city map (transparent for citizens), like layers showing networks of water, gas and electric cables, the sewer network, telephone and cable TV networks etc. Such layers may easily be implemented in a GIS system and can be used for increased transparency, sustainable regional development and innovative applications visualizing the pollution levels.

By collecting data from city and surroundings areas, platforms can identify the city's pollution hotspots (from air quality viewpoint), suggesting alternative positions for fixed stations or the need to introduce new ones. Such data will be valuable for the authorities responsible for air quality monitoring (National Environmental Protection Agency).

Platforms, like the ones described above, may provide real-time monitoring to preserve citizens' health and warn them when permissible level of pollution are exceeded. Platforms equipped with particle detectors may warn citizens about increasing levels of pollen or dust (producing allergies). In such situations, it may advise people to avoid areas that could be dangerous for health conditions and choose another detour and locate the closest pharmacies where antihistamine pills can be bought.

III. Sibiu Case Study

This section presents the case study done as part of a research project conducted jointly by the "Lucian Blaga" University of Sibiu and University College of Southeast Norway and financed by European Economic Area (EEA) grants [18]. The focus is on a specific case for air quality monitoring: the city of Sibiu, Romania. The city is in Transylvania, and has a permanent population of approximately 155.000, and up to 25.000 students and temporary inhabitants. The traffic is high since two national roads, one south-north and one west-east, are meeting in the city. According to technical data obtained from Romanian National Company of Road Infrastructure Management, more than 70,000 cars are crossing Sibiu city every day.

TABLE I. SURVEY QUESTIONS AND RESULTS

Q1: A1:	How interested are you in air quality in general? The citizens of Sibiu have high interest (>85%) in air quality and pollution level
Q2: A21: A22: A23:	How would you describe the air quality in Sibiu in general? The air quality in Sibiu is rather good (70%) The air quality in Sibiu is poor (21%). Uncertain: 9%. Arguments of respondents for "good air quality" consist in: • The air is clean and fresh due to relatively small distance to Carpathians mountains (Păltiniş). • There are enough green spaces in and outside the city ("Sub Arini" large park and "Dumbrava" forest – as known as "the city lung"). • The industrial areas are placed outside, rather to isolate the city by generated pollution. • Sibiu is a small town with relatively small number of inhabitants. • The Sibiu ring road reduced the traffic and contributed to diminish the noxious cars' emissions, even on highly travelled boulevards. Arguments for "poor air quality" are the followings: • The transformation of green spaces in residential districts. • The inefficient modes of transport and traffic. • There are many cars that pollute the air. • 31% of persons over 18 from Sibiu County have own cars (117.663 of 378.382), according to the Public Community Service for Driving License and Vehicle Registration Sibiu. • The number of cars increased in recent years: 6.14% from 2015 to 2016.
Q3: A3:	To what extent do you think that the air quality in Sibiu affects your health? Most subjects (76%) believe that air quality in Sibiu might be an important factor that can influence their health.
Q4: A4:	Do you consider air quality when moving around in Sibiu (e.g. avoid cycling in busy roads or exercising outdoors if air quality is bad)? About one third (35%) think they should avoid activities when pollution levels are high.
Q5: A5:	What do you think about accessibility to air quality information in Sibiu? Or "How often do you consciously look at air quality information (e.g. via television, newspapers, Internet)"? Consciously, people are rarely seeking information on air quality (About once a month 18%). Although interest in environmental quality exists and usefulness of such information is obvious, the biggest problem lies in finding it.
Q6: A6:	Who can improve air quality in Sibiu? And How? The top three groups which can contribute to air quality improvement are: The municipality (e.g., city council): • By not allowing deforestation in the whole county, except dry/sick wood, which should be replaced by other freshly planted trees. • Protecting parks and forests, and developing new green spaces. • Introduction of electric public transport. • Optimize traffic in order to avoid congestion and useless fuel consumption. Industry and commerce: • Industry and commerce can find ways to pollute less by controlling their activities (dematerialization of economy). • Proper management of waste. People who spend most of their time in the city (e.g., residents, workers, students): • Students could participate as volunteers to plant trees in deforested areas. • Large scale use of public transportation or other alternatives (e.g. bicycle) Other groups were regional agencies or research scientists: • Regional and central government agencies must take responsibility to respect the law regarding the maximum level of air pollution, and if this level is overrun by any industrial company take appropriate measures. • Proposing legislation to reduce urban pollution. • Research scientists can contribute by finding new ways to stop air pollution.
Q7: A7:	What steps do you think you would personally take to help improve air quality in Sibiu? The large majority of the respondents are willing to: • use more environmentally-friendly means of transportation (electric bus, bicycle, etc). • involvement in public policy making, of social polls and participating to citizen advisory committees. • use greener systems at home such as renewables energy and electric heating to the detriment of burning wood.
Q8: A8:	In which format would you prefer to receive air quality information? Subjects suggested that an application for mobile phone would be most appropriate since they live in the "Internet of Things" and, nowadays over half of them use such easy accessible technology. Smartphones have excellent processing and storage capabilities and people carry them in their daily lives. Alternatively, information might be exhibited on panels in main public places, in public transport but also using social networks where information dissemination can be done very easily. Websites, TV and radio were also mentioned as alternatives.
Q9:	If you could have an application mobile phone app to inform you about air quality, how important would it be to have the following features?
A9:	See table II.
Q10: A10:	In relation with the previous question, are there any other features you would like to have in a mobile app to be informed about air quality? In addition to the numerical information about concentrations of air pollutants it would be useful that each pollutant to be accompanied by immediate and long-term effects on health. Possibility to select decongested routes to move in the city

A. *Survey about air quality perception of people*

Before starting our project implementation, we developed a survey regarding air quality perception by people, to see the relevance of air quality monitoring in Sibiu and its surroundings. We requested feedback from people working / studying / living in Sibiu (66% being in their twenties, 10% being between 30 and 45, and 24% being older than 45), most of them being students at the Faculty of Engineering. 200 participants were surveyed, 54% men, 46% women. 81% of respondents have secondary level education, 19% have higher education (Bachelor, Master, PhD). In the following we present the most important questions and the answers we received.

Table II lists the possible features of a mobile app to inform about air quality. The most important feature sought was information on how to protect own health. The second important feature sought was information about current air quality, followed by an air quality index to show how air quality improves or degrades.

TABLE II. SURVEY RESULTS (Q9)

No.	Feature	Priority			
		High	Med.	Low	Not a priority
1.	Air quality in your immediate vicinity	58.5	29.3	11	1.2
2.	Numeric information on pollutant	40.2	41.5	14.6	3.7
3.	An *air quality index* indicating if the air quality is poor or good	72	23.2	3.7	1.2
4.	Ability to report what you think the air quality is like	28	45.1	22	4.9
5.	Ability to see what other users have reported	18.3	42.7	26.8	12.2
6.	Information on past air quality	36.6	34.1	22	7.3
7.	Information on *current* air *quality*	75.6	20.7	3.7	0
8.	Information on *forecasted* air quality	43.9	42.7	11	2.4
9.	Information on what to do to protect your health	84	14.8	1.2	0
10.	Notifications in case of increased air pollution	65.9	29.3	4.9	0
11.	Possibility to see the air quality levels in the routes you move around the city	59.8	26.8	12.2	1.2
12.	Possibility to select cleaner routes to move in the city	59.8	25.6	11	3.7

B. Earlier Studies

In Romania, air quality from ambient environment is legislated in accordance with European laws by the Air Act (no. 104/2011) [19], which establishes that the responsibility for air quality monitoring is undertaken by the National Environmental Protection Agency, through the National Network for Monitoring Air Quality [3]. Unfortunately, the number of air quality monitoring stations in Romania is rather small (142 fixed & 17 mobile units). This network includes four fixed stations in Sibiu County, which continuously monitor the air quality (Two are located in Sibiu, one in Mediaş and one in Copşa Mică).

The results presented in Figure 1 and Figure 2 were obtained from the two stationary units located in Sibiu city: SB1 – urban residential station and SB2 – industrial-type station.

The figures show CO and NO_2 concentration levels, for 2016. The agency has also on occasions used mobile units. The monitored parameters are: Sulphur dioxide (SO_2), nitrogen oxides (NO_X), carbon monoxide (CO), ozone (O_3), particles (PM 10 and PM 2.5), benzene (C_6H_6) and lead (Pb).

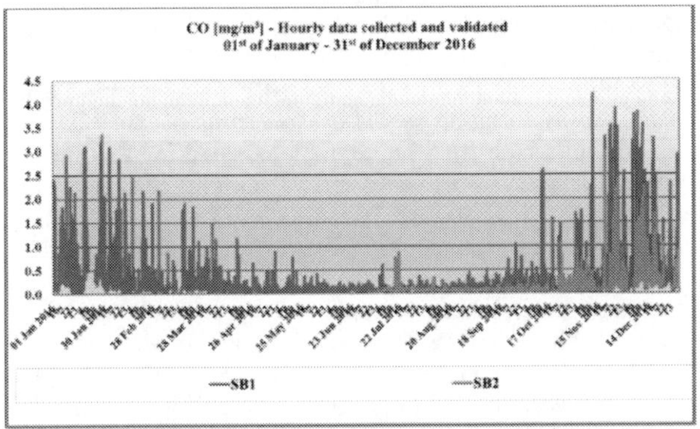

Figure 1. CO concentration levels in 2016

The evolution of values for CO concentration between 1st of January to 31st of December 2016 show that there were no exceedances of the daily limit value for health, taking into account that the daily maximum of averages at each 8 hours is 10 mg/m^3, according to the Air Act 104/2011.

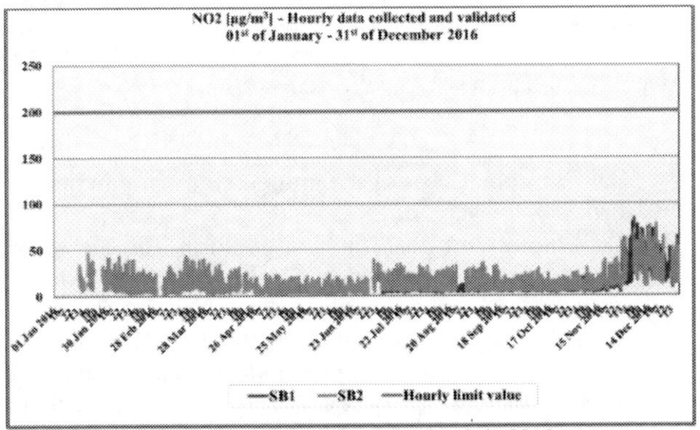

Figure 2. NO2 concentration levels in 2016

The NO_2 pollution indicator has not revealed breaches of the hourly limit of 200 µg/m^3 (the maximum number of exceeding's allowed by Air Act 104/2011 is 18 times yearly / station).

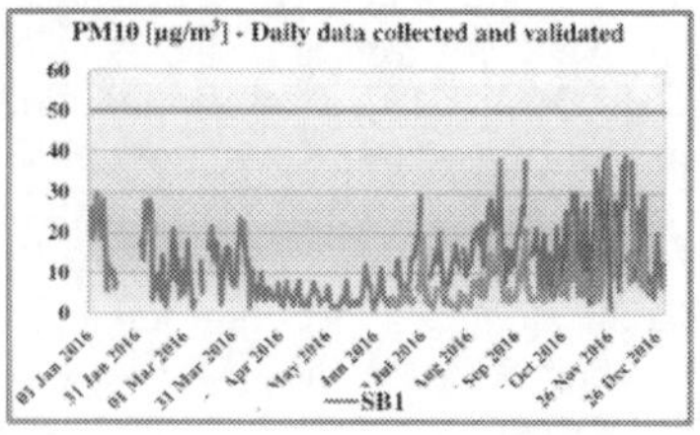

Figure 3. Particle concentration levels (PM10) in 2016

Particles are measured by size. PM 10 is the unit used to measure particles with a diameter between 2.5 and 10 µm. The particles (PM 10) pollution indicator is measured at SB1 station both automatically and manually. Figure 3 shows the daily limit values from SB1 and SB2 obtained in 2016. In 2016, the SB1 station reported 8 overruns of daily limit (50 $\mu g/m^3$) but which is still acceptable considering that the limit set by Air Act is 35 times yearly / station. (Single overruns cannot be seen in Figure 3, due to low resolution in the X-axis). Measurement results indicate that particle pollution is mainly caused by heavy traffic. The maximum (60.28 $\mu g/m^3$) was recorded in a heavily transited location at the entrance to the city where several hypermarkets are in the same area, while in Sub Arini Park (the largest park in the city) the recorded value of 13.93 µg/m3 was far below the daily limit value.

Explanations for this situation are: Apparently, in Sibiu the air quality is rather good, but the results might be pseudo true. The two fixed stations are situated as follows: SB1 is placed in an area where the traffic is relatively low and, SB2 is placed in an area which, on its deployment, in 2007, was heavily industrialized. Today, most industry has relocated (outside the city). Air pollution contributes to climate changes and to the emergence of *urban heat islands* (higher temperatures concentrated in urban areas densely populated and built), which cause temperature increases by up to 5 degrees compared with unaffected areas.

IV. Project Description

The main objectives of the mobile air quality monitoring platform project were to:

- Develop a low-cost mobile platform for air quality monitoring where data are collected through crowdsensing.
- Test the platform in the City of Sibiu, Romania (and other locations) and compare collected data with already existing data, to verify results and extend the number of measurements being made.
- Make the necessary groundwork for establishing a larger project on air quality monitoring, this time with focus on analysis, prediction and visualization.

A. The Platform

The platform has been described in an earlier paper [1]. Shortly summarized the platform consists of a processor unit (LinkedIt Smart Duo 7688 - an open development board with two processors, one running Linux, the other compatible with Arduino), a combined GPS/GSM unit for location and communication, a gas sensor for measuring CO_2 and NO_X (SainSmart MQ135 Sensor Air Quality Sensor and Hazardous Gas Detection Module), a particle sensor measuring PM 10 (Grove Dust Particle Concentration Detection Sensor), and sensors for temperature (DS18B20 Temperature Sensor) and barometric pressure (BMP085 Digital Barometric Pressure Measurement Sensor). The technologies used are: Eagle (for printing the PCB) and Custom Electronic Shields, ASP.NET and Microsoft Azure (for database and cloud), C/C++ (for LinkedIt 8266 programming). 16 prototypes were built for experiments.

B. Hardware and Software Architecture

On the client side, the software will detect when the car is parked, and then start data collection from the sensors at regular intervals. The data are stamped with time and location (both retrieved from the GPS receiver) and sent to a server using a GSM data connection. Figures 4 and 5 show the hardware design of printed circuit board holding the sensors (except the particle sensor which is connected by a wire).

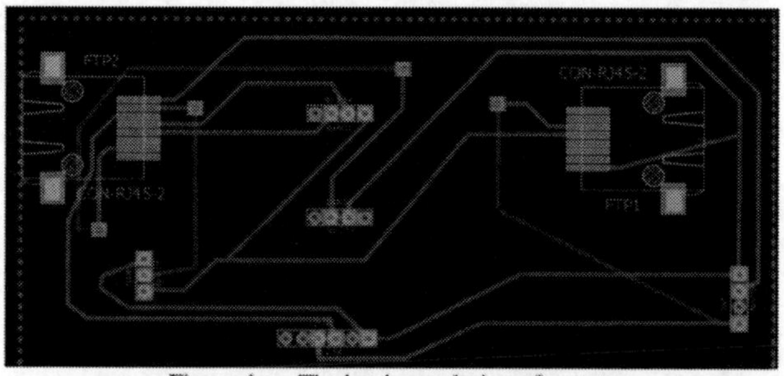

Figure 4. The hardware design of prototype

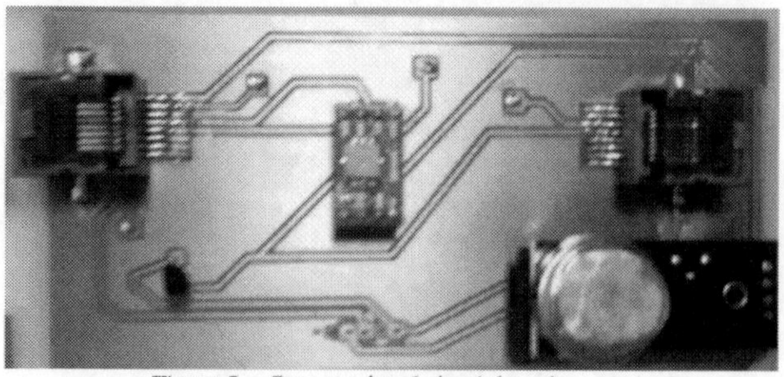

Figure 5. Sensor printed circuit board

On the server side, the data are stored in a database for further analysis. The location of active cars is shown on a map (Google maps) with the possibility to click on one specific car to see the latest data.

C. *Visualizing data*

By clicking on each point from the map, information from each sensor is disclosed. The map is shown in Figure 6.

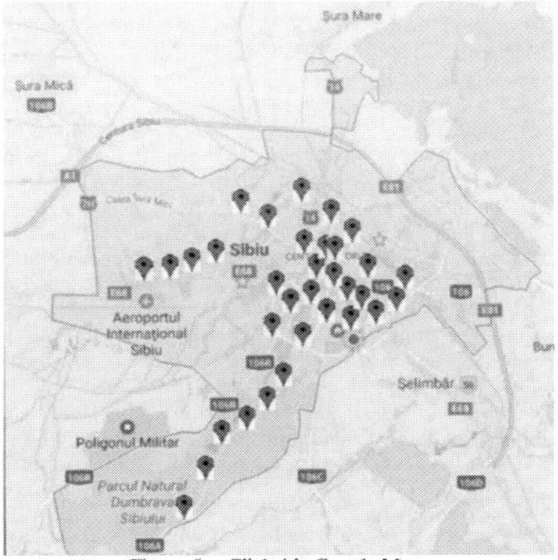

Figure 6. Clickable Google Maps

D. *The Test*

The platform was used for air-quality monitoring in Sibiu first weeks of February 2017. Data were collected from four units, each installed within a car. The data collected generally corresponds to earlier data collected by the National Environmental Protection Agency. At the same time, we showed that granularity has been improved since we could measure from many more locations. Some data were collected from cars driving the same route at different times.

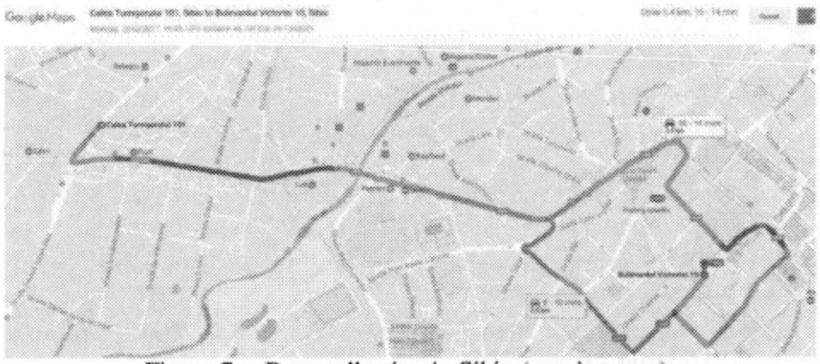

Figure 7. Data collection in Sibiu (moving cars).

Figure 7 illustrates a Google Maps snapshot with the route on which the data were collected at 5 pm when many people return from work. The red color shows heavy traffic because this road is connecting the airport with the city center and represents the single entrance in the city from the west side. In Figure 8, we present the chart with CO_2 variation during the route that takes around 16 minutes. The measurements were done with MQ135 gas sensor set up for CO_2 and the results are exhibited in parts per million (PPM). Regarding the MQ135 sensor and its detection capability, the researchers consider that the general sensitivity is roughly the same for all the gases sensed [14]. Since CO_2 is the fourth most abundant trace gas in the earth's atmosphere they recommend that it is safe to assume that in a normal atmosphere the MQ 135 sensor mostly detects CO_2. The values from Figure 8 somewhat faithfully follows the route from Figure 7, namely, where there is heavy traffic, CO_2 values are higher than 230 PPM. However, the maximum value obtained (277 PPM) is under the highest-ever daily average[2] at planet level (409.44 PPM) reached in 9 of April 2016.

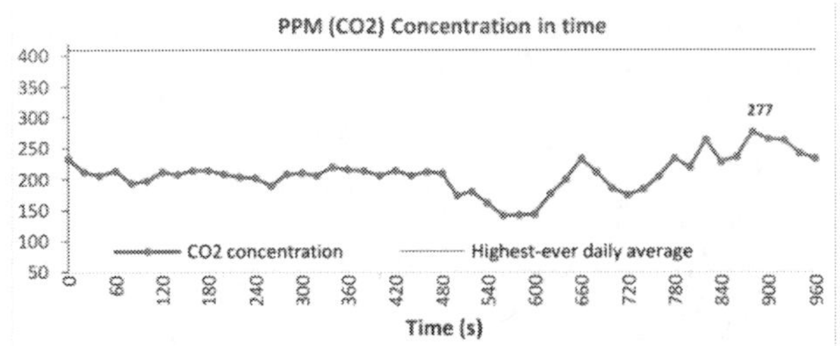

Figure 8. CO_2 values [PPM] collected with MQ 135 gas sensor from a heavy traffic boulevard from Sibiu

Table III presents the range where are situated the measured parameters (gas, temperature, dust and humidity). From a temperature point of view is observed how the heavy traffic produces higher temperature by approximately 2 degrees compared with unaffected areas (urban heat islands effect).

TABLE III. PARAMETERS VARIATION

	CO_2 [PPM]	Temperature [Celsius degree]	Dust [mg/m^3]	Humidity [%]
Maximum	277	2	0.35	87
Average	207.92	1	0.33	87
Minimum	141	0	0.32	87

Measurements were also made from parked cars in an densely populated area close to a major road, and here CO_2 values varied between 200 to 500, depending on the time of the day.

E. *Making Groundwork for a New Project*

EU Research & Innovation program H2020 [3] has allocated 80 billion Euros funding for initiatives related to environmental sustainability and energy efficiency. In a follow-up project, we intend to focus on further developing analytics, prediction algorithms and visualization. By collecting data over a longer period, we will be able to predict when pollution levels reach certain levels. Such information will be useful for decision-making.

[2] https://www.co2.earth/daily-co2

[3] http://ec.europa.eu/research/participants/portal/desktop/en/opportunities/

V. CONCLUSIONS

As mentioned earlier, several cities around the world are restricting car use when air pollution levels are too high. The use of stationary units provides low granularity of measurements, and are expensive. This project has shown that data can be collected by means of crowdsensing, either by using cars of the municipality or calling upon volunteers to accommodate units in their cars.

Largely, the obtained results are consistent with measurements from fixed stations. However, our solution provides much higher granularity of the measurements.

In a longer perspective, our aim is to further develop our platform as part of a system for smart-cities with the purpose of providing insights about people and environmental conditions, and disseminate such information to the public through multiple channels. Such a system will be important for decision making related to environmental issues, and be a measure to increase the transparency of the cities.

ACKNOWLEDGMENT

This work was partially supported by a grant from Iceland, Liechtenstein and Norway, contract type "*Small size bilateral cooperation projects, Scholarships and interinstitutional cooperation program*" - RO15, EEA Financial Mechanism 2009-2014, the Romanian National Agency for Community Programs in the Field of Education and Vocational Training, Contract Nos. 3/07.07.2016, COD: 16-SEE-PCB-RO SIBIU01 / 01.

The authors would like to thank Iosif Băncioiu and Ovidiu Hodorogea, students in the Computer Science and Electrical Engineering Department at "Lucian Blaga" University of Sibiu for providing useful technical help in the hardware and software implementation of the prototypes. We want to express our sincere gratitude to Mr. Liviu Crețu, the Chief of Sibiu National Roads Department, for providing useful information regarding the traffic level in Sibiu County. Last but not the least, our sincere thanks go to Dr. Lucian Roman from SC AutoHaus Huber SRL Sibiu, which has provided relevant insights regarding the influence of fuels and vehicles' operating parameters on air pollution.

REFERENCES

[1] L. Berntzen, M. Rohde Johannessen, and A. Florea, "Smart Cities: Challenges and a Sensor-based Solution," International Journal on Advances in Intelligent Systems 9 (3 & 4), IARIA, pp. 579-588, 2016.

[2] United States Environmental Protection Agency: *Air Pollution: Current and Future Challenges*. [Online]. Available from: https://www.epa.gov/clean-air-act-overview/air-pollution-current-and-future-challenges

[3] Romanian National Network of Air Quality Monitoring. [Online]. Available from: http://www.calitateaer.ro/structura.php

[4] Ericsson: *Ericsson energy, carbon report. On the impact of the networked society*. [Online]. Available from: http://www.ericsson.com/res/docs/2013/ericsson-energy-and-carbon-report.pdf

[5] WHO: *WHO releases country estimates on air polution exposure and health impact*. [Online] Available from: http://www.who.int/mediacentre/news/releases/2016/air-pollution-estimates/en/

[6] Independent: *London's air pollution worse than Beijing's as smog chokes UK capital*. [Online]. Available from: http://www.independent.co.uk/news/science/london-air-pollution-rates-worse-beijing-smog-china-vehicles-weather-a7545446.html

[7] Foxcrawl: *Arctic Ocean could melt in 30 years*. [Online]. Available from: http://www.foxcrawl.com/2016/11/07/arctic-ocean-thawing-ice-cap-melting-30-years/

[8] M. Inta, A. Muntean, C. Purcar, and M. Badescu, "The Study of Traffic Decongestion In A Crowded Intersection," Annals of the Oradea University. Fascicle of Management and Technological Engineering, Volume XII(XXII), ISSN 2285-3278, pp. 367-370, Oradea, 2013.

[9] M. Holder, "Paris, Mexico City, Madrid and Athens to ban diesel vehicles by 2025," BusinessGreen, [Online]. Available from: http://www.businessgreen.com/bg/news/3000622/paris-mexico-city-madrid-and-athens-to-ban-diesel-vehicles-by-2025

[10] European Commission: *A European Strategy for low-emission mobility, European Commission - Fact Sheet, Brussels, 20 July 2016*. [Online]. Available from: http://europa.eu/rapid/press-release_MEMO-16-2497_en.htm

[11] C. Leonardi, A. Cappellotto, M. Caraviello, B. Lepri, and F. Antonelli "SecondNose: an air quality mobile crowdsensing system," In Proceedings of the 8th Nordic Conference on Human-Computer Interaction: Fun, Fast, Foundational (NordiCHI '14). ACM, New York, NY, USA, 1051-1054. DOI: http://dx.doi.org/10.1145/2639189.2670273, 2014.

[12] J. Dutta, C. Chowdhury, S. Roy, A.I. Middya, and F. Gazi, "Towards Smart City: Sensing Air Quality in City based on Opportunistic Crowd-sensing," In Proceedings of the 18th International Conference on Distributed Computing and Networking (ICDCN '17). ACM, New York, NY, USA, , Article 42 , 6 pages. DOI: https://doi.org/10.1145/3007748.3018286, 2017

[13] CITI-SENSE Product Informaton Brochure. [Online]. Available from: http://www.citi-sense.eu

[14] AIRALERT website. [Online]. Available from: http://www.airalert.ro

[15] Z. Pan, H. Yu, H., C. Miao, and C. Leung, "Crowdsensing Air Quality with Camera-Enabled Mobile Devices," Proceedings of the Twenty-Ninth AAAI Conference on Innovative Applications (IAAI-17), pp. 4728-4733, 2017.

[16] C. Migliore, "SwarmBike: an IoT Sensing Platform for Air Pollution," Tesi di Laurea Magistrale. Politechnico di Torino, 2016.

[17] OpenSense website. [Online]. Available from: http://opensense.epfl.ch/wiki/index.php/OpenSense_2

[18] EEA grants website. [Online]. Available from: http://eeagrants.org/

[19] Romanian Parliament: *Air Law, Act no. 104/2011*. [Online]. Available from: http://www.anpm.ro/documents/12220/2049969/Lege+104+aer.pdf/d764d447-baca-448a-9f6d-cfea9bc39252

Online Physical Activity Monitoring From Head Kinematics

Pierre Barralon and Iñigo Dorronsoro
Health Division of Tecnalia
Donostia-San Sebastian, 20009 Spain
Email: pierre.barralon@tecnalia.com

***Abstract*—With older age, people experience increasing hearing loss. With the use of assistive technology systems it is possible to preserve and improve the quality of life of elderly people with hearing losses. The Augmented Hearing Experience and Assistance for Daily life (AHEAD) system, composed of hearing glasses (augmented with Bluetooth audio communication, and physiological sensors) wirelessly connected to a mobile phone also connected to a smart home environment platform, allows to provide services on top of the hearing enhancement provided by the hearing glasses. Beside the health related services that the AHEAD system offers (heart rate monitoring, emergency alarms), a physical activity assistant has been identified to be relevant in order to reduce sedentary behaviours. In this paper, we investigated how accurate fitness algorithms (walking time, step counter, physically active/inactive periods) based on head kinematic data would be. For that purpose we have adapted state-of-the art algorithms. A total of 10 healthy users performed activities of daily living and walking sessions. The results show that the head location is suitable to detect fitness indicators but some personalization of some parameters would be needed to improve the performance of the detection methods.**

Keywords–Active Ageing; Head Kinematics; Walking Detection; Hearing Instrument; mHealth.

I. Introduction

With older age, people experience increasing hearing loss. With the use of assistive technology systems it is possible to preserve and improve the quality of life of elderly people with hearing loss. Currently few hearing aids have a wireless connectivity and for those which support it, it is done through a dedicated physical device which works as a gateway between the hearing aid and the smartphone (Starkey SurfLink Mobile 2 (Starkey, 2015), Phonak ComPilot (Phonak, 2015)). The low usability of such wireless solutions limits the services that can be delivered to the hearing impaired person. The European project Augmented Hearing Experience and Assistance for Daily life (AHEAD) aims to provide a speech-controlled assistive system that supports elderly people in their everyday life as communication tool and healthcare manager, e.g., initiating phone calls, recording vital parameters, performing a audio verification test from home and providing environmental information. The AHEAD system is integrated into hearing glasses that are a combination of traditional hearing aids and eye glasses: two devices elderly people are used to and have accepted already. As health management is especially important for elderly people, the modified hearing aid is able to measure vital signs such as heart rate and body core temperature through sensors that are in contact with the skin of the inner ear and transmit these data for further analysis helping elderly people in self-managing their health. Finally, a 3D inertial sensor embedded into the hearing glasses records the user's physical activity in order to reduce sedentary behaviours. The AHEAD assistant is wirelessly connected to a smart phone

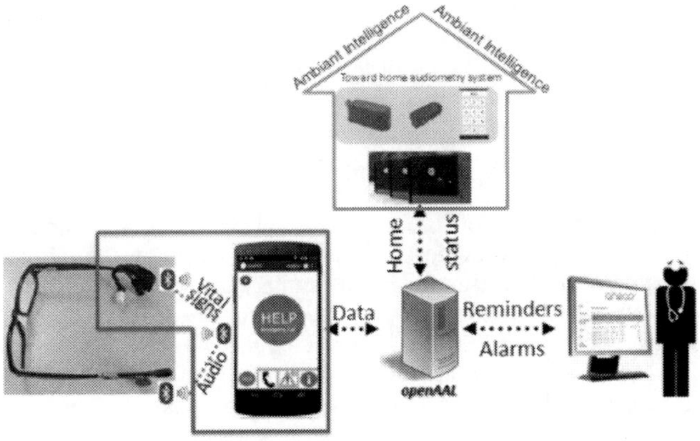

Figure 1. Overall AHEAD components

which is the gateway to the smart living environment and third party services.

Figure 1, depicts the AHEAD system composed by the openAAL platform (back-end and ontology platform), a smartphone, a hearing instrument (either eyeglasses or behind the hear system), hearing verification tools, and embedded physiological and kinematic sensors. For more details regarding the hardware and the services offered, please refer to Barralon [1].

In this paper, we are focusing on a sub part of the AHEAD which is the smartphone and the head mounted physiological and kinematic sensor (red polygon on Figure 1), which are the key components supporting the AHEAD fitness service. This service monitors and provides feedback/recommendation to the user about his/her daily walking time, number of steps and also the duration of physically active and inactive periods with the final goal to reduce the amount of inactivity. This service was considered important within the AHEAD system because the relationship between greater time spent in sedentary behavior and the presence of Activity of Daily Living (ADL) disability has been reported for older adults [2].

Even though they are commercial activity monitors (FitBit, Polar, ActiGraph, Tritrac RT3, Actical, the Actiheart, Activ8) [3] available on the market the AHEAD consortium decided, based on collected user requirements [4], not to add any another body sensor (e.g., watch) to promote physical activities but rather investigate and use the sensor embedded into the hearing glasses. In this case a 3D accelerometer already integrated into the Cosinuss device [5]. The question was, however to investigate whether the head was a suitable location for detecting walking events. It is known that the head vertical position is very well regulated during walking in order to maximise the visual input quality [6]. Brajick [7] investigated different smartphone locations (hand held, backpack, handbag, trousers back pocket, trouser front pocket, and handheld using). They, obviously, did not study the head location.

Since the AHEAD smartphone is the gateway between the hearing glasses (microphone, speaker, physiological sensors) and the back-end platform (openAAL) we have investigated which are the available algorithms supporting the detection of walking events, the calculation of the daily number of step and the duration of physically active and inactive periods with low computation power. We have found the Jigsaw Continuous Sensing Engine for Mobile Phone Applications [8] from which we adapted the method to track the amount of physically active and inactive events. We have used the frequential Short Time Fourier Transform (STFT) method proposed by Barralon [9] and confirmed by Brajick [7] to be better than other alternatives such as thresholding time series (acceleration magnitude, acceleration energy, mean crossing counts, etc.). For reference, the following papers estimate walking detection event but also gait authentication and identification [10] [11], stride and heading determination for pedestrian navigation system [12], and gait event detection for Functional Electrical Stimulation (FES) actuation [13]. Recently, a novel confidence-based multiclass boosting algorithm for mobile physical activity monitoring has been proposed by Reiss [14] to improve the classification performance on most of the evaluated datasets, especially for larger and more complex classification tasks.

Since the AHEAD system includes a smartphone anyway, we have selected four mobile applications (Pedometer, WalkLogger, Pacer, Google Fit) to compare our results with.

The rest of the paper is structured as follows. Section 2 describes the materials and methods offering the aforementioned services. Section 3 reports on the performance achieved by the system in comparison with other applications. Conclusions are drawn in the Section 4.

II. Measurements and Methods

A user experiment was performed in Tecnalia HomeLab, to test the accuracy of the AHEAD fitness algorithm (including walking time, number of steps and active/inactive duration), and compare with other commercially available Android apps.

A. Subjects

10 Healthy subjects were involved in the test, all Tecnalia employees (5 males, 5 females; 25-64 years old, mean 35.8 years, standard deviation 11.3 years).

B. Experimental protocol

In order to test the sensitivity (Se) and specificity (Sp) of both the Active/inactive and Walking/non Walking detection methods the users were asked to perform the following activities during the test:

1) Spending 2 minutes in sitting position reading the newspaper (in this situation the user should be detected as "inactive" and "non walking").
2) Standing up and arranging the kitchen during 3 minutes (should be detected as "active". The evaluation of the performance (e.g Se, Sp) of the walking detection algorithm was never performed on this part of the recording since some few and sporadic steps happened and were not counted by the experimenters because of the complexity to define what is a step in this context).
3) Standing up and still standing for 2 minutes watching a video on TV (should be detected as "inactive" and "non walking").
4) Sitting down and remaining sited for 4 minutes watching a video on TV (should be detected as "inactive" and "non walking").
5) Initiating gait and walking for 5 minutes (should be detected as "active" and "walking"). In this phase the number of steps performed by the users was counted and reported by two observers.

C. Materials

1) Hardware: For this experimentation we used a Nexus 5 smartphone [15] running an Android operating system (version 5.1, released on December 2014. API 22). The Nexus 5 is powered by a 2.26 GHz quad-core Snapdragon 800 processor with 2 GB of RAM. The smartphone was connected to a Cosinuss One device [5] in charge of measuring physiological parameters (e.g., heart rate, oxygen saturation, body surface temperature) but also the head motion using a 3-axis accelerometer. The component is an integrated circuit which records an analog accelerometric input and returns a digital signal with 12 bits resolution. The sampling rate was set to $100Hz$. The accelerometer data (packet of the five last measurements) was sent by Bluetooth Low Energy (BLE), RAW Data Service (UUID 0xA000), RAW Data characteristic (UUID 0xA001), every 50ms to the Nexus 5.

2) Software: During all the trials, five mobile applications were running in parallel and recoding the tasks.

- AHEAD app: This app has been developed by Tecnalia within AHEAD project. It provides different services as already explained above. One of the services provided by AHEAD app is the Fitness service, that is being analysed in this publication. It monitors and provides feedback to the user about his/her daily walking time, number of steps and also the duration of physically active and inactive periods. The algorithms estimating these variables are analysed in the next section. The Fitness service is connected by BLE to Cosinuss One device, and receives x and y axes accelerometer data in the RAW Data Service every 50ms, including 5 x and 5 y axis data per package. This data is buffered, and then analysed in a period of 1 second. So, updated information about active/inactive time, walking time and number of steps is provided every 1 second.
- Pedometer (tayutau) [16]
- WalkLogger pedometer [17]
- Pacer [18]
- Google Fit [19]

D. Detection and classification methods

The first version of fitness algorithms have been developed in Matlab. This first development was validated in [9]. To implement these algorithms in AHEAD, we translated them into Java. Due to the processing limitation of a smartphone compared with a computer, and the fact that other AHEAD services are concurrently running in parallel in the smart phone, a loss in the algorithm performance could be considered. We therefore compared on pre-trial data the Matlab and Android outputs (Figure 3 and Figure 4).

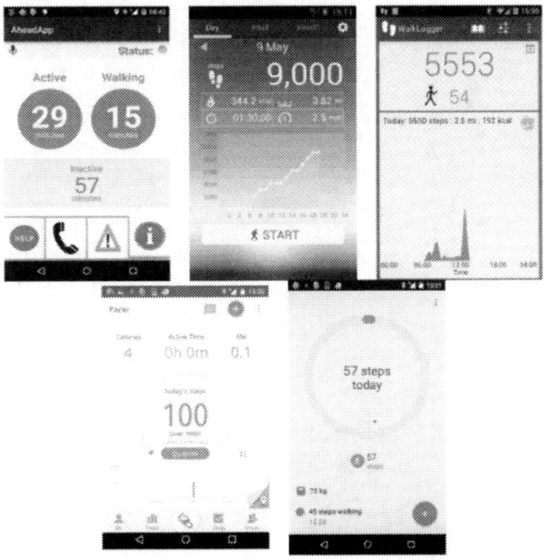

Figure 2. AHEAD app (top left) ; Pedometer (top center) ; WalkLogger (top right) ; Pacer (bottom left) ; Google fit (bottom right)

In a second step we have compared the AHEAD app methods with other Android apps. However, some of the selected apps (Google Fit, Pacer) do not detect (at least display) the physically active (or inactive) periods. For example when the user is not walking but still performing an activity of daily living (e.g., cleaning the dishes) no information is shown. In AHEAD these active periods are also detected and counted, with the aim to reduce the amount of inactivity of the user.

1) Physically active or inactive: In order to detect whether the user is physically active or not we have followed the approach of Lu and collaborators [8]. A stationary state detector is used to select qualified $\overrightarrow{a_i^s} = (a_{x,i}, a_{y,i}, a_{z,i})$ (i.e.,stationary accelerometer readings). Our stationary detector begins by dividing raw data into candidate frames each contain M successive samples. For each frame, the mean and standard deviation are calculated for the three axes. If all three standard deviations fall below a percentage threshold σ of the mean, we assume the device is stationary. In the AHEAD case and in order to alleviate the communication bandwidth between the mobile and the hearing glasses, we stream only two dimensions of the accelerometric components (vertical (a_v) and antero-posterior (a_{AP})). Instead of applying a threshold on each standard deviation of each component [8], we rather calculate the acceleration magnitude (AM) $AM_i = \sqrt{(a_{AP,i}^2 + a_{v,i}^2)}$ of the candidate frame and apply a threshold (named *minVariation*) on the standard deviation of the AM. The length of the candidate frame was set to one second (100 samples).

2) Walking duration and number of steps: Recently Brajdic has reported a comparison of different walking detection algorithms (MAGN_TH, ENER_TH, STD_TH, NASC+STD_TH, STFT, CWT, DWT, HMM) [7]. His conclusion was that the best performing algorithms for walk detection were the two thresholds based on the standard deviation (STD_TH) and the signal energy (ENER_TH), STFT and NASC, all of which exhibited similar error medians and spreads.

As explained in Barralon [9] and Brajdic [7], the walking detection is performed as follows: signal was split into successive time windows using SFTF of size *DFTwin* and labelled as walking if it contained significant (greater than a threshold: *DFTthresh*) spectral energy at typical walking frequencies *freqwalk*.

For the *DFTthresh* threshold, we used what was proposed by Barralon [9]:

$$DFTthresh = \frac{1}{pFactor}\left[\frac{b.DFTwin}{2}\right]^2 \quad (1)$$

where $pFactor$ is an attenuation coefficient, b the amplitude of the input signal (a_V or a_{AP}).

However, since the value of *DFTthresh* is adapted according to the amplitude b of the input signal, a noise with a small amplitude can be classified as walk if its frequency content is included within the frequency range of interest. To overcome this problem, Barralon [9] defined a constant threshold (T_b, named *minAmp* in this paper) to test b. If the amplitude of the input acceleration is too low then the algorithm will never classified the candidate frame as "walking".

The step counting is then only computed when walking has been detected and we compute a fractional number of strides for each window by dividing the window width by the dominant walking period it detected. These fractional values were then summed to estimate the total number of step taken.

During daily life activities, the fastest body movements occur when walking which corresponds to accelerometric signal ranging from 0.6 Hz to 2.5 Hz [20]. However Brajdic [7] has extended it to [0.01-7] Hz for the Short Term Fourier Transform (STFT) method.

For the walking and active/inactive detections we used the following parameters (see section III-B):

- $pFactor = 0.03$
- $freqwalk = [0.8 - 5]Hz$
- input accelerometer axis: vertical
- $minAmp = 0.1g$
- $minVariation = 0.13g$

III. Results

A. AHEAD algorithm - Comparison between Matlab and Smartphone

In figures 3 and 4 the results of the comparison between fitness algorithms running in Matlab and in AHEAD app are shown. Figure 3 shows the results during activities of daily living (e.g., cleaning up the kitchen table) and inactive episodes (reading and watching TV). Minor differences can be identified between the two implementations, surely due to the mislaid of some accelerometer data packages. Figure 4 shows the results of a walking sequence, where the results are the same for both Matlab and Android algorithms of walking detection and active/inactive detection. Step counting has not been included in this Matlab vs smartphone comparison, because it requires very few processing resources; the key point to correctly count the steps is the correct detection of walking episodes.

B. Thresholds identification

As presented in section II-D, several parameters have to be defined to detect the user activity. Even if values of these parameters have been reported for trunk mounted devices in various publications [9][7], we investigated how the change of some of them impact the performance for head mounted device which is the case of the AHEAD solution.

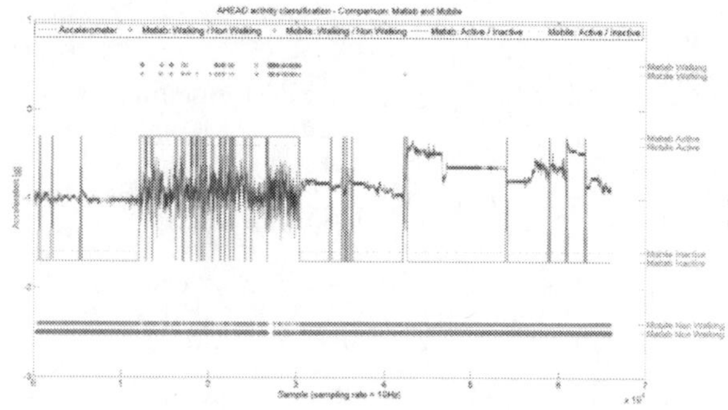

Figure 3. Illustration of AHEAD classification (walking/non walking, active/inactive) durind daily life activities

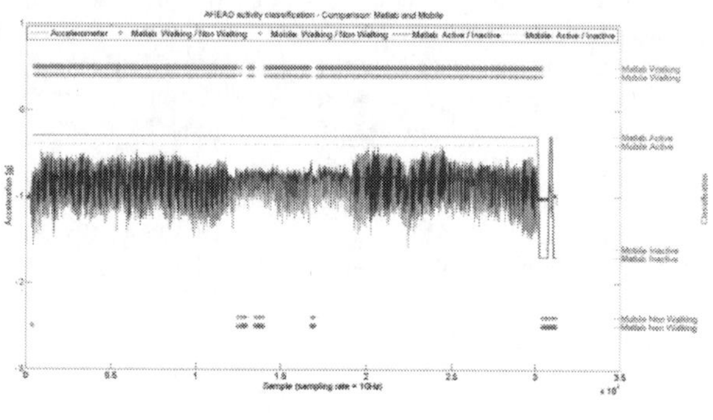

Figure 4. Illustration of AHEAD classification (walking/non walking, active/inactive) durind a walking sequence

In total, 10 subjects have performed the trial. Data from the first 3 subjects has been used to study and select the inner thresholds/values of the algorithms. The other 7 subjects' data has been used to validate the algorithm. The first three users have been selected to be representative of the whole set of subjects, and so we tried to include variation in gender and age: 2 males, 1 female; mean age 42.7 years, standard deviation of age 19.8 years.

1) Active/Inactive: The threshold to identify in the active/inactive detection algorithm is the threshold *minVariation* to which the standard deviations are compared with. Figures 5 and 6 show the results of this identification, with the Receiver operating characteristic (ROC) curve and the maximum accuracy with different threshold *minVariation* values. The best accuracy of 89% was obtained for $minVariation = 0.13$.

In the threshold identification process, data from tasks 1, 3 and 4 (sitting or still reading or watching TV) were tagged as inactive, and data from tasks 2 and 5 (arranging the kitchen and walking) were tagged as active.

2) Walking: Walking detection algorithm has three parameters that can be adjusted (and will affect the sensitivity and specificity). We therefore tested several combinations of those three parameters and analysed how they affect the performance of the walking detection algorithm:

- Walking detection algorithm is based on acc data from only one axis. So, the best axis (V or AP) to be used should be defined. V is the vertical axis, and AP is the anteroposterior axis.
- The highest peak on frequencies between 0.8Hz and 5.0Hz should be bigger than a percentage of the theoretical maximum frequency. This attenuation coefficient *pfactor* (1) should be defined.
- The amplitude of the acc signal above the mean should be bigger than a threshold *minAmp* to be defined (see section II-D2).

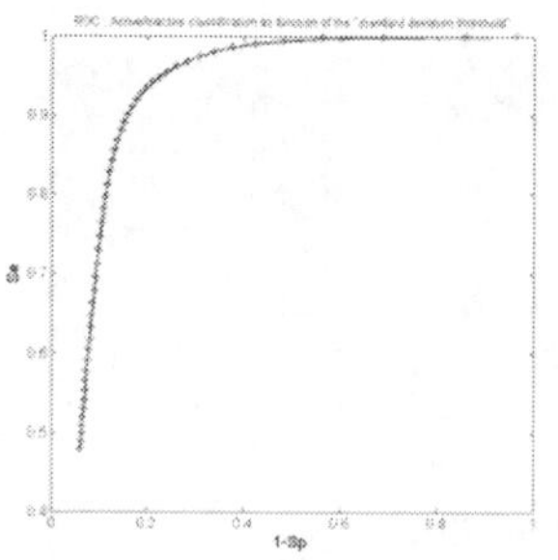

Figure 5. Active/inactive ROC curve as a function of the $minVariation$ parameter

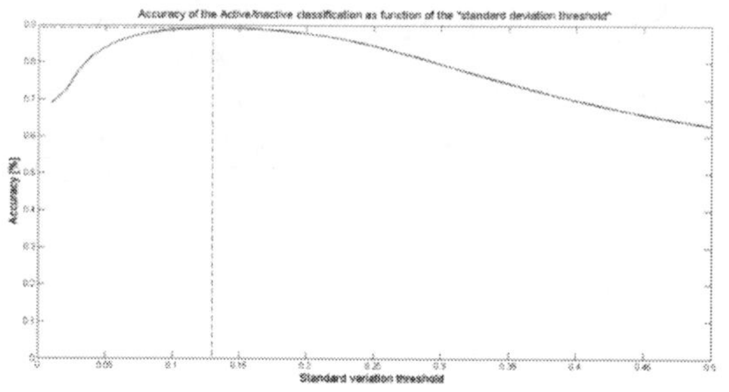

Figure 6. Active/inactive accuracy as a function of the $minVariation$ parameter

Figures 7 and 8 show the results of the identification of these 3 parameters. When selecting these values, a better sensitivity has been prioritized at the expense of poorer specificity. The best results were obtained for the vertical axis. We selected an attenuation coefficient $pFactor = 0.03$ and the minimum amplitude of the acc signal above the mean $minAmp = 0.1$.

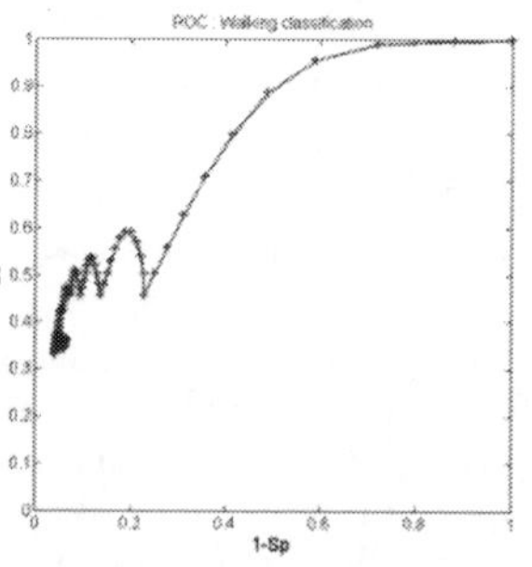

Figure 7. Learning: Walking - ROC as function of $pFactor$, $minAmp$ and acceleration axis (V or AP).

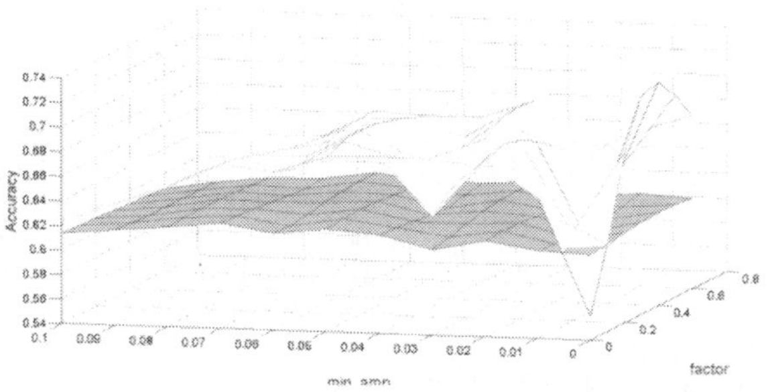

Figure 8. Learning: Walking Accuracy as function of $pFactor$, $minAmp$, and $axis$. The blue plot represents the AP axis and the white one the V axis

For this threshold identification process, data from tasks 1, 3 and 4 (sitting or still reading or watching TV) were tagged as non walking, and data from task 5 (walking) was tagged as walking. Data from task 2 was excluded from this section, because some few and sporadic steps happened and were not counted by the experimenters because of the complexity to define what is a step in this context.

C. Results on seven subjects

After setting the required parameters (see previous section), the configured algorithms were validated with the remaining 7 users: 3 males, 4 females; mean age 32.9 years (standard deviation 5.3 years).

Table I shows the overall results of the test, comparing AHEAD fitness service with the true values and the results obtained with other Android apps available in Google Play.

- Active/Inactive time detection algorithm has a sensitivity of 89 percent.
- Walking time algorithm has a sensitivity of 86 percent for all 7 users. For the 4 users where the algorithm has a better performance, the sensitivity is 96 percent, while it is of 72 percent for the other 3 users.
- Step counter has also a sensitivity of 86 percent for all 7 users. For the 4 users where the algorithm has a better performance, the sensitivity is 93 percent, while it is of 77 percent for the other 3 users.

In Figures 9 and 10, the walking time and number of steps information is shown. Numbers correspond to average values of the 7 users, and associated standard deviation in brackets.

AHEAD walking detection and step counting algorithms clearly had much worse performance with 3 of these 7 users. In Table I and in Figures 9 and 10, new columns were added to distinguish the algorithms good performance in 4 users and bad performance in 3 users.

IV. Conclusion

A new approach for fitness activity detection has been presented in this paper. The main novelties presented here are 1) the head location of the accelerometer sensor embedded into a pair of hearing glasses, and 2) the detection of physically active episodes that do not necessary imply a walking event. The integration of additional sensors into the hearing instruments will facilitate the user acceptance while offering additional services with the aim to increase the autonomy level of the users and reduce the amount of sedentary behaviours.

The results presented support that the head kinematics is a suitable location for physical activity monitoring. The results are promising, with a sensitivity higher than 85% for all 3 algorithms (active detection, walking detection and step counter). Even though the user trial was designed to cover sequentially inactive, active, and walking phases, the test was performed in a Homelab and the users executed those tasks in a very natural manner. As a consequence, sequences that were supposed to be "inactive" sometimes include "active" events (postural re-adjustment on a chair, head and trunk motion to scratch a leg, ...). Similarly, during walking we observed large head movements to either look around or talk to the experimenter. Besides, the Cosinuss sensor was placed by the user him/herself on the hear, and therefore the sensor placement was not identical for all users. All these elements contributed to reduce the performance of the implemented algorithms. The raw acc data of the 3 users with worse walking detection performance show some similarities, e.g., changes in the Cosinuss sensor orientation during the trial. Finally, the three users selected for the learning stage of the algorithm were chosen based on general characteristics (gender and age), but we did not take into account other gait related features such as body mass, leg or step length.

The promising results presented in this publication may require some more research so that the algorithm could be more independent of various gait patterns or gait styles.

The AHEAD subsystem presented in this paper is a potential candidate to be used in the ACTIVAGE project (European Large Scale Pilot on Smart Living Environments) where the main objective is to build the first European Internet of Thing (IoT) ecosystem across 9 Deployment Sites (DS) in seven European countries.

Acknowledgment

The research presented in this paper is partially funded by the European project ACTIVAGE (grant agreement 732679) and the European AHEAD project (AAL-2012-2-167), which is partially funded by the European Ambient Assisted Living Joint Programme and the National Funding Agencies from Austria, Denmark, Germany and Spain (Ministerio de Industria, Energa y Turismo). The authors would like to thank the AHEAD partners Atos, Auditdata, Austrian Institute of Technology, Bruckhoff hannover, Forschungszentrum Informatik am Karlsruher Institut fr Technologie, Innovationsmanufaktur, Johanniter, and particularly Cosinuss, the manufacturer of the ear sensor used in this experiment.

References

[1] P. Barralon, I. R. M. Martins, N. Merkle, and S. Schwarz, "Augmented hearing assistance for elderly people - from requirements to implementation," in ICT4AgeingWell 2015 - Proceedings of the 1st International Conference on Information and Communication Technologies for Ageing Well and e-Health, Lisbon, Portugal, 20-22 May, 2015., 2015, pp. 59–66. [Online]. Available: http://dx.doi.org/10.5220/0005445900059006, [retrieved: June, 2017]

[2] D. D. Dunlop et al., "Sedentary time in us older adults associated with disability in activities of daily living independent of physical activity." J Phys Act Health, vol. 12, no. 1, Jan 2015, pp. 93–101.

[3] D. P. Heil, S. Brage, and M. P. Rothney, "Modeling physical activity outcomes from wearable monitors." Medicine and science in sports and exercise, vol. 44, no. 1 Suppl 1, 2012, pp. S50–60.

[4] A. Rashid, L. Wulf, and M. Garschall, "Augmented hearing for elderly people user requirements and use cases," in Mensch & Computer 2014 - Workshopband, A. Butz, M. Koch, and J. Schlichter, Eds. Berlin: De Gruyter Oldenbourg, 2014, pp. 075–082.

TABLE I. RESULTS OF THE TRIALS PERFORMED BY HEIGHT HEALTHY SUBJECTS

Feature	Truth	Pacer	Pedometer	Walklogger	Google fit	AHEAD	AHEAD 4 best users	AHEAD 3 worst users
Walking time (s)	299 (2.2)	240 (34.6)	298.4 (5.7)	299.9 (5.6)	300 (60.0)	257.0 (39.9)	287.75 (11.9)	216 (12.5)
Number of steps	490.1 (33.8)	506.9 (46.0)	493.3 (33.5)	506.6 (45.6)	471.7 (78.7)	422.1 (51.7)	456 (35.5)	377 (28.2)
Active time	481 (2.8)	NA	NA	NA	NA	429.2 (23.6)	NA	NA
Inactive time	480.8 (1.0)	NA	NA	NA	NA	542.2 (31.8)	NA	NA

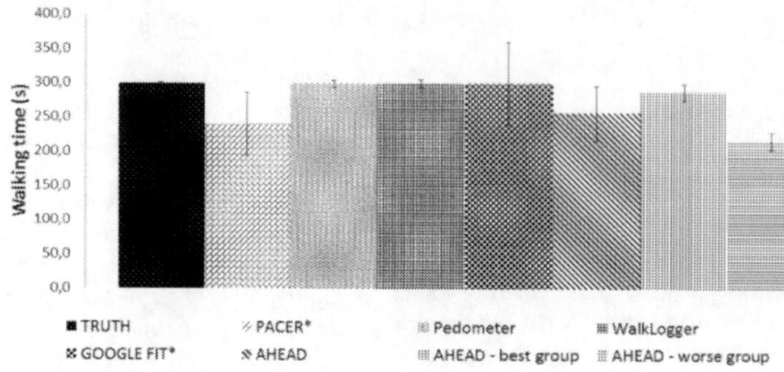

Figure 9. Testing Walking Time

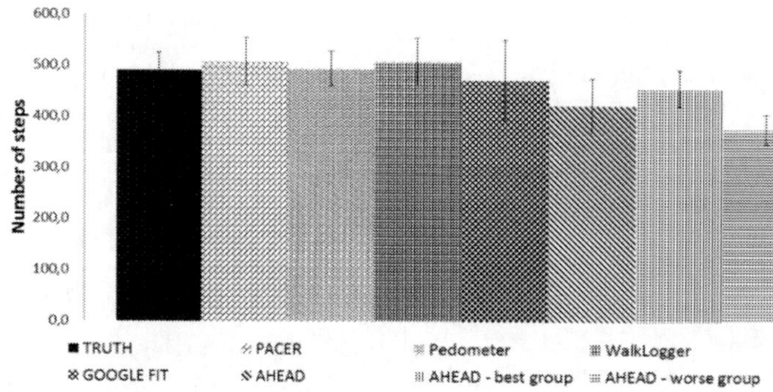

Figure 10. Testing Walking number of steps

[5] [Online]. Available: http://cosinuss.com/en/ [retrieved: June, 2017]

[6] E. Hirasaki, S. T. Moore, T. Raphan, and B. Cohen, "Effects of walking velocity on vertical head and body movements during locomotion." Exp Brain Res, vol. 127, no. 2, Jul 1999, pp. 117–130.

[7] A. Brajdic and R. Harle, "Walk detection and step counting on unconstrained smartphones," in Proceedings of the 2013 ACM international joint conference on Pervasive and ubiquitous computing. ACM, 2013, pp. 225–234.

[8] H. Lu et al., "The jigsaw continuous sensing engine for mobile phone applications," in Proceedings of the 8th ACM conference on embedded networked sensor systems. ACM, 2010, pp. 71–84.

[9] P. Barralon, N. Vuillerme, and N. Noury, "Walk detection with a kinematic sensor: Frequency and wavelet comparison," in Proc. 28th Annual International Conference of the IEEE Engineering in Medicine and Biology Society EMBS '06, Aug. 30 –Sept. 3 2006, pp. 1711–1714.

[10] J. Rueterbories, E. G. Spaich, B. Larsen, and O. K. Andersen, "Methods for gait event detection and analysis in ambulatory systems," Medical engineering & physics, vol. 32, no. 6, 2010, pp. 545–552.

[11] D. Gafurov, E. Snekkenes, and P. Bours, "Gait authentication and identification using wearable accelerometer sensor," in Automatic Identification Advanced Technologies, 2007 IEEE Workshop on. IEEE, 2007, pp. 220–225.

[12] J. W. Kim, H. J. Jang, D.-H. Hwang, and C. Park, "A step, stride and heading determination for the pedestrian navigation system," Positioning, vol. 1, no. 08, 2004, p. 0.

[13] M. Hanlon and R. Anderson, "Real-time gait event detection using wearable sensors," Gait & Posture, vol. 30, no. 4, 2009, pp. 523 – 527. [Online]. Available: http://www.sciencedirect.com/science/article/pii/S0966636209003373, [retrieved: June, 2017]

[14] A. Reiss, G. Hendeby, and D. Stricker, "A novel confidence-based multiclass boosting algorithm for mobile physical activity monitoring," Personal Ubiquitous Comput., vol. 19, no. 1, Jan. 2015, pp. 105–121.

[15] [Online]. Available: https://store.google.com/product/nexus5 [retrieved: June, 2017]

[16] [Online]. Available: https://play.google.com/store/apps/details?id=com.tayu.tau.pedometer [retrieved: June, 2017]

[17] [Online]. Available: https://play.google.com/store/apps/details?id=com.walklogger.pedometer [retrieved: February, 2017]

[18] [Online]. Available: https://play.google.com/store/apps/details?id=cc.pacer.androidapp [retrieved: February, 2017]

[19] [Online]. Available: https://play.google.com/store/apps/details?id=com.google.android.apps.fitness [retrieved: February, 2017]

[20] M. Henriksen, H. Lund, R. Moe-Nilssen, H. Bliddal, and B. Danneskiod-Samsøe, "Test–retest reliability of trunk accelerometric gait analysis," Gait & posture, vol. 19, no. 3, 2004, pp. 288–297.

Real-Time Monitoring of Heart Rate by Processing of Near Infrared Generated Streams

Ilaria Bosi, Chiara Cogerino, Marco Bazzani
ISMB - Istituto Superiore Mario Boella
Turin, Italy
e-mail: {bosi, cogerino, bazzani}@ismb.it

Abstract—**This paper presents a novel solution for non-invasive real-time heart rate monitoring by processing of Near Infrared (NIR) generated streams, provided by a low-cost, easy-to-use sensor, such as Microsoft Kinect™. The standard method to monitor physiological information exploits photoplethysmographic images. In fact, the changes in blood volume can be determined from the spectra of radiation reflected from (or transmitted through) body tissues. Using a mathematical processing, the study shows how it is possible to real-time estimate the heart rate of people sitting for 1 minute in front of the sensor at distance 1 meter by analysing the NIR stream and without wearing any other sensors. In order to prove the correctness of the method proposed, 35 different subjects are involved in the test phase. During the tests, each subject wears also a pulse oximeter for comparing the values calculated by our method.**

Keywords: Heart rate; Near Infrared channel; real-time; Kinect™ 2.0.

I. Introduction

The scope of this work is to present a new solution for non-invasive remote monitoring of vital signs (in particular heart rate), using an algorithm that processes the data acquired by the NIR channel of the Kinect™ sensor at medium distance (1 m). By analysing the raw signals with an appropriate mathematical elaboration, the cardiac pulse is extrapolated in "real-time" mode. In this way, it is possible to monitor the heart activity during playing games or during the execution of training programs (e.g., rehabilitation programs), even when light conditions are not optimal, without having to combine additional medical devices that are often invasive.

The Kinect™ 2.0 sensor, by combining a HD camera and an infrared camera (to estimate the depth), uses a human morphological model to match the silhouette seen through the infrared camera and to provide the position (X,Y,Z) for each one of 25 joints. In addition, each data stream (RGB, infrared) could be autonomously gathered for more accurate data analysis [1][2].

By thoroughly analyzing the work and the criticalities that have emerged in the previous tests on real-time heart rate determination via RGB channels [3], one of the key requirements for proper setup is the right lighting (natural or artificial). For this reason, it has been decided to take advantage of the supplied sensor at Kinect™ to use the near-infrared imaging technique (NIR) [4]. NIR is a source of electromagnetic radiation at the beginning of the infrared spectrum range and borders on the spectrum of visible light. Its benefits include the ability to be reflected from objects, penetrating glass and serving as an active source of illumination [5]. While most face sensors use color images as inputs, lighting variance remains a challenge because lighting can alter the color intensity in an image.

Especially in low light conditions, some faces may have a minimum contrast of intensity with the dark background, resulting in facial detection. IR images, on the contrary, remain the same despite the changes in lighting. Even in the dark, IR images can capture distinct details of the face [6].

The paper is organized as follows. The study begins in Section II with a general overview of the devices available on the market and referring to the telemedicine and various sensors for cardiac monitoring. In Section III, the analysis of the state of the art of the already implemented methods for remote monitoring of vital signs is presented. The core of this work is descripted in Section IV and the developed algorithms with the procedures adopted for their validations and tests are presented in Section V. In Section VII, the discussion of the results of the entire work and the conclusions are proposed in Section VIII.

II. Background

The topic of non-invasively detection of vital parameters has been successful increased in the last few years, in part due to the use of new technologies in hospital wards and surroundings, in part because the majority of patients is in favour of personalized assistance instead of health care services provided up to now [7][8].

The market is witnessing the continuous spread of new devices and software systems that allow monitoring the vital parameters (e.g., heart rate, oxygen saturation, respiratory rate) or setting personalized triggered alerts. In this perspective, in order to enhance the daily management of diseases by facilitating self-care, e-Health and related personalized health services are steadily growing [9][10].

A further step towards non-invasive systems has been taken with the introduction of the pulse oximeter, an instrument that, thanks to the principles of photoplethysmography, is able to detect the oxygen saturation of the blood and the heart rate simply by exploiting the changes in blood volume in the microcirculation of the human tissues [11].

Considering the Physiology, the impulse of cardio-vascular wave that flows through the body periodically, causes stretch in the vessel walls. The volumetric changes due to fluctuations in the amount of blood or air contained within the human body can be measured by photoplethysmography (PPG) [12].

These fluctuations modulate the absorbance of light passing through a given volume of tissue, so it is possible to evaluate the variation of light during a normal cardiac cycle. If these changes are recorded, they originate a waveform that corresponds to the changes in the pulsatile arterial blood in the tissue [13].

It is worth noting that the PPG is usually performed with a dedicated light's source and it considers environmental light as a source of noise. Then, applying the PPG at medium/long distance (2.5m - 3m) implicates that the environmental noise becomes more relevant.

The absorbed light of a human in NIR consists of two components [14]: one static absorption constant from muscles, fat, bones and venous blood (de-oxyhemoglobin) and one varying component from arterial blood (oxyhemoglobin). As the heart beats, the concentration of oxyhemoglobin will fluctuate in the body and effect the light absorption subsequently [15]. The red color of the blood is caused by the fact that absorption coefficient is low for the red wavelengths (620 - 700nm) and high for the other wavelengths of visible light, meaning that only the red light is reflected. The light absorption coefficient in NIR (700 - 1400nm) is very low: 5.7 cm^{-1} in 850nm. The wavelength of 540nm (green light) has around a 50 times higher absorption coefficient than what NIR has [16]. Another difference between RGB-videos and NIR-videos are the number of wavelengths captured. An RGB-camera records three wavelengths simultaneously while a monochrome NIR-camera only records one. The benefit of having more than one frequency is to use the other wavelengths that have a lower oxyhemoglobin absorption as reference to cancel out ambient light and noise as Verkruysse et al [17].

III. State of the Art

In recent years, there has been a growing interest in the study of remote monitoring of vital signs using webcam and algorithms with computational software.

One of the first experiments to extract heartbeat from video (with a webcam) was conducted by Poh at al. [18] in 2010 at MIT in Boston: they have recorded videos of a minute and then completed processing of signals from the RGB channels by computer's webcam. The results obtained from MIT are based on studies conducted few years before: Verkruysse et al. [17] had demonstrated that the blood absorbs light more than the surrounding tissues and this application can also be used to evaluate the heart rate and breathing (photoplethysmography).

Moreover, the studies conducted by Takano et al. [19] considered the use of a charge coupled device (CCD) camera for the acquisition of the person's face every 30 seconds: from these studies, it was possible to extract the heart rate and respiratory rate.

Another webcam-based heart rate measurement method, was studied in 2013 using Laplacian Eigenmap (LE) [20]: this technique is used to extract the volume of blood pressure (BVP) from subjects' videos acquired.

In recent publications [21], different tests has been conducted in order to change the technology used, by adopting a camera with five channels and demonstrating that the alternation of the frequency bands, in particular the orange band, allows a physiological measurements much more correlated to the values obtainable with a classic pulse oximeter. However, this type of camera is not included in most of the commercial devices.

The use of the Microsoft Kinect™ device is certainly linked to gaming platforms, rather than to other areas [22]. Recently, the Polytechnic University of Marche has presented a method for measuring heart and respiratory rate [23] by using the Kinect™ 1.0 sensor. The study has been based on the detection of micro-movements of the neck, abdomen and chest of supine subjects, placed a short distance (<1m) from the sensor.

In the Healthcare Innovation Conference (HIC) [24] it has been presented a study that uses a Kinect™ camera mounted on the car's dashboard in order to collect video and to calculate the driver's heart rate in real time.

Finally, our paper presented at SpliTech 2016 [3] described the implementation and the tests of a novel methodology for evaluating the heart rhythm by a non-invasive monitoring system based on Kinect™ 2.0 sensor, acting at medium/long distance (2.5 m). Furthermore, this work highlights the capability to monitor the cardiac pulse rate during the performance of physical exercises.

About Infrared system, in 2015 Zeng presented in a paper a non-invasive heart rate detection process using Kinect™ to measure the heart rate via the obtained near-infrared video, in order to decrease the interference from light and establish a non-invasive system via near-infrared camera [25].

Procházka [26] detect possible medical and neurological disorders using Microsoft Kinect™ sensors for non-contact monitoring of breathing and heart rate estimation: video sequences of facial features and thorax movements are recorded by device image, depth and infrared sensors to enable their time analysis in selected regions of interest. Spectral analysis of the time evolution of the mouth area video frames (infrared data) was also used for heart rate estimation.

IV. Methods

The combination of the Depth camera of the Kinect™ sensor and the information contained in the signal emitted by the major surface vessels is the base of the real-time method developed for monitoring the heart rate without the direct contact between the instrument and the patient. The solution proposed is able to solve some of the problems related to an invasive monitoring system, ambient light conditions and, at the same time, to ensure the reliability of the results from a physiological point of view. In these terms, the Kinect™ camera detects the changes of blood flow (and thus the work done by the heart) by collecting the mixture of the reflected photoplethysmographic signal (with the fluctuations based on the amount of reflected light) and the volumetric changes of the blood vessels.

In order to choose the region of interest (ROI), the most suitable areas for the detection of heart rate are the forehead and cheeks [27][28]. A rectangle (size 100x140 pixels) that includes the person's face and tracks it during movements is designed from the neck joint. The sizes of the ROI are the best compromise in order to reduce the background noise and analyse the most significant pixels. Furthermore, it is decided to use the neck joint because the Kinect™ has encountered problems in identifying and tracking the face of people wearing glasses with anti-reflective lenses.

The software developed for this study, integrates a C# code able to activate the Kinect™ sensor, to detect the person's face and to proceed with the acquisition of the raw signals from the NIR channel and a Python code used for the data processing and the analysis of the signals. In this way, the Kinect™ sensor is able to maintain the 30 fps real-time images acquisition and to implement the mathematical algorithm processing, without creating duplication or data loss. Indeed, the raw IR data, i.e., the intensity average of the pixels of the ROI, are sent to the Python processes, while the Kinect™ sensor continues the real time acquisition of the frames. In order to mitigate the background noise, a bandpass Butterworth filter with infinite impulse response, double-pass, 7th order, and bandpass [0.85 ÷ 3.5 Hz] is applied.

Then, the spectral analysis (by Fast Fourier Transform) of the average of the filtered IR pixels is applied in order to represent the distribution of the power of the signal itself.

The FFT of the IR signal allows deciding the frequency corresponding to the maximum peak's intensity in the same band of the filter [0.85 ÷ 3.5 Hz], that corresponds to the range [51 to 210 bpm] of the heart rate: in this interval it is surely contained the normal range of physiological heart rate values for healthy people [60÷100 bpm] [29]. The average beats per minutes are obtained by the multiplication by 60 of this value of frequency. Every new 60 frames acquired, this analysis is re-performed. In this way, a new heart rate value is generated every two seconds. In Figure 1, the block diagram of the whole implemented algorithm is reported.

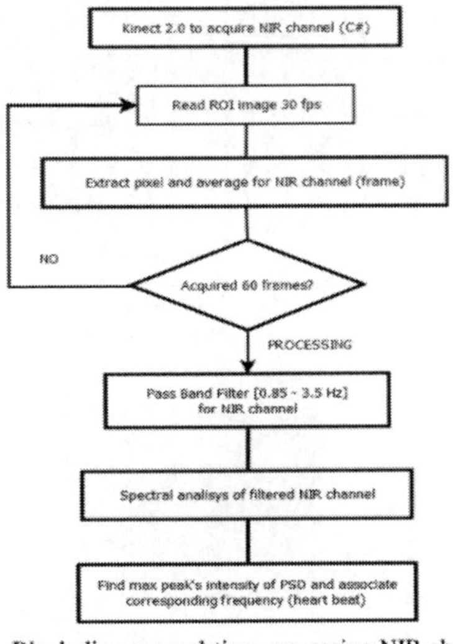

Figure. 1. Block diagram real-time processing NIR channel.

V. EXPERIMENTAL SETUP

The technical equipment used for performing the test is based on the Microsoft Kinect™ 2.0 sensor. All the videos are acquired in NIR (8-bit IR) at maximum frame rate available (30 fps - sufficient to generate a valid real time value for the heart rate) and with a resolution of 512x424 pixels.

A test is performed by 35 participants (18 men and 17 women), between the ages of 24-60 years, in good health (some of which are also well-trained) and with different features (beard, moustache, glasses, foundation creams). During tests, they wear a GIMA OXI-10 pulse-oximeter (in order to make a later comparison of the obtained values) [30].

The distance between the subject and the sensor is approximately set to 1 meter. The choice of the distance is given after a pre-test where the subjects are placed to different distances: 1m, 2m and 3m. It is worth noting that there are not any relevant deviations of the heart rate values calculated from the Kinect™ sensor due to the distances [31].

Figure 2 well represents the experimental setup created during tests in laboratory environment.

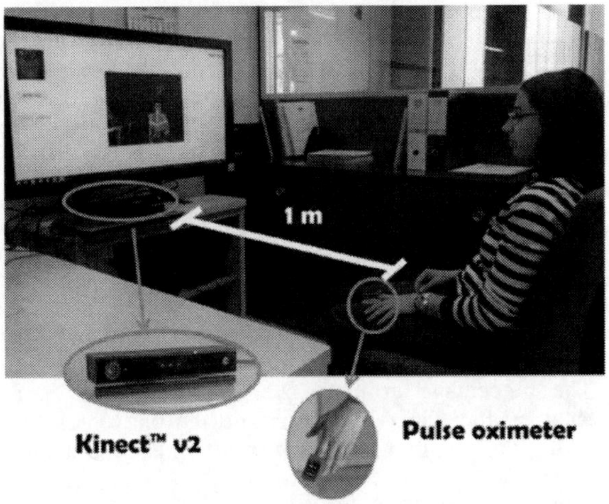

Figure. 2. Experimental Setup.

During the different tests to find the right setup of Microsoft Kinect™, is used a dual data acquisition that involves real-time heart rate detection using the RGB channels and infrared channel available to device.

By analyzing the Microsoft device used, Figure 3 compares the infrared sensor with the RGB channels of Kinect™ [32].

As shown in Figure 4, the two cameras are placed few centimetres far. This implicates that also the sensor area of coverage is slightly different: for this reason it is necessary to proceed with a pre-calibration to align as much as possible the size of the ROI gained through RGB and the ROI gained through NIR, especially if the facial rectangle is constructed following the skeleton joint's trend.

	Camera Name			
	Kinect 2.0 RGB Camera		Kinect 2.0 IR Camera	
	Imaging Sensor			
Type	-		-	
Resolution (pixels)	1920 × 1080		512 × 424	
Pixel size (μm)	3.1		10	
	Interior Parameters			
	Value	St. Dev	Value	St. Dev
Focal length (mm)	3.291	1.0e−3	3.657	5.2e−4
Format width (mm)	6.00		5.12	
Format height (mm)	3.38		4.24	
Image width (pixels)	1920		512	
Image height (pixels)	1080		424	
Principal Point x (mm)	−0.005	5.6e−4	0.032	3.5e−4
Principal Point y(mm)	−0.016	6.9e−04	0.033	3.9e−4

Figure 3. Sensors and IO parameters of RGB and IR cameras estimated during the camera calibration procedure for Kinect 2.0.

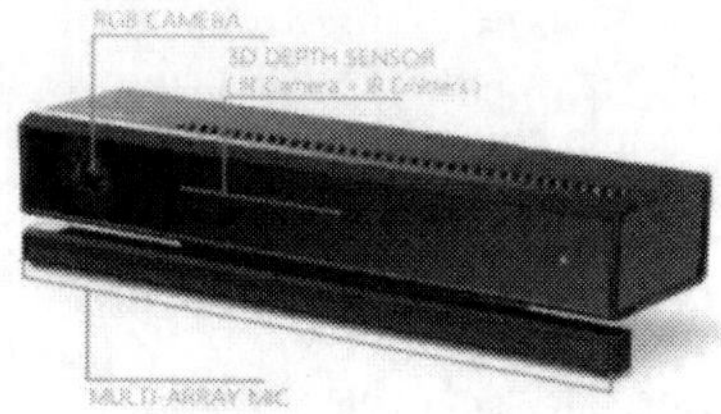

Figure. 4. Kinect™ features.

After all these considerations, to choose the best setup, the participants are standing and sitting in front of the Kinect™ sensor, at approximately 1 meter far from the built-in camera, while the system calculates the heart rate in real time mode using the NIR channel.

VI. RESULTS

For each subject, the graph comparing the timely progression of the heartbeat detected both by Kinect™ sensor and the pulse oximeter has been plotted. Then, it has been decided to calculate the heartbeat's average in the time interval considered.

The percentage error of the mean of heart rhythm detected by the Kinect™ sensor and the one obtained by averaging the incoming values from the pulse oximeter are also calculated.

Plots in Figure 5 show the graphs of heart rate value acquired by the Kinect™ based system (red line) and gathered by pulse oximeter (blue line) during the test.

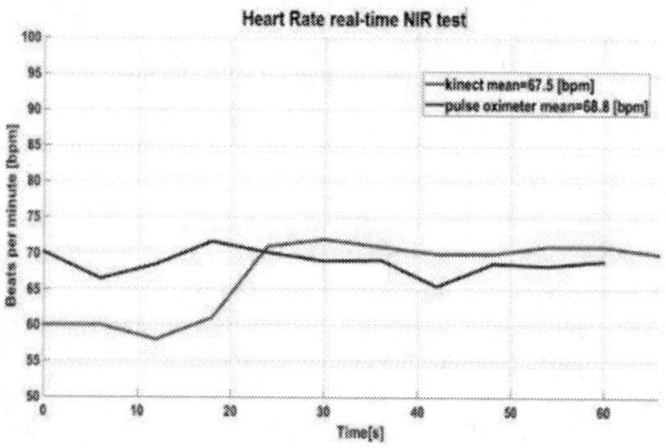

Figure. 5. Representation of heart rate-time during two different tests.

In Figure 6, the scatter graphs of mean value between Kinect™ and pulse oximeter are plotted for each test conducted: a linear trend line has been added for better understanding the graphs and the correlation coefficient (R) and the level of significance (p) are also calculated.

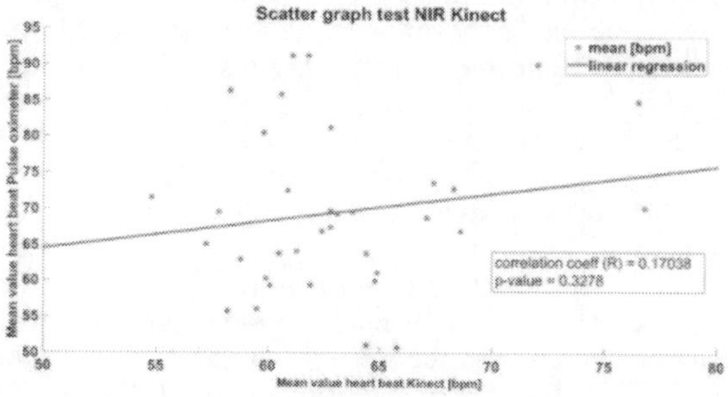

Figure. 6. Representation of scatter plot Kinect™/pulse oximeter.

The correlation coefficient (R) is a number between –1 and 1 that determines whether two paired sets of data are related: the weakest linear relationship is indicated by a correlation coefficient equal to 0. So the coefficient for the test shows a moderate positive correlation between data of heartbeat from Kinect™ and from the pulse oximeter. The p-value is a number between 0 and 1 that determines whether the correlation between variables is significant. A p-value (as calculated for the still test) of 0.30 indicates that the risk of concluding that a correlation exists—when, actually, no correlation exists—is about 30%. [33].

For each tester the average heart rate (HR) calculated is also reported in Figure 7, considering the device used and the type of the test performed. The table well summarize the comparison of the mean heart rate values obtained from Kinect™ and from pulse oximeter, according with the relative percentage error calculation.

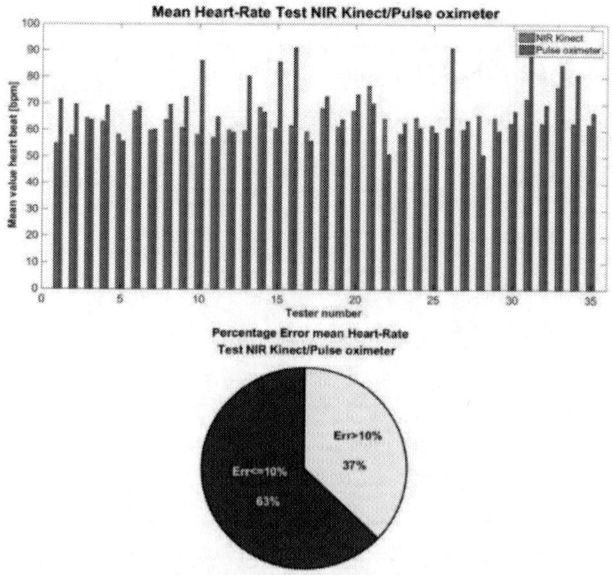

Figure. 7. Results of (HR) average of different tests and relative error.

By considering these three factors, i.e., value of correlation coefficient (R), the p-value and the relative errors (acceptable within 10%), it is possible to say that, the values of the heart rate calculated with this novel solution are comparable with the values gathered by the medical device only during the still tests. Moreover, the obtained values are also comparable with the previously acquired data and analyzed through RGB channels of the Kinect™.

VII. DISCUSSION

As discussed above, it is possible to consider the system implemented as a valid system for gathering the real-time heart rate values in static position, even when light conditions are not optimal. While considering the pulse oximeter as a reliable system, the device used has inherent accuracy ±2%. For these reasons, part of the deviation between the values gathered by the Kinect™ sensor and the GIMA oximeter should be related to a non-correct use of the oximeter.

Finally, not significant variations of the results are due to gender, age and fitness status of the testers.

VIII. CONCLUSION

This work describes the implementation and the tests of a novel methodology for evaluating the heart rhythm acting at medium distance (1 m), by analysing the NIR stream. The performance of the proposed method (applied in real-time) is tested in adverse situations, such as in the dim light condition. The study starts showing the real-time processing of the video acquired by the Kinect™ built-in NIR camera. The procedure begins with the automatically choice of the ROI with a strong passage of blood modulation and with the reduction of the background noise with a band-pass filter. Then, it continues with the analysis the signals coming from the IR channel of camera and it finishes by creating an ad-hoc algorithm for accurate heart rate detection using FFT.

The system and the algorithm implemented are validated by 35 participants sitting in front of the sensor at approximately 1 meter.

As described in the results, the study has shown a quite good reliability in detection of heartbeat at distance and in real-time, when the subject is in a static position in front of the sensor.

As a future development, it could be considered the possibility of applying this heart rate detection solution using infrared sensor, in situations where it is difficult to wear sensors for a long period of time (e.g., driving, neonatal department, etc.). Generally this type of monitoring can be useful in all the situations in which acquiring remote vital parameters is easier than wearing medical devices.

After the results obtained with a sufficiently reasonable number of testers, as a future work, it is designed to continue the study with large-scale testing to validate and perform the entire algorithm in a robust manner.

ACKNOWLEDGMENT

This work was supported by the European Union through the my-AHA project (H2020 - PHC 21 – 2015, grant agreement no. 689592).

REFERENCES

[1] I. Bosi, C. Cogerino, and M. Bazzani, "Real-time monitoring of heart rate by processing of Microsoft Kinect™ 2.0 generated streams." Computer and Energy Science (SpliTech), International Multidisciplinary Conference on. IEEE, 2016.

[2] R.Tranfaglia, U. Bracale, and M. Bracale, "E-Health systems for the continuity of care from the hospital to the home care."

[3] F. Han, B. Reily, W. Hoff, and H. Zhang, "Space-time representation of people based on 3D skeletal data: A review". Computer Vision and Image Understanding, 158, 85-105, 2017.

[4] X. Zou, J. Kittler, and K. Messer, "Illumination invariant face recognition: A survey." Biometrics: Theory, Applications, and Systems, 2007. BTAS 2007. First IEEE International Conference on. IEEE, 2007.

[5] S. Z. Li, R. Chu, S. Liao, and L. Zhang, "Illumination invariant face recognition using near-infrared images." IEEE Transactions on pattern analysis and machine intelligence 29.4 (2007).

[6] Fong, K. KaYan, "IR-Depth Face Detection and Lip Localization Using Kinect V2". Diss. California Polytechnic State University, San Luis Obispo, 2015.

[7] S. Cook, M. Togni, M. C. Schaub, P. Wenaweser, and O. M. Hess, "High heart rate: a cardiovascular risk factor?." European heart journal 27.20 (2006): 2387-2393.

[8] I. Korhonen, J. Parkka, and M. Van Gils, "Health monitoring in the home of the future." IEEE Engineering in medicine and biology magazine 22.3 (2003): 66-73.

[9] S. Kwon, H. Kim, and K. S. Park, "Validation of heart rate extraction using video imaging on a built-in camera system of a smartphone." Engineering in Medicine and Biology Society (EMBC), 2012 Annual International Conference of the IEEE. IEEE, 2012.

[10] M. Lewandowska, J. Rumiński, T. Kocejko, and J. Nowak, "Measuring pulse rate with a webcam—a non-contact method for evaluating cardiac activity." Computer Science and Information Systems (FedCSIS), 2011 Federated Conference on. IEEE, 2011.

[11] M. Garbey, N. Sun, A. Merla, and I. Pavlidis, "Contact-free measurement of cardiac pulse based on the analysis of thermal imagery." IEEE Transactions on Biomedical Engineering 54.8 (2007): 1418-1426.

[12] I. Pavlidis, J. Dowdall, N. Sun, C. Puri, J. Fei, and M. Garbey, "Interacting with human physiology." Computer Vision and Image Understanding 108.1 (2007): 150-170.

[13] J. Allen, "Photoplethysmography and its application in clinical physiological measurement." Physiological measurement 28.3 (2007): R1.

[14] A. Lindqvist and M. Lindelow, "Remote Heart Rate Extraction from Near Infrared Videos."

[15] L. J. Mengelkoch, D. Martin, and J. Lawler, "A review of the principles of pulse oximetry and accuracy of pulse oximeter estimates during exercise." Physical therapy 74.1 (1994): 40-49.

[16] S. Prahl, "Molar extinction coefficients of oxy and deoxyhemoglobin." URL:http://omlc.org/spectra/hemoglobin/ (2017).

[17] W. Verkruysse, L. O. Svaasand, and J. S. Nelson, "Remote plethysmographic imaging using ambient light." Optics express 16.26 (2008): 21434-21445.

[18] M. Z. Poh, D. J. McDuff, and R. W. Picard. "Non-contact, automated cardiac pulse measurements using video imaging and blind source separation." Optics express 18.10 (2010): 10762-10774.

[19] C. Takano and Y. Ohta, "Heart rate measurement based on a time-lapse image." Medical engineering & physics 29.8 (2007): 853-857.

[20] L. Wei, Y. Tian, Y. Wang, T. Ebrahimi, and T. Huang, "Automatic webcam-based human heart rate measurements using laplacian eigenmap." Asian Conference on Computer Vision. Springer Berlin Heidelberg, 2012.

[21] D. McDuff, S. Gontarek, and R. W. Picard, "Improvements in remote cardiopulmonary measurement using a five band digital camera." IEEE Transactions on Biomedical Engineering 61.10 (2014): 2593-2601.

[22] D. Haas, S. Phommahavong, J. Yu, S. Krüger-Ziolek, K. Möller, and J. Kretschmer, "Kinect based physiotherapy system for home use." Current Directions in Biomedical Engineering 1.1 (2015): 180-183".

[23] N. Bernacchia, L. Scalise, L. Casacanditella, I. Ercoli, P. Marchionni, and E. P. & Tomasini, "Non contact measurement of heart and respiration rates based on Kinect™." Medical Measurements and Applications (MeMeA), 2014 IEEE International Symposium on. IEEE, 2014.

[24] T. Smilkstein, M. Buenrostro, A. Kenyon, M. Lienemann, and G. Larson, "Heart rate monitoring using Kinect and color amplification." Healthcare Innovation Conference (HIC), 2014 IEEE. IEEE, 2014.

[25] A. C. Burton, "The range and variability of the blood flow in the human fingers and the vasomotor regulation of body temperature." American Journal of Physiology--Legacy Content 127.3 (1939): 437-453.

[26] W. Zeng, Q. Zhang, Y. Zhou, G. Xu, and G. Liang, "Infrared video based non-invasive heart rate measurement." Robotics and Biomimetics (ROBIO), 2015 IEEE International Conference on. IEEE, 2015.

[27] A. Procházka, M. Schätz, O. Vyšata, and M. Vališ, "Microsoft Kinect Visual and Depth Sensors for Breathing and Heart Rate Analysis." Sensors 16.7 (2016): 996.

[28] A. V. J. Challoner, "Photoelectric plethysmography for estimating cutaneous blood flow." Non-invasive physiological measurements 1 (1979): 125-151.

[29] [Online] Avaible: http://www.livescience.com/42081-normal-heart-rate.html (2017).

[30] [Online] Avaible: http://www.gimaitaly.com/default.asp (2017).

[31] A. Shagholi, M. Charmi, and H. Rakhshan, "The effect of the distance from the webcam in heart rate estimation from face video images." Pattern Recognition and Image Analysis (IPRIA), 2015 2nd International Conference on. IEEE, 2015.

[32] D. Pagliari and L. Pinto, "Calibration of kinect for xbox one and comparison between the two generations of Microsoft sensors." Sensors 15.11 (2015): 27569-27589.

[33] N. Fenton and M. Neil, Risk assessment and decision analysis with Bayesian networks. Crc Press, 2012.

Supporting Active and Healthy Aging - An Assistive Process Improvement Approach

Gerhard Chroust
Johannes Kepler University Linz
Email: gerhard.chroust@jku.at
Georg Aumayr
Johanniter Oesterreich Ausbildung und Forschung gemeinnuetzige GmbH
Email: georg.aumayr@johanniter.at

***Abstract*—Active and Healthy Aging (AHA) is one of the growing concerns and aims of a sustainable society and of the European Union. In many business and industrial enterprises, the adoption of a process view and the analysis of the processes to be performed has brought about numerous advantages, ranging from clarity and understandability to increased efficiency due to assessment and measurements of quality and capability. In this paper, we apply the process view concepts to the processes needed for Assisted Healthy Aging. The necessary activities are described on an abstract level (i.e., as activity types) and organized in a Process Model. Individual processes are derived (instantiated) from the AHA-model to be enacted by the aging persons, the Seniors, utilizing the human and technical support structure. We discuss the application of the concept of process view in the AHA-environment, especially pointing out the difference from classical business/industrial processes. A discussion about the possibilities to assess the quality of AHA-processes and their support by a Model Interpreter closes the paper.**

Keywords*–*Seniors; Process View; Process management; Maturity; Capability; Assessment

I. INTRODUCTION

Active and Healthy Aging (AHA) is one of the growing concerns and aims of a sustainable society and the central theme of the EU Project My-AHA [1]. Supporting Active and Healthy Aging is an ethical, an economic and finally also an organizational issue, especially due to the demographic changes in the Western World. Most Seniors will become involved in active and/or passive roles in activities related to AHA, if they like it or not. Usually, support is needed to compensate for lack of Seniors' sufficient capability to perform simple or complex necessary processes on one's own. This deficit in capability has to be overcome by a human support environment (consisting of persons from many different disciplines: family, doctors, nurses, service personal, helpers, etc.) and the technological support system (consisting of gadgets, tools, computers, robots, etc.). Automation will be a key factor in providing an effective and also economic support.

Based on the advantages and the success of the process view in industry ("Industry 4.0"), i.e., an increased autonomous intercommunication behavior of multiple machines, we suggest adopting a process view of supporting AHA. This will be a good basis for including technological means and tools. We believe that applying a process management approach can help to improve the quality, efficiency and understandability of AHA-projects. We will use the terminology and concepts of system development processes (e.g., ISO/IEC (International Organization for Standardization / International Electrotechnical Commission) 12207 [2] and ISO/IEC 15288 [3]) for describing the AHA-support processes, their interfaces and the necessary requirements. Quality assessment will be based on the ISO/IEC 33000 family of standards [4].

In this adoption process, we have to be aware that an obvious key difference is that the 'objects' of software processes are innate artefacts and not living beings, human Seniors. This will impose strong implications and limits with respect to aspects of humanity, morality, ethics, and risks.

The paper will be structured as follows: In Section II, we will describe the basic concepts and terminology of a process view, i.e., the structure of processes with activities and tasks and their interrelations and the Process Models. While this discussion is applicable essentially to all processes we will specifically discuss the requirements, challenges, and differences introduced by considerations of AHA, especially in comparison with 'pure' technical processes in Section III. In Section IV, we will again be inspired by software engineering with respect to discussing means to measure, control and even improve the quality of AHA-processes. At last, Section V will be devoted to the technological support to enact, assess, control, and measure the maturity of the AHA-processes leading to concepts for an AHA-Process Interpreter.

Statements and observations specific to AHA will be emphasized by printing them in italic and preceding them by "AHA:".

II. THE PROCESS VIEW

A. Activities and Tasks

The process view decomposes a complex undertaking into a set of processes, activities and tasks, which interact and exchange information and work products ("inputs" and "outputs"). The Software Engineering Standard ISO/IEC 12207:2017 [2] defines:

- process : set of interrelated or interacting activities that transforms inputs into outputs
- task : a requirement, recommendation, or permissible action, intended to contribute to the achievement of one

or more outcomes of a process. (In the management literature a task is often considered an uninterruptible unit of doing to be performed in one go.)

- activity : a set of cohesive tasks of a process. Despite the fact that the above distinctions are important for the structuring of Process Models, we will in most cases simply speak of 'activities', encompassing also tasks and sometimes also processes.

The division of an activity into different tasks (the granularity) will depend on the nature of a task and also on the capability/knowledge of the performing person [5][6]. A Process Model designer must strike a good balance between too coarse a granularity (leaving to much open and some users helpless) and too fine a granularity (boring some users with unnecessary and/or' obvious' details of tasks).

AHA: *This issue will receive special attention in this paper (see Section III). Activities can be assigned to be performed by the Senior himself/herself, by various helpers from different professions and machines (computers) of diverse capability and diversity. One consequence is that the same support activity task has to be divided differently depending on the capability of the individual Senior.*

B. What is a Process Model?

A Process Model defines and documents the activities, their contents, their meaning, and their interaction (input and output) with other activities. For Software Engineering, the key documents are ISO/IEC 12207 [2] and ISO/IEC 15288 [3].

The Process Model abstracts from idiosyncrasies of a single process and describes the process 'in general', independent of the enacting person or the object of the activity. It describes in an abstracted form all necessary activities (e.g., 'evaluate health status' or 'perform operation') and their logical dependencies (e.g., 'measure blood pressure' before 'perform operation') and the necessary work products (e.g., 'blood pressure values', 'description of previous treatments') to be produced and used by these activities. When modelling a process, all semantically equivalent activities are abstracted into one "activity type" [7], e.g., measuring blood pressure in the morning, the afternoon and the next day are abstracted to one activity type 'measure blood pressure' (Figure 1). Similarly, the work products are abstracted into "work product types", e.g., to a work product type "blood pressure".

The logical dependencies between activities are also expressed on the 'type'-level and have to be applied for the individual activities (instances). This leaves still considerable freedom to "navigate", i.e., to choose the next task [9], see Figure 2. A Process Model contains in abstracted form the experiences of many preceding processes combined with theoretical considerations and desirable improvements. By updating the Process Model, newer experiences and best practices can also be added to it. Different methods and strategies will distinguish themselves, both in the activities and work products, but especially in the sequence the various activities are to be performed in.

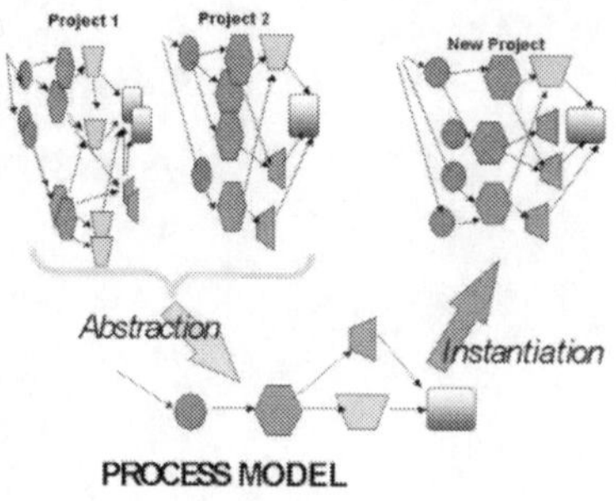

Figure 1. Process Abstraction and Instantiation [8].

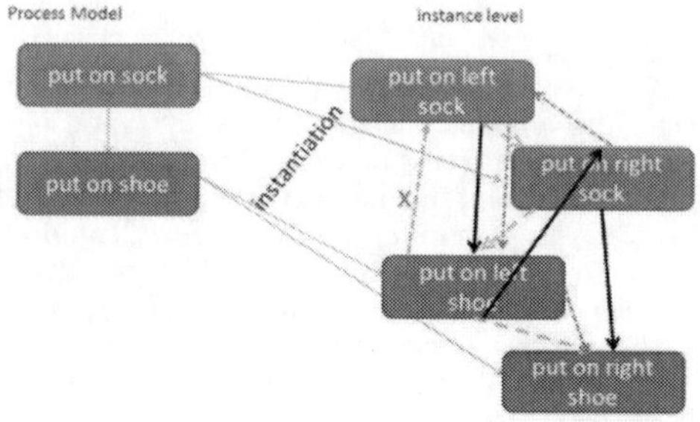

Figure 2. Instances of activity-types and work-product-types for AHA.

Figure 3 shows the extended meta-model of a software Process Model, also showing additional components: tools, roles, input/output relations, and structural information [9].

C. Advantages of the Process View

Key advantages of a formal Process Model are [9][10] :

- from implicit to explicit definition : A formally described Process Model can be recorded, standardized, transmitted to others, stored and taught, thus converting implicit knowledge into explicit knowledge [11].
- Storing Best Practices : It also acts as a repository for new best practices, thus preserving experience, but also allows audits and recording of inadequacies. One can also identify essential or usefully subprocess ex-post [6].
- Standardization : It provides standardization across different persons, projects and applications. This is of special value for the cooperation of heterogeneous teams.
- Quality assessment : The process can ex-post be evaluated, improved [12], its capability and maturity assessed (e.g., by the ISO/IEC 33000 family [4]. For details see Section IV.
- Audits, Tracing and Recording of Resources : Computer support allows the automatic recording of enacted activities and accounting of used resource (personnel, volunteers, operational material, etc.)
- Computer Support : A formally described Process Model can be supported by a Process Interpreter, see Section V.

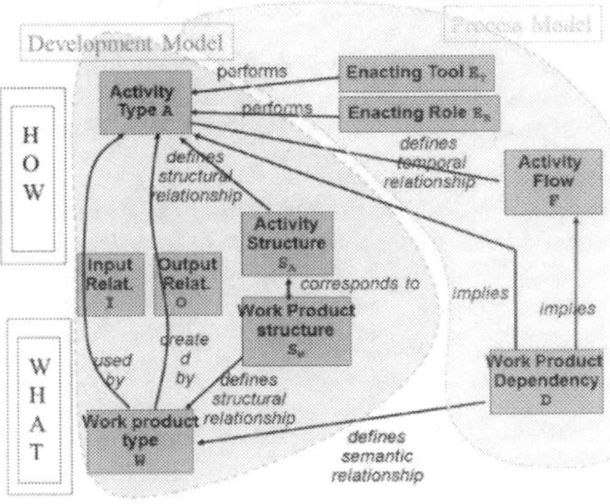

Figure 3. A Process meta-model.

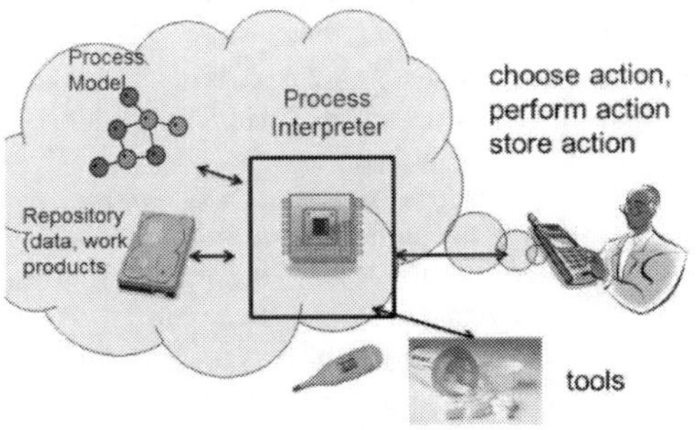

Figure 4. Interfaces for AHA.

D. Enacting a Process Model

When performing a project (or actually any activity based on the Process Model (Figure 3)) the model has to be 'enacted'. An appropriate 'Interpreter' of the Process Model (Figure 4), be it a human or a computer programs has numerous different activities to perform.

- Instantiation and administration of activity types : Instances of activity types must be created, shown to the user, worked on by the user, and their status remembered (planned, started, finished, under rework, etc.). Access to the needed inputs must be provided, outputs identified. AHA: *In many cases a Senior has to initiate and/or perform specific activities. The Process Interpreter can ask the Senior to do so. It is difficult to check whether the actions have been performed, see Section III-B.*
- Instantiation and administration of work products : All work products (documents or pointers to external artefacts) must be created (are 'replicated'), i.e., instantiated as often as necessary (Figure 2)), administered and related to the appropriate activities.
- Navigation : The enactment of an activity (an instance) must honour restrictions and dependencies within and between all other activities (e.g., sequence constraints between activities, common start or end of activities, exclusion of parallelism between them, etc.).

  The sequence in which activities are to be performed (the 'navigation information') is partially defined in the Process Model. The Model (as a construct on the 'type' level) leaves considerable freedom.
  AHA: *For example, a Process Model for a Senior might contain two activity types "put on socks" and "put on shoes" (see Figure 2). Actually, each of these two activity types identifies two activities (one for the right and one for the left foot) and thus would result in 8 different activity sequences.*
- Pre-emption and Resumption : Sometimes processes have to be urgently interrupted in order to assign resources to other activities, typically for emergencies.
  AHA: *An unexpected heavy bleeding has to be handled immediately, probably pre-empting another activity. After the emergency has been taken care of it is often difficult to decide how to handle the interrupted activity (start anew, continue at point of interrupt, abandon the rest of the activity). In all cases the Process Model Interpreter has to be informed and the necessary status set.*

III. System Development and Supporting AHA

In this section, we will expand on the use of the Process View in AHA and use the experience and know-how from Software Engineering. See also a similar comparison between Software Engineering and Disaster-Management in [13].

A. AHA as a Collection of Processes

The processes performed in AHA are in many aspects similar to systems engineering. A Senior himself/herself is a very complex system. The processes, which try to improve his/her status and/or situation must - as consequence - also be very complex, as the Law of Requisite Variety postulates [14]. Support for Seniors by humans and machines (including computers) must enact a large variety of support processes.

Health care processes diverge in their properties in several ways from the classical systems engineering processes. The reason lies in the different focus of these two types of processes: the 'objects' of AHA are living humans with their will, personality and idiosyncrasies while the objects of systems engineering processes are usually inert software objects. Humans are flexible, variable, sometime irrational, and provided with a free will, with moods and variations. This has to be considered when discussing the various components of the AHA-process. We restrict ourselves to My-AHA, i.e., supporting individuals in living through their aging process in an acceptable and healthy status.

All activities must be designed with strong consideration of human factors with respect to all involved persons [15][16]. This includes observation of cultural differences between ethnic groups [15] with respect to contents, form and differences as far as believing in and interpretation of warnings and instructions and the willingness to obey them [17].

B. Challenges in AHA

Considerable differences exist between the situation in a system engineering situation as compared to a AHA-situation (see also [13]) . Many of them challenge our creativity.

- Completion Control : In a 'regular' system development project guided by a Process Model each task or activity has at least one outcome in tangible form (a piece of document, finished intermediate product etc.), which is expected (and needed) by a successive task. In most cases a different person will be in charge of the successive task and therefore will 'ask for' the result - quality might be lacking, but a document is expected.
  AHA: *In most cases this is not true. Most 'outputs' of an AHA-process are triggers for another activity or acknowledgements ('take medicine XYZ' , 'morning gymnastics done', ...). In the Process Model only surrogates for these 'outputs' are created. Whether the Senior has cleaned his/her teeth, or drank enough liquid is very difficult to control. The simple solution that the Senior has to acknowledge the completion of the task is of little use since a Senior can (and often will) easily fake the acknowledgement.*
  Two approaches are promising:
  Internet of Things: Utilizing the concept of the Internet of Things one can equip essential gadgets (e.g., the tooth brush or the jug) with active sensors and thus recognize the completion of an activity (at least to a certain extent). However, experience also tells us, that many Seniors dislike this type of control and will be very creative in circumventing and faking completion (e.g., watering the flowers instead of drinking, etc.)
  Gamification: A more promising approach seems to be the concept of Gamification [18]: the recognized successful completion of an activity will produce of visible 'achievement mark' on a prominently visible display. Psychologically this is more promising, but can only be used in certain environments.
- Misplacing and Searching : In a Software Engineering Environment the Process Interpreter stores, administrates and makes available the work product.
  AHA: *Seniors are generally plagued by misplacing things and having problems finding them later. To a certain extent an Internet of Things approach could help, one would need to equip all important object with sensors. In this case the system could indicate where to find the necessary objects or documents*
- Forgetfulness : Depending on the specifics of the chosen Project Interpreter, users will be reminded of pending activities and deadlines
  AHA: *Seniors tend to become forgetful. A Process Interpreter can bridge and alleviate much of this forgetfulness by registering activities and dates to remind the Senior.*
- Time variability : While mechanical systems show a reasonable predictability and stability this is not true especially of Seniors.
  AHA: *This means that one cannot make reliable assumptions about the physical or mental status of a Senior. It can change any time. Therefor the AHA-processes must be carefully double checking the situation etc.*
- Lack of full knowledge of the history : In Software Engineering lots of the information is not provided explicitly but hidden in the code and documentation (as far as trustworthy).
  AHA: *Similarly historical data documented about a Senior is full of hidden facts, omissions, mistakes, misunderstanding and unknowns - often due to privacy considerations. Treatment has to take this into account, especially if certain activities are performed by computers.*
- Pre-emption of activities : One often has to interrupt an activity in favour of performing another one.
  AHA: *A well-ordered enactment of a Process Model is often not possible. Activities have to be started suddenly due to an emergency (e.g., "severe coughs"). Other activities have to be interrupted and later taken up at the point of interrupt, or repeated.*
- Pressure of Time and Success : The production of software seems to be notoriously under performance pressure.
  AHA: *For Seniors the time very often 'runs away'. Hazards appear suddenly and have to be taken care of immediately. Life-saving activities often have a very narrow time window to be successful.*
- Stress and psychological pressure : Helpers are often under stress due to the responsibility in view of unclear situations [19][20].
  AHA: *This problem often is more pronounced due to the close relations between Seniors and personnel.*
- Systemic problems : Health problems are usually the result of several interacting causes.
  AHA: *Illnesses and hazards often have highly interrelated causes and reciprocal influences, often showing new symptoms (emergence [21]) like allergic reactions against some medicine. Domino-effects of existing illnesses, side effects of medication need to be considered*
- Cultural "blockages" and taboos : When treating Seniors, social taboos and conventions have to be kept in mind (no blood transfusion for Jehovah's Witnesses, no male personal for Muslim women, etc.).
  AHA: *Seniors often have their own mind, long established peculiarities and often no understanding for the necessities of treatment. They also often object to being 'led' by a 'machine' despite the lack the capability to manage themselves.*

IV. CAPABILITY ASSESSMENT OF THE AHA-PROCESSES

One of the key advantages of defining and following a Process Model is the possibility to assess the capability of the performing organization: to what extent can the organization provide the services and products intended to be provided based on a standardized and accepted Process Model (cf. [4])?

In the 1980s, the Software Process Program was founded at the Software Engineering Institute (SEI) at Carnegie Mellon

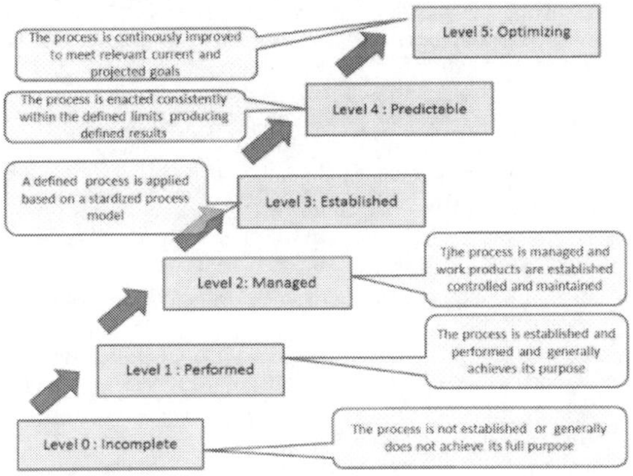

Figure 5. Levels of Process Capability (ISO/IEC 33000 [4]).

University under the leadership of Watts Humphrey. This program resulted in the development of the Capability Maturity Model [22][23][24]. A prerequisite is a comprehensive, generally agreed-upon Process Model containing all the key processes needed for software engineering. [2] identifies some 40 individual processes. These processes are rather comprehensive with many individual tasks. Each process is evaluated to what extent it is performed by the organization (N..not performed, P..partially performed, L..largely performed, F..fully performed). This yields a profile as shown in Figure 6. This profile can be compared to other Process Models, to an industry average and also compared with the profile needed for the specific project.

AHA: *A Senior who is able to walk alone, does not need certain processes irrespective of their performance level.*

In order to characterise a complete enterprise (be it a software house or - in our case - a senior home) its overall maturity is of high relevance for future planning and can be measured. Figure 5 is the basis for assessing an enterprise. In software engineering the levels (see Figure 5) run from incomplete (where the process is mostly unsuccessful) up to 'improving' (where the process is continually adapted to new needs and challenges). In a nutshell the maturity of an enterprise to produce good software can be assessed and measured using a two dimensional graph (capability versus individual relevant processes), see Figure 6. The Assessment can also be used for the improvement of the processes [10][12].

AHA: *One needs a comprehensive, agreed-upon Project Model and historical records of what has worked in the past. Then one can identify deficiencies in the Process Model, compatibilities and differences of various processes (since not all Seniors need all processes), and identify the improvement potential.*

V. A Process Interpreter

Computer support is the key for efficiency and effectiveness of the AHA-processes. It has to show two different faces:

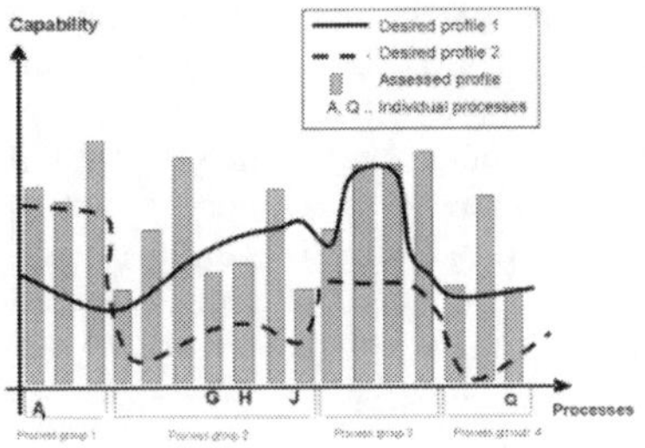

Figure 6. Comparing different profiles.

One is directed to the Senior, the aging person. It has to be empathic, helpful and tries to explain/show the situation in a way a Senior can understand. The other one is technological and effective and provides a stable, effective infrastructure for the other interface.

A. User Interface

The system helps the user to enact the processes he/she is supposed or intended to perform. It also allows the user enter processes of his/her own (things to do, things not to forget and be reminded, deadlines...) Considering the challenges listed in Section III-B a Process Interpreter for AHA-purposes must fulfil several somewhat contradicting properties:

- strict : Certain activities must be performed exactly as prescribed, often even within a very narrow time window.
- tolerant/flexible : Some activities may be performed not at all or very loosely, depending on the specific situation, especially in view of the varying psychical and mental situation of a Senior.
- robust : The system must be robust against disturbances of various kinds (be it changes in the well-being of the Senior, computer failures, cultural differences, sudden unexpected changes in the behavior or the situation, ...)
- agile : Handling of Seniors must be highly flexible (especially due to inflexibilities, which come with old age.)
- user-friendly : The interfaces must be easy to understand and show "good behavior with the sensitivity of an intuitive, courteous butler" [25]. They should take into account the personal and cultural differences as defined in [26]
- unobtrusive and non-stigmatic : The Senior must feel confident, that his/her use of the assisting system is accepted by his/her peers and neighbours without negative feelings.

B. The Role of Tools, Machines and Robots

In many ways, robots can even replace humans. For this to happen, it is necessary to have a clear, unambiguous and formal description of the processes to be performed (the Process Model), plus a characteristic of machine environments. Thus it is possible to allocate processes to persons or machine, whatever is the better choice, also for the Senior. Robots can relieve helpers from chores, which do not really require human understanding and human empathy versus the Seniors. A Process Interpreter (Figure 3) is an ideal tool and infrastructure to automatically include the access to tools into the AHA-processes.

VI. Conclusion and Future Work

Adopting a process view for supporting Assisted Healthy Aging (AHA), like in other business and industrial areas, promises an improvement in clarity, understanding, and efficiency: The necessary processes are defined and documented in a Process Model, which is the basis for automatically guiding the execution of the individual processes by a so-called Process Interpreter. It helps all stakeholders, Seniors, human support personnel to follow the processes and use technical support. This approach also allows a better control of the execution of these processes and assess the quality and capability of the defined processes. Implementing such a scenario requires a deep understanding of the behavior, the limitations and idiosyncrasies of Seniors.

Obviously, the work described here is only a beginning. More work has to be done to understand the requirements of Seniors with different social, cultural and economic background. This strongly affects the 'look and feel' of interfaces, especially with respect to ease of use and empathy. We hope that our contribution will trigger further research and useful result for Assisted Healthy Aging of Seniors.

Acknowledgment

This the research behind this paper was supported by the EU Horizon-2020 project No 689592 My-AHA: all /stadarMy Active and Healthy Aging, 2016-2019.

References

[1] Univ. Torino(ed.), "My-aha - my active and healthy ageing," http://www.activeageing.unito.it/home, [retrieved: May, 2017], 2016.

[2] ISO/IEC, "ISO/IEC cd 12207.4 Systems and Software engineering - Software life cycle processes," Internat. Org. for Standarization, ISO, Tech. Rep., 2016.

[3] ——, "ISO/IEC 15288:2006: Systems Engineering - System Life Cycle Processes," Internat. Org. for Standarization, ISO/IEC JTC 1/SC 7/WG 7 (Jan 2006), Tech. Rep., 2006.

[4] ——, "ISO/IEC 33001:2015 : Information technology – process assessment – concepts and terminology," International Organisation for Standarization, Tech. Rep., 2015.

[5] F. Milani, M. Dumas, R. Matulevicius, N. Ahmed, and S. Kasela, "Criteria and heuristics for business process model decomposition," Bus Inf Syst Eng, vol. 58 (2016), no. 1, 2016, pp. 1–17.

[6] W. van der Alst and S. Dustdar, "Process mining put into context," IEEE Internet Computing, March 2012, pp. 82–87.

[7] G. Chroust and G. Aumayr, "Process models for disaster management - standardization and assessment," in EMCSR 2014 - book of Abstracts, W. Hofkirchner and S. Blachfellner, Eds. BCSSS 2014, p. 5.

[8] G. Chroust, N. Sturm, M. Roth, and P. Ziehesberger, "Regional disasters and systemic reactions," in ISSS 2011 and ISKSS 2011: All Together Now: Working across Disciplines, J. Wilby, Ed. (CDROM) Int. Systems Science Society, UK, 2011, p. 15 (paper no 1631).

[9] G. Chroust, "Software process models: Structure and challenges," in Feng, Y. and Notkin, D. and Gaudel, M.C.(ed.): Software: Theory and Practice - Proceedings, IFIP Congress 2000, Aug. 2000, Beijing. Kluwer, 2000, pp. 279–286.

[10] SPIRE Project Team, The SPIRE Handbook - Better, Faster, Cheaper - Software Development in Small Organisations. Centre of Software Engineering Ltd, Dublin 9, Ireland, 1998.

[11] I. Nonaka and H. Takeuchi, The Knowledge Creating Company. Oxford University Press, New York 1995.

[12] W. van der Alst, M. La Rosa, and F. M. Santoro, "Business process management - don't forget to improve the process!" Bus Inf Syst Eng, vol 58 (2016), no. 1, 2016, pp. 1–6.

[13] G. Chroust, G. Aumayr, G. Haider, R. Randus, and A. Thür, "Prozessmanagement im Katastropheneinsatz: agil, strikt, tolerant und robust? (Process management in disaster management: agile, strict, tolerant and robust?)," in Projektmanagement und Vorgehensmodelle 2016 - Arbeiten in hybriden Projekten: Das Sowohl-als-auch von Stabilität und Dynamik, M. Engstler, M. Fazal-Baqaie, E. Hanser, O. Linssen, M. Mikusz, and A. Volland, Eds. Lecture Notes in Informatics (LNI), vol P-263, Gesellschaft für Informatik, Bonn 2016, pp. 93–107.

[14] W. Ashby, "Requisite variety and its implications for the control of complex systems," Cybernetica 1:2, p. 83-99. (available at http://pcp.vub.ac.be/Books/AshbyReqVar.pdf) [retrieved: May 2017], 1958, pp. 83–99.

[15] D. McEntire, Disaster Response and Recovery: Strategies and Tactics for Resilience. Wiley, USA 2007.

[16] ISO, "ISO 22320:2011, Societal security – emergency management – requirements for incident response," International Organization for Standardization, 2011, Tech. Rep., 2011.

[17] K. Haddow and G. Haddow, Disaster Communications in a Changing Media World. Butterworth-Heinemann Homeland Security, kindle-book, 2008.

[18] S. Deterding, D. D., R. Khaled, and L. Nacke, "From game design elements to gamefulness: defining gamification," in Proceedings of the 15th International Academic MindTrek Conference: Envisioning Future Media Environments. ACM 2011, pp. 9–15.

[19] D. Duckworth, "Psychological problems arising from disaster work," Stress Medicine vol. 2 (1986), no. 4, 1986, pp. 315–323.

[20] Bundesamt f. Bevölkerungsschutz und Katastrophenhilfe, Psychosoziales Krisenmanagement in CBRN-Lagen / Psychosocial Crisis Management in CBRN Incidents. Bundesamt f. Bevölkerungsschutz und Katastrophenhilfe, Germany 2011.

[21] G. Chroust, "Feature interaction and emergent properties," in Feature Interactions: The Next Generation (Dagstuhl Seminar 14281), S. Sven Apel, J. M. Atlee, L. Baresi, and P. Zave, Eds. Dagstuhl Reports, vol. 4 (2014), no. 7, Schloss Dagstuhl–Leibniz-Zentrum fuer Informatik, 2014, pp. 15–16.

[22] W. Humphrey, Managing the Software Process. Addison-Wesley Reading Mass. 1989.

[23] ——, "A discipline for software engineering," SEI Series in SW Engineering, Addison Wesley, 1995.

[24] H. van Loon, Process Assessment and ISO/IEC 15504. Springer, New Aork 2004.

[25] C. Miller, Ed., Human-Computer Etiquette: Managing Expectations with Intentional Agents. Comm. ACM vol. 47 (2004), No. 4, 2004.

[26] G. Hofstede, G. J. Hofstede, and M. Minkov, Cultures and Organizations - Software of the Mind, 3rd edition. McGraw-Hill, NY 2010.

Development of an Intelligent Drinking System for the Prevention of Dehydration in Old Age

Elisabeth Haslinger-Baumann, Anneliese Lilgenau, Katharina Gugenberger
Department Nursing Science, FH Campus Wien
Vienna, Austria
e-mail: elisabeth.haslinger-baumann@fh-campuswien.ac.at, anneliese.lilgenau@fh-campuswien.ac.at, katharina.gugenberger@fh-campuswien.ac.at

Gernot Korak, Sebastian Geyer, Udo Unterweger, Stefan Tiefenbacher
Department Engineering, FH Campus Wien
Vienna, Austria
e-mail: gernot.korak@fh-campuswien.ac.at, udo.unterweger@fh-campuswien.ac.at, sebastian.geyer@fh-campuswien.ac.at, stefan.tiefenbacher@fh-campuswien.ac.at

Franz Werner
Department Health Sciences, FH Campus Wien
Vienna, Austria
e-mail: franz.werner@fh-campuswien.ac.at

Abstract— **This paper describes the user needs analysis for a system that supports the professional management of fluid balance in older people to prevent dehydration. Dehydration is a frequent age related issue that typically leads to a steep decrease in physical and / or mental performance. Severe cases are life threatening due to risks of circulatory collapse or loss of consciousness. Hence, the prevention of dehydration is of particular importance. For data gathering, social-scientific methods (individual interview, focus group interview, cultural probes and documentary research) were implemented. The survey involved primary end users (elderly, dependent people), secondary end users (informal and formal caregivers), experts from ethics and the analysis of care documentation from older users. The main results were derived from the data by using a thematic analysis and subsequent data fusion as well as consolidation concepts on result level. As a conclusion, aside of valuable system-specific recommendations, a concept for reminding and motivating could be designed and will be implemented.**

Keywords: Active and Assisting Living; health care and nursing; dehydration prevention; interdisciplinary research

I. INTRODUCTION

Ensuring a sufficient supply of fluids to the body is a major challenge for the elderly, or the caregiving family members or nursing staff in a mobile care setting. With increasing age, the water content of the body, as well as the feeling of thirst decreases significantly [1-3]. This makes elderly people particularly vulnerable to dehydration. The effects of dehydration are extremely serious. Impairment of consciousness, fatigue and weakness, dizziness, muscle cramps and headaches are possible symptoms. With old people even a minor water deficiency leads not only to a drop in salvia production with mouth dryness, but also to reduced urine production and dry skin, which, in turn, can easily break up or develop pressure sores. In case of an even greater water deficiency, an accelerated pulse, an increase in body temperature, dizziness, weakness, impairment of consciousness and a decrease in physical and mental performance occurs. The onset of disorientation, states of confusion, apathy and a life-threatening circulatory collapse with loss of consciousness are possible consequences [1]. In elderly people, other causes such as heart disease or dementia are erroneously suspected without considering an insufficient supply of fluid as a possible cause. The consequences can also be life-threatening in the case of unconsciousness, circulatory or renal failure. Frequently, hospital admission is required. According to a study conducted in two English hospitals, 6.5 and 22.5 of 1,000 hospitalizations are based on dehydration. The mortality rate of hospitalized elderly people with dehydration symptoms is 45-46% [2].

The prevention of dehydration is therefore particularly important in mobile as well as in stationary care. Particularly in mobile care, the estimation of the quantity of liquid intake can only be carried out inaccurately, as the often very dependent clients live alone at home and are not supervised continuously. This means that elderly people cannot be cared for adequately in mobile care.

The presented research was conducted within the experimental research project "DrinkSmart" (2016-2018), which has the main aim to support the autonomy of elderly people with and without chronic diseases in order to facilitate their living in their own environment. The project led by the University of Applied Sciences "FH Campus

Wien" was funded by the Austrian research promotion agency (FFG) and carried out in interdisciplinary cooperation with the software company "akquinet ristec", the plastic mug manufacturer "Schorm" and the home care provider "MIK-OG".

II. STATE OF THE ART

Technical solutions for adequate hydration are already being developed in this field. They are mainly advertised as lifestyle products and are aimed at a young IT-savvy user group. These include the "Pryme Vessyl [1]" and "hidratespark[2]" systems. Apart from the pure analysis of the drinking quantity, these systems also offer the analysis of the liquid inside the drinking cup. Further they provide an optical warning function when too little liquid was drunk. In addition, a connection with a smartphone app for iOS or Android is to be made via "Bluetooth low energy", which should enable the future entry of individual data of consumed fluid quantities and body data like weight and size combined with GPS function. Alternatively, a lid cap has been designed for a cup, which measures the amount of fluid drunk with different sensors. This information should be transferred to a PC.

All described products focus on the needs of a young target group, not on older, dependent people and care contexts. Specifically those systems were not designed to transfer data to an electronic care documentation system. Such systems are important to assure the quality of care and are typically used to document the health status of the patient and the activity of nurses. Both aspects are core concepts of the here presented approach.

III. METHOD

For the survey of user needs and the development of the intelligent drinking system with appropriate sensors in the drinking vessel, which is used to measure the daily liquid consumption, qualitative scientific methods were used. The needs assessment in the primary and secondary target group was conducted using different socio-scientific survey and evaluation methods: guideline-specific individual [4] and focus group interviews [4][5]. For all interviews and focus group interviews guides including the structure, timing and detailed open and closed questions were developed. The data was analysed according to Mayring [5]. Furthermore, the ethnographic method of "Cultural Probes" [6] was used to obtain detailed insight into the existing drinking habits of the target group. A documentation analysis [7] of the existing care documentation completed the survey. The methods were chosen based on the individual research questions. Focus groups and individual interviews were chosen based on the individual timing possibilities of the recruited participants. A wide mix of methods was chosen to become able to conduct cross-method triangulation [12] of results. Researcher triangulation was undertaken for further quality assurance.

[1] https://myvessyl.com/prymevessyl, last checked on 2017.5.10
[2] https://hidratespark.com, last checked on 2017.5.10

The data gathered showed clear signs of saturation, which was to be expected considering the large user base.

TABLE I. OVERVIEW ON DATA COLLECTION METHODS

Data collection methods implemented		
Data collection method	*User group*	*Number of users involved*
Literature research	-	-
Discussion and interviews with experts from ethics [4]	Ethics experts	2
Cultural probe studies [6]	Primary users	6
Single-user, semi-structured interviews [4]	All user groups	40
Focus-group interviews [4][5]	Secondary users	22 (in 4 groups)
Analysis of care documentation [7]	Older dependent users and formal caregivers	5 documentations

The development of the intelligent drinking system, which is based on the summarized user requirements and follows the product specifications, adheres to the user-centered design approach [8] combined with the phase model on product development according to Glende [9]. The implementation of the user studies with selected participants was accompanied by a process- and result-oriented evaluation approach [10][11] with regard to the technical and social-scientific aspect.

IV. RESULTS

The summary from interviews and cultural probes shows the following common aspects despite the heterogeneous user groups involved.

The material should be comfortable to touch and not breakable. A modular design is desirable, that is, the drinking cup should be adaptable to different end user requirements. Care dependency may be a fluctuating phenomenon, which means that in the case of an acute disease, independent drinking might only be ensured with devices on the cup itself, such as the handle, or the spout, which might not be necessary in the further course of the disease.

An important additional component is the design of reporting functions. With the help of acoustic and optical signals, reminder functions should be realized, which remind the user of drinking. At the same time, the cups should facilitate a motivating design or component for motivation as users often knowingly object drinking.

The system should provide an overview of the quantity of liquid that has been drunk. It is important that the signals issued by the system (e.g. to remind or motivate drinking) should not be irritating and the optical and functional design of the system should appeal to different senses. This was considered in particular regarding used colours, materials and the design of the user-system interaction.

The results of the cultural probes studies with a duration of one week each and involving a subset of the primary user group (n = 6), underline the complexity of existing drinking habits. For example, drinks were consumed in parallel from several vessels; several differently shaped vessels were preferred in the course of the day or "favourite cups" were used which cannot easily be replaced by a single new system. As a consequence, the planned drinking system is limited in practice regarding the accuracy of the measurement of the total amount of liquid intake during a day, due to the users' habits. Further due to ethical concerns we found a need for a system that does not force users to change previous habits through alarms.

The analysis of nursing documentation shows that with many clients the focus is on the description of the risk of dehydration in terms of symptoms and causes. On this basis nursing measures and resources are formulated for the nurses to carry out. The objective of this standardized approach is to mitigate the symptoms of dehydration, to eliminate the causes, if possible, and to strengthen the resources of the clients by direct and indirect measures.

Based on the results of the conducted user need analysis a non-functional mock-up was created within a rapid prototyping process using the generative production method of Selective Laser Sintering (SLS). Due to the consistent consideration of the user needs, a simple and handy mug with clearly visible and intuitive visual and acoustic signals could be developed and is depicted in figure 1.

Figure 1. Mock-up of the modular system based on the user needs analysis. Comprised of a cup (inside), a plastic cup holder with electronics compartment and a grip. Acoustic and optical motivational and reminder functions are not yet visible. (left design-study showing the motivational component, right 3D printed system).

The optical components were realized as a dynamically growing seedling with seven leaves. Depending on the daily volume drunk, the leafs light up simulating a growing plant. This gives users a definitive feedback on the drinking volume reached up to the time X. By holding the system, the current drinking quantity status is displayed; otherwise the cup does not produce any acoustic or optical output to minimize potential irritations during night-time. The liquid within the cup forms a second optical component. It can be illuminated with an LED and in this way acts as a reminder for the users. This visual reminder is displayed when, within a predetermined interval, no liquids have been consumed.

At the end of the research project in 2018, the crucial result will be a market-oriented prototype (hardware and server / application software) for a smart drinking system. For the design of the corresponding sensors in the drinking cup, the liquid intake is measured via the Drink Smart Mug and controlled by means of reminder signals (visual and acoustic) and notification functions (e.g. SMS / E-mail). By connecting to a computer-aided care documentation already used in nursing care companies, the collected data can be recorded and documented. The caregivers are thus informed promptly and can react accordingly in acute cases.

The system is going to be evaluated within a home care setting including around 20 users for the duration of 4 weeks. Data gathering will be undertaken by implementing questionnaires, diaries, individual interviews and participatory observation. This qualitative research approach is important taking the complexity of the system and early prototype phase into account. The used social-scientific methods focus on the users' perspective and the nursing result quality, including also a risk-assessment for technology aversion. Technical evaluation methods test the efficiency, ease of use and technical practicability.

V. CONCLUSION

The consistent user-oriented approach ensures that the needs of the users and their relatives, as well as their caregivers, are largely covered in the development of the intelligent drinking system. The use of the documentation analysis method, as well as several different survey methods for the primary and secondary target groups, and the Cultural Probes method form a comprehensive data material, which clearly identifies the needs of the user groups by data fusion and structuring and greatly facilitated the design of the drinking system.

In the current technical implementation phase, the requirements generated from the results have been implemented as far as technically possible, and the resulting first prototypes (mock ups) have been subjected to further testing by the clients.

Thus the drinking system can be used as a supplementary aid in the future to prevent dehydration in old age and thereby it can be used in a low-threshold manner as a contribution to the management of chronic diseases. Consequently, elderly people are supported to live autonomously in their own homes, and help by caregivers can be targeted.

ACKNOWLEDGMENT

This research is sponsored by the Austrian research promotion agency (FFG) under grant number 856166. Projectpartners are: MIK-OG (Austria), Schorm (Austria) and acquinet ristec (Germany).

REFERENCES

[1] Bigorio, "Hydration in der palliativen Betreuung". Consent on best practices for palliative care in Swizerland, 2009. [Online]. Available from: http://www.palliative.ch/de/fachbereich/arbeitsgruppen-standards/best-practice 2017.05.10.

[2] B. Hodgkinson, D. Evans, and J. Wood, "Maintaining oral hydration in older adults: A systematic review." International

Journal of Nursing Practice, pp.19–28, 2003, doi: 10.1046/j.1440-172X.2003.00425.x.

[3] D. Bunn, F. Jimoh, S. H. Wilsher, and L. Hooper, "Increasing Fluid Intake and Reducing Dehydration Risk in Older People Living in Long-Term Care: A Systematic Review.", Journal of the American Medical Directors Association, vol.16, pp. 101–113, 2015, doi: 10.1016/j.jamda.2014.10.016.

[4] R. Bohnsack, "Gruppendiskussion." in Qualitative Forschung, U. Flick, from E. Kardorff, and I. Steinke, Eds. Reinbek bei Hamburg: Rowohlt, pp. 369–384, 2009.

[5] P. Mayring, Qualitative Inhaltsanalyse, Beltz Verlag, Weinheim and Basel, 2010.

[6] W. Gaver, A. Boucher, S. Pennington, and B. Walker, "Cultural probes and the value of uncertainty." Interactions vol.11, 5, pp. 53-56, 2004, doi: 10.1145/1015530.1015555.

[7] A. Salheiser, "Natürliche Daten: Dokumente," from Methoden der empirischen Sozialforschung, N. Baur and J. Blasius, Eds. Wiesbaden: Springer VS, pp. 813–829, 2014.

[8] D. A. Norman, Emotional Design: Why we love (or hate) everyday things. New York: Basic Books, 2004.

[9] S. Glende, Entwicklung eines Konzepts zur nutzergerechten Produktentwicklung - mit Fokus auf die „Generation Plus". Genehmigte Dissertation, TU Berlin, Fakultät V – Verkehrs- und Maschinensysteme, Berlin, 2010. doi.org/10.14279/depositonce-2367

[10] G. Vitt, Pflegequalität ist messbar. Schlütersche Verlagsdatenbank, Hannover, 2002.

[11] A. Donabedian "The Definition of Quality and Approaches to Its Assessment, Explorations in Quality Assessment and Monitoring." vol.1, Health Administration Press, pp. 166ff, 1980.

[12] V. A. Thurmond, "The point of triangulation." Journal of nursing scholarship" pp. 253-258, 2001.

Evaluation of Architectural Backbone Technologies for WINNER DataLab A Project Focused Point of View

Sebastian Apel, Florian Hertrampf, and Steffen Späthe

Chair for Software Engineering
Friedrich Schiller University Jena
D-07745 Jena, Germany
Email: florian.hertrampf|sebastian.apel|steffen.spaethe@uni-jena.de

Abstract—**The WINNER DataLab aims to collect, evaluate and forecast load data used to optimise the first-hand consumption of locally generated energy within buildings, by rentee, as well as electric vehicles. Every actor within a residential area has to be considered, and integration into a centralised data stream process is necessary. As a non-hard real-time system, the WINNER DataLab has to solve enterprise application integration problems, looking at complex event processing and knowledge discovery in data. This paper targets to analyse possible architectural backbone technologies. Out of a wide range of potential technologies Node-Red, WSO2 CEP and Apache Camel are selected and compared. Those technologies with a diverse field of application are used to implement a comparable test setup. Furthermore, they are analysed through their characteristics of processing, execution, usability and simplicity. As measured, Node-RED, Apache Camel and WSO2 indicate stable and fast message processing, especially in the case of raising message throughput. Node-RED surprises with constant memory and CPU loads and seams to be exciting option in rapid prototyping.**

Keywords–System Architecture; Stream Processing; Message Routing; Complex Event Processing; Renewable Energy; Smart Grid.

I. Introduction

Research on the smart grid has become a well-known task over the last years. Our research project WINNER [15] aims to integrate electromobility, the energy consumption within residential areas and the local production of electricity by, e. g. photovoltaic systems. We do not look for electric vehicles (EVs) as consumers only. They are used via the carsharing approach so that it is possible to gain booking data. Knowing the start and stop times of rides we can schedule the charging or discharging process or create prognoses on it. Summarised EVs can contribute to the stability of the power grid and help to handle load variations and load peaks. If the EVs are not used within the next hours, you can take the electric energy from their batteries and supply it to the local power grid. Additionally, it is possible to decide when to charge the car based on available information like current energy production as well as energy market prices.

Therefore, three main tasks have to be considered and brought together within our so called WINNER DataLab (WDL). At first, we collect all the produced data and store them in a meaningful way. After that, potentials have to be found, e. g. correlating weather forecasts, electricity consumption, specific time information, and the usage characteristic of EVs to optimise external energy purchase for charging batteries. In the end, we have to optimise operation. So we could control accumulate electric energy locally or supply it to the grid. Maybe it is superior or necessary to get energy from another grid operator, e. g., in case of too less output of the local energy production.

The above-mentioned facts imply an information flow managed by data streams. These must be routed and checked for mistakes. Beyond various data sources have to be integrated, like Representational State Transfer (REST) interfaces based on Hypertext Transfer Protocol (HTTP) or mail services. Out of that, we have to integrate devices using the System, Mess- und Anlagentechnik (german solar energy equipment supplier) (SMA) protocol or other TCP-based protocols.

According to backbone technologies, we have to discuss the potentials of tools made for message routing and analysing within the WDL. We focus on event-based approaches and easy integration of external components. In the end, we ask for a tool that offers the possibility of routing messages and analysis of the contained data without dropping information. This publication summarises our decision process.

In Section II, related work about terms and projects related to our approach are discussed. Section III presents the level 0 view of our WDL, and the following Section IV lists the requirements we impose on this system. As a result of that, a short overview of possible tools is presented in Section V. Furthermore, three tools are used to implement a uniform task in Section VI and compare them in Section VII by using measurement values of latency, memory consumption and CPU load. Finally, we discuss the results in Section VIII.

II. Related Work

The WDL seems to be far away from traditional database management systems. The WDL should be usable as a platform for data scientists for mining knowledge as well as a platform to attach analyses for already known behaviours and relationships directly on data streams. Furthermore, the WDL should consume data from different kinds of systems as well as produce data to optimise the usage of those systems.

Connecting various types of applications by using their provided data and processes belongs to the term of enterprise application integration (EAI) [23, P. 3]. Within the area of application integration terms like message-oriented middleware (MOM) and service-oriented architecture (SOA), as well as enterprise service bus (ESB), describe how to challenge those use cases [17, S. 1][24]. As a traditional approach, MOM describes how to use asynchronous messages to decouple applications based on messaging systems [24]. SOA, on the other hand, represents an architectural concept where applications publish their precisely defined functionalities within reusable services [24]. Finally, ESB draws an open standard, which merges those ideas and defines a distributed architecture usable to integrate applications. The architecture itself describes calls and distribution of messages between integrated applications [24].

Within the scope of EAI, the enterprise integration patterns (EIPs) are the base of tools to solve integration problems. The EIPs describe a set of reusable patterns without a particular technology reference. Base concepts within these patterns are the usage of "routing" and "messages" [22].

Beside the application integration itself, activity tracking, sensor networks and analysing of market data is a central topic within the so-called complex event processing (CEP). CEP describes a general term for methods, techniques and tools. CEP helps to process events while they happen [20, S. 163].

Bringing together EAI, MOM, SOA, ESB and CEP seem to be not clearly possible. Currently, there are multiple terms to describe the problem of integration, routing, processing and analysing. The first one, Information Flow Processing, is described in [19]. This term focuses on event processing in combination with data management to "collect information produced by multiple, distributed sources, to process it in a timely way" [19]. Another term, streaming data system, focuses on processing data streams within "a non-hard real-time system that makes its data available at the moment a client application needs it" [25].

While EAI, MOM, SOA, ESB and CEP are concepts to assemble setups based on already known behaviours and relationships between messages (or events), data sciences utilise tools to mine knowledge based on already available data. This part within the WDL uses concepts from knowledge discovery in databases (KDD), which describes methods to statical analyses, applications within the field of artificial intelligence (AI), pattern recognition and machine learning [21, S. 3].

In addition to this classification of concepts within our field of application, related work targeting onto architectural drafts in data grids and smart grids can be used. Chervenak et al. [18], e. g. describes basic principles for designing data management architectures and Tierney et al. [27] introduce concepts how to monitor such grids. Furthermore, Appelrath et al. describe in [16] the process of developing an IT-architecture for smart grids as a result of a German research project, and Rusitschka et al. [26] present a computing model for managing real-time data streams of smart grids within the scope of the energy market. Unfortunately, these approaches are not directly applicable to our use case. Either they are large scaled, or focusing on data storing and mining. However, they can be considered within our architecture, which has to fill the gap between smart grids, data storing, possibilities for data mining as well as non-hard real-time event processing.

III. Architectural Draft

At this point, the level 0 view of the WDL is discussed. Taking a look at the data sources and data sinks you can get a better understanding of what the WDL should do.

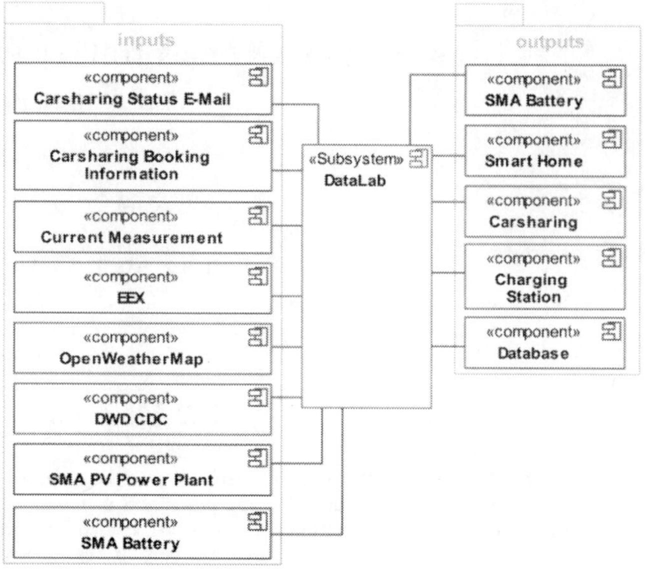

Figure 1. Level 0 view of the WDL.

At first, there are external services. They are sending messages to the WDL, or it acquires data from them. These data packages have to be assumed as inhomogeneous, e. g. carsharing data of a booking system the WDL is connected to. That means the WDL gets information on bookings like start time and end time. Out of that current state updates on a reservation such like an earlier beginning or a defect vehicle can be received. Another data source offers messages containing information on the current electrical power consumption. The actual electricity price is obtained by an interface of European Energy Exchange (EEX). Data of photovoltaic systems or batteries are gained through SMA interfaces. The German Meteorological Service [1] offers historical information on the past weather, an application programming interface (API) of the online service OpenWeatherMap [11] is available for weather forecasts.

A system working with time series, forecasts and master data must be created. As you can see in Figure 1, the WDL is positioned between the aforementioned sources and at least five data sinks. These refer to controllable devices like a charging station, a battery or Smart Home systems. On the other hand, data is delivered to the car sharing service and dumped to a database. Within our setup, a KairosDB is used as data storage as it is suitable for working with larger time series and quite easy to use.

An unanswered question is how the different components can be integrated and how analysis as well as event processing can be handled. The WINNER project focuses on the intelligent integration of components of the residential area into the Smart Grid. That means predictions must be made to get an overview of the future power consumption and the electricity production. Either one charges the batteries or one uses the stored energy to overcome load peaks. The prediction mechanism might be implemented by using artificial neural networks (ANNs) or regression methods. Thinking about energy production predictions, you might need to receive information from hardware components like SMA-devices and weather services. These specific data formats require reshaping to use them in prediction mechanism. Using input filters, output filters, and stream routing the arriving information is transformed and sent to the prediction and dump units. These units save the data, send commands or just forward information to external devices.

IV. Requirements

One can divide up the list of requirements into three subsets. The first one refers to the system in general; the second touches the various components and the third covers the aspects of architecture and functional groups.

Thinking of the system in general shows that the ability to process time series data is required. An incoming message contains a time value referring to a point and a value e. g. the result of a measurement. The WDLs task on an incoming message is to associate the arriving values with a data source. Possible data sources are photovoltaic installations, batteries, power consumption measurement devices or actual weather data. Out of that, the system must handle forecast data. They are special because a complete time series and a time value, which refers to a validity point are included. At the time this point describes the time series is valid. Contemplable data sources are weather forecast services or EEX. The last category covers master data without time dependencies. Booking information or general data on devices and services belong to this group. This data may be very unstructured like text-only entries.

Focusing on technical aspects derived from our architectural draft in Section III, the WDL needs the ability to process JSON, XML and CSV values. Out of that proprietary formats have to be handled as well. Especially photovoltaic and smart metering installations tend to send production data in proprietary formats.

Central non-functional requirements are scalability and reliability. The latter refers to interfaces receiving data from external services and devices. On occurring errors incoming and shortly arrived messages should not get lost.

Keeping the interfaces in mind, one has to think of the necessary contact points to other services or the environment in general. The consumer interfaces of the WDL have to accept HTTP requests, especially while communicating with REST services. Similarly, FTP servers must be communicated with. The WDL must receive and process e-mails as well. Likewise, a file-based data transfer is needed. Finally, there are interfaces to external services using proprietary communication formats via TCP or UDP. The developed system has to enable the reception of messages sent by them. In contrast, the message producing components of the WDL primarily need to communicate via HTTP. Particularly the interface to a database can be made up of simple REST client services sending HTTP-based messages.

After paying attention to input and output components, the internal processes of routing and filtering shall be characterised. Asynchronous processing describes the most important requirement. Message queues or small buffer databases may decouple various components so they can work without waiting for each other to terminate. Furthermore, incoming messages caused by occurring events have to be converted into an internal format. To achieve this the WDL can extend these data packages with additional information. But after processing unneeded contents must be removed as well. Alongside external descriptors have to be mapped to internal descriptors and vice versa.

TABLE I. Tool overview and classification. Classification is based on tools to handle application integration (AI), stream processing (SP) and knowledge discovery (KD).

Name	AI	SP	KD
Apache Camel	✓	✗	✗
Apache Storm	✗	✓	✗
Apache Spark	✗	✗	✓
Apache Hadoop	✗	✗	✓
Apache ServiceMix	✓	✓	✗
Siddhi	✗	✓	✗
ESPER	✗	✓	✗
WSO2 CEP	✓	✓	✗
RapidMiner	✗	✗	✓
KNIME	✗	✗	✓
Node-RED	✓	✗	✗
JBoss Fuse	✓	✓	✗

The WDL has to transform the incoming data into an internal format for further processing. Additionally, the WDL has to be capable of providing data for doing manual statistical evaluations and analysis. Furthermore, the WDL has to be capable of triggering automatic evaluations and forecasts as additional components. This work is done while keeping the CEP pattern in mind.

Within this paper, we leave out the specific aspect of data storage. That means different databases are not discussed or compared. The built prototype uses a KairosDB to persist time series data. It was chosen because of an existing simple HTTP-based interface that provides easy access.

V. Tool Overview

The WDL requirement analysis illustrates an EAI task with KDD topics. Furthermore, results gathered from KDD could result in CEP related tasks, which have to be considered as well. The following list of tools covers these tasks. Of course, this list is not complete. There are a lot of tools available to handle specific tasks within the area of EAI, KDD or CEP. Our selection focuses on widely used, platform independent and easily accessible tools with suitable licenses models. Thus, the list of our selection contains mainly open source tools.

Selected tools will be classified into at least one of our primary topics: (1) tools to handle KDD related tasks, (2) tools to solve EAI related tasks and (3) tools to implement CEP related tasks. Additionally, there are (4) tools providing runtime environments to execute solutions solved with tools from class (1), (2) and (3).

Table I lists our selection of considered tools. Furthermore, this table classifies them within our previously identified main topics. Apache Camel is an open source lightweight framework to solve EAI problems based on an implementation of EIPs in [22]. Furthermore, a lot of components are available to extend the functionality of Apache Camel [4]. Apache Storm is an "open source distributed realtime computation system" with

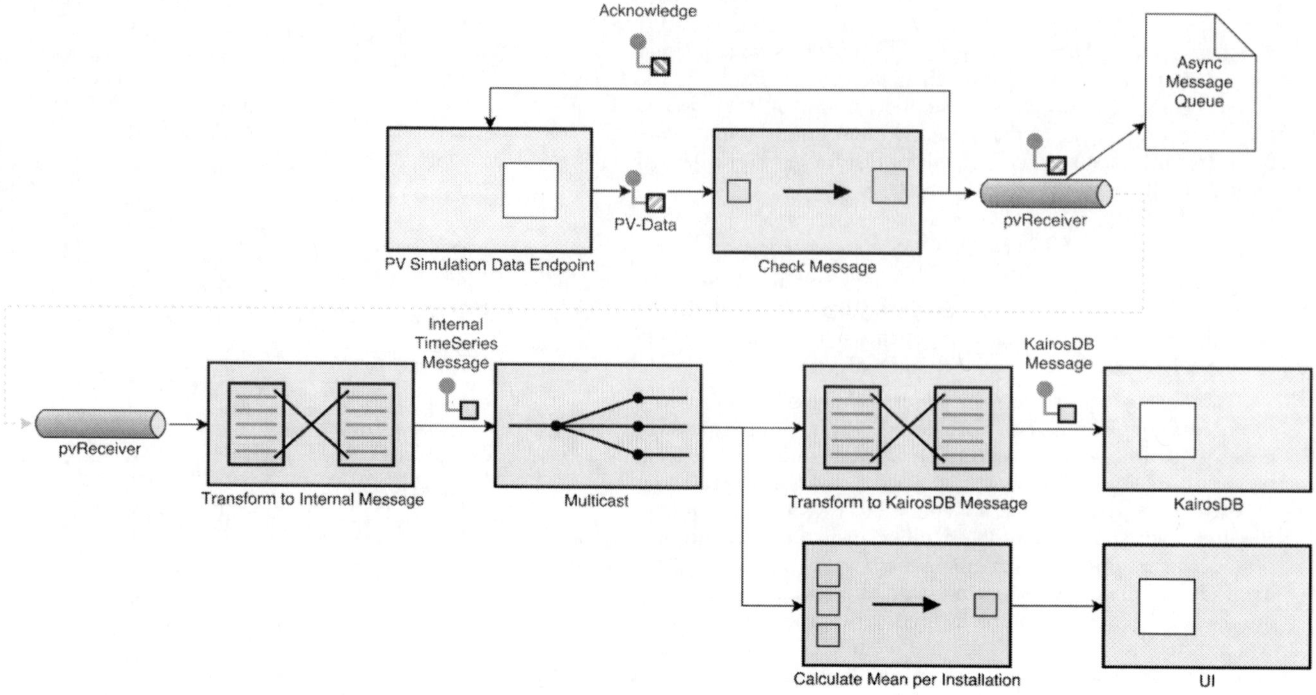

Figure 2. Visualization of our general prototype based on EIP notation.

a lot of use cases like "realtime analytics, online machine learning, continuous computation". This scalable environment can handle a lot of data streams within a specific Storm topology [5]. Apache Spark [6] and Apache Hadoop [3] are tools for knowledge discovery in data. They differ in performance as well as their internal approaches in data storage and processing. Apache Service Mix [2] and JBoss Fuse [8] are integration containers, which include other tools like Apache Camel. Siddhi [14] and ESPER [7] are CEP engines and can be used as standalone tools as well as an integration within tools like Apache Camel. WSO2 CEP is a runtime environment for the CEP engine Siddhi, which adds user interfaces for external and internal usage [13]. RapidMiner [12] and KNIME [9] are tools for knowledge discovery in already existing data. It is also possible to integrate interfaces to access data streams and use a wide range of algorithms to analyse collected data. Finally, Node-RED is a message processing framework with internet of things (IoT) roots and can be used to solve application integration problems quicklys. This framework is based on Node.js, can be extended with additional packages and deployed into cloud services like Bluemix [10].

VI. Prototype

We have selected three tools based on our preselection in Section V, which we want to use within a uniform test setup. This selection focuses on tools from different fields of application: (1) Node-RED because of its simplicity within the field of IoT, (2) WSO2 CEP because of its Siddhi engine for complex event processing and (3) Apache Camel as the reference implementation for EIPs in combination with Wildfly as Java EE based runtime environment.

The comparison is done with an uniform test setup with a simplified task, which combines the integration of a REST-based data source which encodes data with JSON, a KairosDB based data sink with HTTP interface which consumes JSON encoded data as well, and a calculation of the mean according to a particular sender device, e. g. a photovoltaic station, has to be calculated across multiple messages. The time window of these multiple messages is ten seconds. That means if sender "Station A" sends a message at 10:00:00 am the values "Station A" sent between 09:59:50 am and 10:00:00 am are used for calculating the mean. The result is delivered via HTTP request to an external service which consumes JSON encoded data as well as the data source and KairosDB.

The data source in our test setup gets its messages from a generative photovoltaic data endpoint in configurable timings. This source device transmits structured data like the tuple "(time,energy,station,id)". The first value of the generated data tuple represents a long value as a point in time, the second value a double based energy value of solar insolation. Furthermore, a tag containing the string based station name is included. Finally, the last value is a string based identifier of this single message for further time measurements. The identification value does not contain any relevant information in the context of energy data aggregation. It is only used to register and match the outgoing and incoming messages on the peripheral systems around the measurement environment.

The KairosDB endpoint of this setup gets its message as structured data like the tuple "(name,value,tags,time,id)". This tuple corresponds to the structure of data that are sent to a KairosDB instance for storing also. The included ID is not needed for the process of storing the data but necessary for matching the messages afterwards. Finally, the aggregation endpoint of this test setup gets its message as the same structured data like the data source tuple "(time,station,energy,id)".

The internal message routing has to be implemented across Node-RED, WSO2 CEP and Apache Camel as shown in Figure 2. This figure illustrates the test setup and its components by using the notation of EIPs. The selected transformation and routing steps refere to the already mentioned requirements in Section IV and architectural draft in Section III to cover some kind of data source, transformation, processing, reverse transformation as well as dumping.

A. Node-Red

Node-RED is a JavaScript based message processing framework with IoT roots and can be used to solve application integration problems quickly. The framework is executed with Node.js and uses NPM for dependency management. Implementing the test setup mentioned above within Node-RED web client can be done by using a bunch of function nodes, nodes to create HTTP endpoints as well as change nodes. Change nodes are designed to modify the structure of our currently handled message object. Function nodes, on the other hand, are designed to execute custom scripts onto a particular message. Finally, nodes to create HTTP endpoints ranges from HTTP server nodes to some path which can be called, HTTP response nodes which have to be placed within a message processing path which starts with an HTTP server node and HTTP client nodes to call external resources.

The implemented setup is shown in Figure 3. As mentioned, the messaging pipe starts with "PV Receiver" to create an HTTP server endpoint for "/endpoints/pvenergy". The message is piped onto an HTTP response node as well as to the primary processing path. The path starts with a function node to clean, enrich and transform incoming messages into the internal format. The result is forwarded to the database handling as well as the aggregation processing. Our database handling creates KairosDB compatible messages by using a template node and submits the resulting message by using an HTTP client node. The aggregation processing utilises the other function node to implement the aggregation function. This function node describes a simple memory to persist messages within a time window of ten seconds as well as calculating the mean within this window for the particular installation. The aggregation handling is finalised with a switch node to determine "NaN" values and an HTTP client node.

Summarising, Node-RED is a quickly providable platform for fast prototyping which can integrate various data sources as well as data sinks. Unfortunately, it is tricky to develop collaboratively. Well, each developer can maintain its environment, but Node-RED-Flows are managed by Node-RED itself; synchronising them between different development platforms is hard. Furthermore, any particular use case, e. g. aggregate values from messages have to be implemented manually or by using additional NPM-based components which can be added directly in Node-RED. However, it is possible to integrate a broad range of endpoints with standardised formats and protocols. Handling proprietary endpoints requires more efforts in development.

B. WSO2 CEP and Siddhi

WSO2 CEP is a tool that runs within a Java Virtual Machine (JVM). This CEP-environment offers a graphical user interface within a web browser. Using this an input receiver (named "SolarReceiver") and two output publishers (named "AveragesLog" and "SolarPublisherDB") are created (Figure 4). The receiver accepts data if they are JSON-formatted and sent via "HTTP-POST" request. The HTTP request is answered automatically if it is sent to the right unified resource locator (URL) of the mentioned receiver i. e. "HTTP://localhost:9763/endpoints/SolarReceiver". The messages arriving at "SolarReceiver" are redirected to the data stream "SolarRaw". From this queue, the data packages are picked by a so-called execution plan named "toInternalFormat" and inserted into stream "SolarIn".

The syntax of Siddhi can be used within execution plans just as JavaScript functions. e. g. incoming string objects can be converted to timestamps. Starting with message stream "SolarIn" the internal workflow begins. Splitting is necessary because two output publishers are required. The lower branch from Figure 4 just processes the messages by adding a metric attribute and sending them to an HTTP interface of a KairosDB instance.

In contrast, the upper branch from Figure 4 performs a more complex task. The average of the last ten seconds must be computed corresponding to the last station that sent a value. This is done by taking messages from "SolarIn" and sending them to a helper stream if they are not to old. Beforehand an id for one measurement is added matching the time of arrival. If a new message arrives the helper stream is matched against it by using the station name. The average is calculated over the resulting messages and put to the output stream "averagesclean".

The measurement values are discussed later. But some facts need to be mentioned at this point. WSO2 CEP offers a graphical user interface that aims to provide access to some script files. Out of that data streams are illustrated. The direct manipulation of data streams happens while editing script files. Other options like tracking of messages or a CPU log provide support for software engineers.

C. Apache Camel and Wildfly

Apache Camel is a Java-based EAI-framework, which is lightweight and extendable. It can be executed as a standalone routing system or within middleware infrastructures like Spring, Java EE, Apache ServiceMix or JBoss Fuse. Implementing the test setup mentioned above within Apache Camel can be done by utilising a REST endpoint and describing a route which channels incoming messages to our HTTP database and aggregation endpoints. Apache Camel offers a large number of implemented patterns, which are described within [22], as well as the option to implement custom processes, for example within "Beans". Furthermore, it is possible to extend the framework with own components for further functionalities.

Figure 2 visualises general and the finally implemented route within Apache Camel. Its components are shown in Figure 5. The route itself is implemented by using the so-called "Java Domain Specific Language (Java DSL)" in Apache Camel. This route is implemented within "DataLabRouteBuilder" and describes the REST endpoint, which uses a servlet to process a specific resource and utilises SEDA to decouple incoming message flows from database and aggregation flows locally. SEDA is a lightweight in-memory message queue component within Apache Camel. The decoupled route

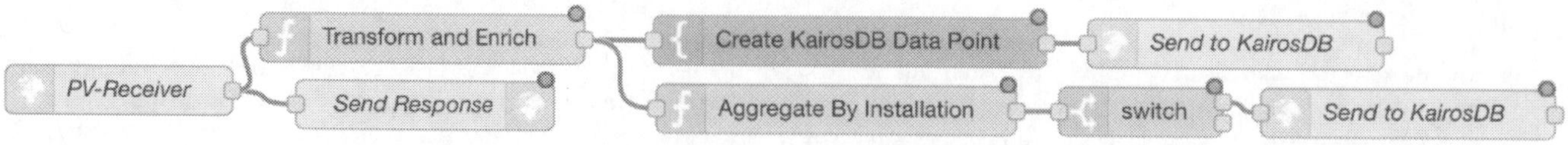

Figure 3. Node-RED implementation of the example from Section VI.

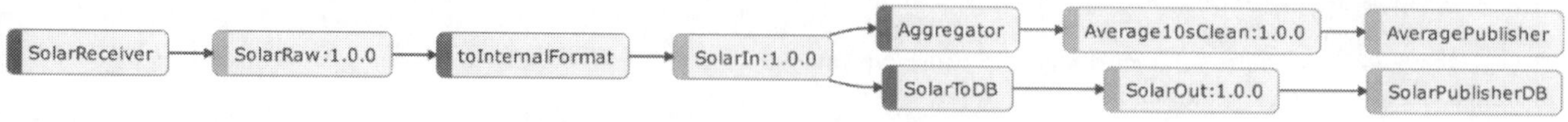

Figure 4. Message processing using WSO2 CEP.

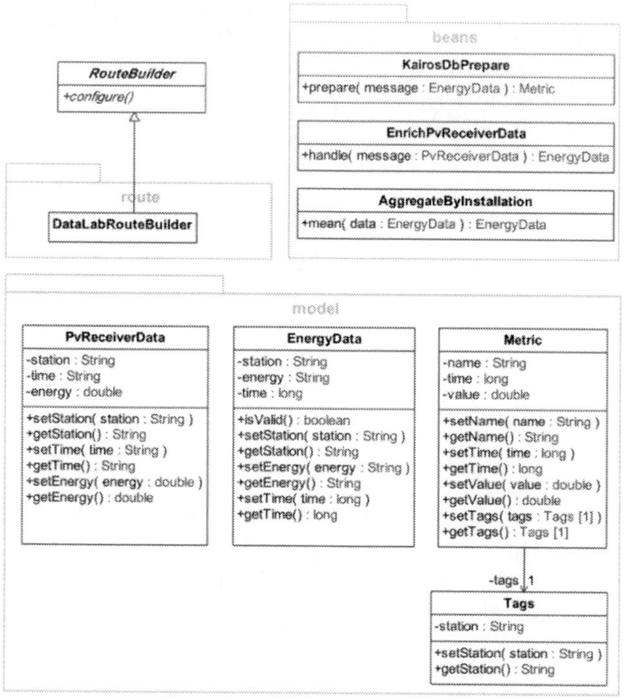

Figure 5. Apache Camel implementation of the example from Section VI.

contains the transformation and enrich bean "EnrichPvReceiverData" to transform external "PvReceiverData" into internal "EnergyData" as well as a multicast to handle the database and aggregation route. The database route contains another bean "KairosDbPrepare" to transform internal "EnergyData" into "Metric" datatypes for "KairosDb". The aggregation route includes the aggregation bean "AggregationByInstallation" itself, which is implemented as stateful bean to save messages within a time window of ten seconds and finally calculate the mean for a particular installation. Both routes are completed with an HTTP client call onto the respective external endpoint.

Finally, Apache Camel is easy to use, especially when used in combination with Maven as build and deployment tool. It is possible to describe routes within Java DSL as we did or use XML-based description to build those routes. Furthermore, Apache Camel is primary a routing engine. Any particular use case, e. g. aggregate values from messages, has to be implemented manually or by using additional libraries.

VII. EVALUATION

In this section, we want to test the aforementioned prototypes. To guarantee the same conditions for every application Docker containers are used on the same machine. These containers encapsulate the runtime environment as well as the prototype itself. Our test machine runs on Debian GNU/Linux 9.0 Stretch using an Intel(R) Core(TM) i5-4570 CPU @ 3.20GHz. Because of the main task of our prototypes is routing messages some exclusions are necessary. First, the application sending information to the routing engine is installed on another machine. Furthermore, the service which receives information the routing engine sends is placed on another machine too. This setup admits for quantifying the response time, memory consumption and CPU load of the various Docker containers or the applications within them omitting the aspect of additional load of sending and receiving applications.

The sending device transmits JSON-based structured data tuples like "(time,energy,station,id)". One could think of a solar system with a particular station identifier sending the actual energy production. The frequency of sent messages is configurable and initially set to 10 per second for the first measurements. Later we will increase them multiple times up to 200 messages per second.

The JVM for our WSO2 CEP instance and the Apache Camel prototypes are fixed to use 1024 MB of memory. We use the measured values of "jstat" for calculating the memory consumption of the tools mentioned above with a time resolution of one second. Furthermore, we sum up the usage of survival space ("S0U" and "S1U"), eden space ("EU"), old space ("OU"), metaspace space ("mu"), and compressed class space ("ccsu"). A node.js module measures the memory consumption of Node-RED, i. e. the "heapUsed" value. Out of that, the CPU load is measured by the "top" command every second. We get the response times of the various systems by measuring the time of sending and the time of receiving messages in milliseconds. The arrival timestamps of messages corresponding to database operations and aggregations are measured separately.

A. *Results*

At first, we want to describe and discuss the respond time, the memory consumption and the CPU load. As you can see in Figure 6(a) and Figure 6(b) the mean time between sending and receiving never increases up to more than 1 second.

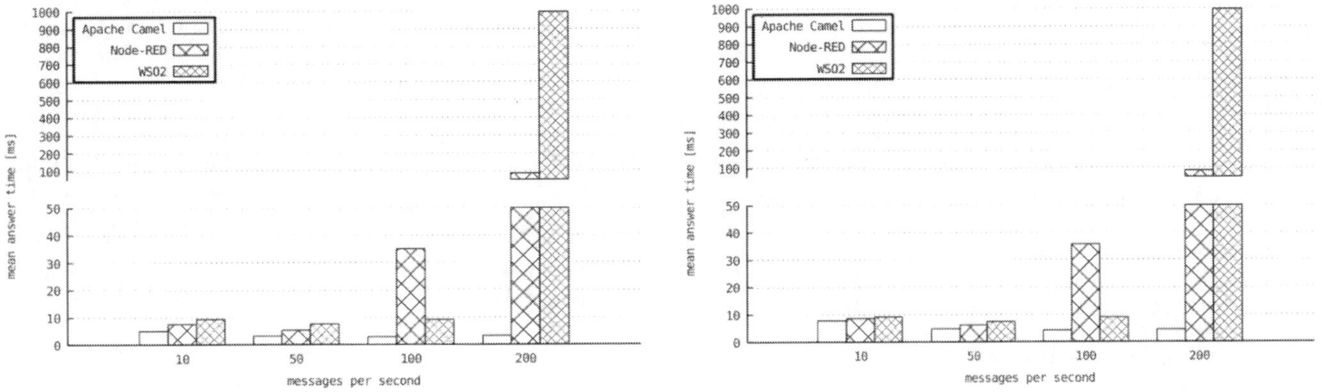

(a) (b)

Figure 6. Mean response times of tested systems with various message frequencies for database (a) and aggregation (b) messages.

Apache Camel shows a mentionable effect of becoming faster by receiving more messages. All considered tools exhibit the same behaviour on database and aggregation messages. Out of that, we have to mention, that there is no significant difference between the response times of aggregation 6(b) and saving processes 6(a). The progressions of both cases are similar.

Figure 7 shows four segments separated by vertical dotted lines: The left one refers to the message frequency of 10 messages per second, the right to 200. In between, there are parts with increasing message rate (50 and 100). Watching the CPU load, we see an expectable process. The more messages are sent, the more CPU load is reached. WSO2 CEP uses the processor the most at least while processing 100 messages per second or more.

Figure 8 describes the memory consumption of the evaluated tools. The segments are placed according to Fig 7. We identify a memory peak for Node-RED at the beginning of the 100 messages per second section. Apache Camel presents a trend of using the less memory, the more messages arrive. WS02 CEP shows fluctuation in metaspace, which may be caused by runtime generated classes per message to execute JavaScript based functions.

B. Comparison

Watching only memory consumption in Figure 8 Node-RED works with the lowest. Apache Camel uses three to four times as much memory as Node-RED but does not demand the CPU that much (Figure 7). The less memory consumption of Apache Camel while processing a larger amount of messages is caused by the "eden space utilisation". Measuring this, we see that the consumed memory decreases down to a constant minimum. WSO2 CEP shows characteristic minima of memory consumption and CPU load (Figure 7, Figure 8). Garbage collections cause these. Especially the memory graph indicates that the points of lower consumption values can be located in the middle of a sending phase not only between them.

For further evaluation, the response times can be compared. All test messages were answered. That means database information, as well as aggregation information, was not dropped. Figure 6 illustrates the fact that messages of both categories

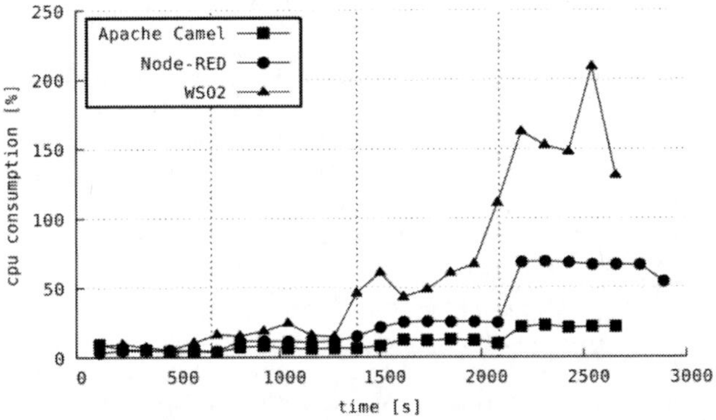

Figure 7. CPU load within four phases of sending (100 values aggregated).

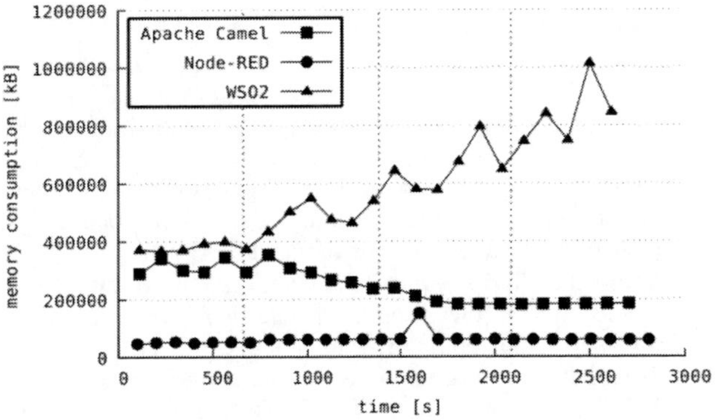

Figure 8. Memory consumption within four phases of sending (100 values aggregated).

are sent with the same time delay. WSO2 CEP reaches a limit when receiving 200 messages per second. At this point, only applications allowing a time delay of one second can be built. Up to a message frequency of 100 messages per second, WSO2 and Apache Camel show a solid response time below ten milliseconds. Especially Apache Camel becomes faster while handling more messages. This may be caused by the decreased overall usage of memory.

VIII. Discussion

Thinking about the main goal focusing on the architectural backbone technologies for our WDL the selected technologies cover different aspects as required. WSO2 CEP, Apache Camel and Node-RED are not directly comparable. WSO2 CEP is an environment for handling complex events, which use Siddhi to redirect message flows as well as creating high-level events based on multiple low-level events. Apache Camel, on the other hand, is an implementation of EIPs which also allows to route message. Its advantage is primary to solve integration problems, which results in much more effort to handle complex events. Finally, Node-RED is an readily usable environment to create message flows within the scope of IoT. The environment enables developers to easily integrate endpoints and handle related tasks in case of occurred events.

Apache Camel seems to be an efficient framework in case of routing messages. It is usable as a standalone application, and it is possible to use this framework within a wide range of environments like Spring, Java EE (e. g. Wildfly), Apache ServiceMix and JBoss Fuse. Our measurements show a quiet strange behaviour when raising the amount of messages per second, which cannot be comprehended fully. Taking a closer look onto the measurements show, that the eden space within the JVM is not used that much which may save garbage collection time. This might be an explanation for our strange behaviour. However, it is possible to quickly setup new routes and integrate them with a broad range of potential endpoints.

Node-RED, on the other hand, seems to be an easy to use prototyping platform at least because of its graphical user interface. This easiness applies as long as the integrated endpoints use standard formats and protocols. CEP has to be handled separately, in the case of clean code development processes it is necessary to implement additional nodes. Surprisingly, Node-RED runs quietly efficiently. The memory consumption, as well as the CPU load and response times, illustrates that, despite JavaScript, all messages are handled fast and efficiently.

Watching WSO2 CEP, there are some remaining challenges. The complexity of using windows and aggregation functions on one stream with messages from different logical sources forces the user to research intensively. A desirable feature is missing. There is no opportunity to create own objects and saving them. The included event tables only offer the option of saving whole messages. The feature of adding custom JavaScript functions cannot be used in its entirety (at least not in the release we used). A weird phenomenon shows up when comparing long values. Even if you declare all variables of streams using matching types the log of WSO2 CEP shows parsing errors. These refer to string-to-long conversions, which actually should not happen.

Finally, the evaluation lack discrete measurments on usability and simplicity. Usability and simplicity are rated, within the discussion, based on our development experience while implementing the described prototypes.

IX. Conclusion

The WDL has to be able to handle data streams as mentioned in different manners. Beside the integration and routing itself, there are tasks in the area of complex event processing as well as knowledge discovery in data. Our first reflection of architectural backbone technologies covers those aspects. Based on our experiences and measurements gathered from this test setup, we can make some decisions. In the case of a complex heterogeneous environment with different kinds of interfaces, Apache Camel seems to be a right choice. It is usable within a wide range of conditions and able to handle a lot of technologies to cover integration problems. Furthermore, in the case of handling complex events, WSO2 CEP seems to be the right choice. Unfortunately, its surrounding environment does not cover our requirements. So there are three possible approaches: (1) build CEP algorithms based on beans manually within Apache Camel; (2) integrate WSO2 CEP as a backend system; (3) extract Siddhi and integrate its functionalities into Apache Camel. However, Node-RED has its advantages in rapid prototyping and fast message processing. It might be usable as front end system to easily integrate standardised external interfaces as well as an additional platform for experiments within a productive setup. Nevertheless, everything you can do with Node-RED seems to be possible with Apache Camel too. The main difference can be found within the usability, the deployment process and the underlying language. Adapting knowledge discovery in such setups, independent of which routing engine is used, should be possible by using a database and route messages as required or by integrating available public interfaces from tools for knowledge discovery within Apache Camel or Node-RED.

However, next steps might be a final concept for the WDL by using results of this analyse as well as the implementing of this concept. Further, it is neccessary to integrate mentioned data sources into this finally implemented WDL-prototype, e.g., PV, weather forecasts, booking information, and electricity consumption.

Related implementations and instructions for further analyses of this test setup can be found within a public repository[1].

X. Acknowledements

The research project Wohnungswirtschaftlich integrierte netzneutrale Elektromobilitat in Quartier und Region (WINNER) is funded by the Federal Ministry for Economic Affairs and Energy of Germany under project number 01ME16002D.

References

[1] Climate Data Center. URL http://www.dwd.de/DE/klimaumwelt/cdc/cdc_node.html.
[2] Apache ServiceMix, 2011. URL http://servicemix.apache.org.
[3] Apache Hadoop, 2014. URL http://hadoop.apache.org.
[4] Apache Camel, 2015. URL http://camel.apache.org.
[5] Apache Storm, 2015. URL http://storm.apache.org.
[6] Apache Spark, 2015. URL http://spark.apache.org.
[7] Esper, 2016. URL http://www.espertech.com/esper/.
[8] Jboss Fuse, 2016. URL https://developers.redhat.com/products/fuse/overview/.
[9] KNIME, 2017. URL https://www.knime.org.
[10] Node-RED, 2017. URL https://nodered.org.

[1] https://github.com/winner-potential/smart-2017

[11] OpenWeatherMap, 2017. URL http://openweathermap.org/price.
[12] RapidMiner, 2017. URL https://rapidminer.com.
[13] WSO2, 2017. URL http://wso2.com/products/complex-event-processor/.
[14] Siddhi Complex Event Processing Engine, 2017. URL https://github.com/wso2/siddhi.
[15] WINNER, 2017. URL http://www.winner-projekt.de.
[16] Hans-Jürgen Appelrath, Petra Beenken Ludger Bischofs, and Mathias Uslar. *IT-Architekturentwicklung im Smart Grid*. Springer Gabler, Heidelberg, Germany, 2012.
[17] David Chappell. *Enterprise Service Bus*. O'Reilly, 2004.
[18] Ann Chervenak, Ian Foster, Carl Kesselman, Charles Salisbury, and Steven Tuecke. The data grid: Towards an architecture for the distributed management and analysis of large scientific datasets. *Journal of Network and Computer Applications*, 23(3):187 – 200, 2000. ISSN 1084-8045. doi: http://dx.doi.org/10.1006/jnca.2000.0110. URL http://www.sciencedirect.com/science/article/pii/S1084804500901103.
[19] Gianpaolo Cugola and Alessandro Margara. Processing flows of information: From datastream to complex event processing. *ACM Computing Surveys*, 44(3):1–70, 2012.
[20] Michael Eckert and François Bry. Complex event processing (cep). *Informatik Spektrum*, 32(2):163–167, 2009.
[21] Christian Gottermeier. Data mining: Modellierung, methodik und durchführung ausgewählter fallstudien mit dem sas enterprise miner. Diplomarbeit, Universität Heidelberg, 2003.
[22] Gregor Holpe. Enterprise integration patterns. In *Proceedings of 9th Conference on Pattern Language of Programs*, September 2002. URL http://hillside.net/plop/plop2002/final/Enterprise%20Integration%20Patterns%20-%20PLoP%20Final%20Draft%203.pdf.
[23] D.S. Linthicum. *Enterprise Application Integration*. Addison-Wesley information technology series. Addison-Wesley, 2000. ISBN 9780201615838. URL https://books.google.de/books?id=LIYadz3qEyEC.
[24] Falko Menge. Enterprise service bus. In *Free and Open Source Software Conference*, 2007.
[25] Andrew G. Psaltis. *Streaming Data - Understanding the real-time pipeline*. Manning Publications Co., 2017.
[26] S. Rusitschka, K. Eger, and C. Gerdes. Smart grid data cloud: A model for utilizing cloud computing in the smart grid domain. In *2010 First IEEE International Conference on Smart Grid Communications*, pages 483–488, Oct 2010. doi: 10.1109/SMARTGRID.2010.5622089.
[27] B. Tierney, R. Aydt, D. Gunter, W. Smith, M. Swany, V. Taylor, and R. Wolski. A grid monitoring architecture, 2002.

Smart Mobility and Cultural Tourism: The Termini-Centocelle Train Museum, an Example of "Smartourism" Project in Rome

Michele Angelaccio, Berta Buttarazzi and Marco Marrozzini
Department of Enterprise Engineering, University of Rome "Tor Vergata", Rome, Italy
Email: angelaccio@dii.uniroma2.it, buttarazzi@dii.uniroma2.it,marco@marrozziniengineering.it
and Claudio Gnessi, Romina Peritore
Associazione per l'Ecomuseo Casilino
Email: claudio.gnessi@gmail.com, rperitore@gmail.com

***Abstract*—Many recent trends in mobile Web and context aware applications are leading to consider new applicative scenarios including the so called smart services which are characterized by the use of autonomous devices connected to the Internet (sensors, beacons, etc.) and cooperating with user personal mobile devices (tablet, smartphone, etc.). In the case of urban mobility management, several issues are related to local mobility especially for tourism and cultural cases. We consider one of this related to old train re-using in Rome which has been selected as a pilot test for future sustainable transportation systems. We are able to show that, in this case, an effective system with mobile applications could leverage a real contribution both for mobile museums and for geo annotation of peripherical urban lands.**

Keywords*—*Internet of Cultural Things, Internet of Things, Mobile First, Mobile Web, Smart City, Smart Mobility.

I. Introduction

With the continuous development of Information and Communication technologies and Smart City for Cultural heritage, it is possible, thanks to the Internet of Things (IoT) implementation, to have smart systems connected to Wi-Fi, to revolutionize the management of tourism, promoting sustainable economic development, engaging the citizens effectively, as well as reducing mobility costs and resource consumption. To this purpose, we proposed the first applicative framework for Smart City named STREET WEB [1]. STREET WEB is a platform to distribute tourist information "on the road" without Internet connection. The physical architecture of STREET WEB is composed of a network of different nodes called Smart Box (SB), each representing a complete working station linked to a node sensor station to improve locality visibility. It is based on the Mobile First paradigm for adapting graphical user interface to multiple browsers and device sizes. In this paper, the purpose is to extend STREET WEB functionality to provide cultural contents and services to all visitors in the context of Smart Mobility (an important field belonging to the ecosystem of the Smart Cities). The fundamental issues of this approach, based on the integration of tourism, cultural heritage and mobility, are not only to enhance the cultural heritage present in the territory, but also to increase the tourists flow (cultural, scenic, artistic, gastronomic, etc.) and finally, to create new conditions for sustainable territorial socio-economic development. The paper is organised as follows: Section II introduces the Smart Mobility Context of the Mobility Project and the main issues of the Architectural Design. Section III gives the detailed description of the Platform used to distribute tourist information "on the road", based on Digital Niches Model and Microservers System. Section IV concludes the paper introducing implications and potential results yielding in the field of Sustainable Transport and Smartourism for obtaining information related to touristic Point of Interests in the land.

II. Scenario Overview

The use case scenario is related to a mobile system for exploring the "Ecomuseo Casilino", a type of museum [3] managed by the "Association Ecomuseum Casilino - Ad Duas Lauros" which aims to show and protect the cultural area [2] named "Comprensorio Casilino - Ad Duas Lauros"." The Ecomuseo Casilino hosts many archaeological resources, such as: Mausoleum of Elena (the mother of Emperor Constantine), the Catacombs of Marcellinus and Peter, the Roman villas in the Park of Centocelle, the Park of Villa dei Gordiani, and various Roman tombs. The archaeological and green area of the Ecomuseo Casilino includes two ancient Roman roads: via Casilina and via Prenestina and is traversed by the railway Roma-Giardinetti. Since 2012, the Association "Ecomuseum Casilino Ad Duas Lauros" promoted the use of the train as a cultural and tourist discovery tool. To enhance the public transport infrastructure and at the same time to enhance the area in which it travels, it was necessary to equip the train with a technological tool that can "augment" the features as a comprehensive virtual guide.

These reasons motivate the use of an ad hoc mobile system designed for such cultural train. To this purpose, we combined STREET WEB architecture with Digital Niches Model to implement a mobile cultural info-system. As shown in Figure 1, each train stop is represented by a sensor included in a Digital Niche and managed by a devoted Web-gis (Microserver Niche). Through a set of train stops and urban surroundings, which are geo tagged and linked to a mobile cultural info-system, it is possible to notify passengers and citizen in Ecomuseo Casilino while walking close to train stops. As referred in [9], a Digital Niche includes a set of sensors managed by a devoted Web-gis microserver.

To our knowledge, our proposed solution is a new wireless mobile system which differs from others due to the following reasons:

- It is the first mobile Web gis which is configurable and tailored to the scenario
- It will integrate map based on the wi-fi location system working on the train
- It is a complete Web based app connected to a local server providing up to date information

III. The Mobile Cultural Transport Digital System Overview

This section gives the detailed description of the platform used to distribute tourist information useful for exploring the "Ecomusem Casilino" by using the the railway Roma-Giardinetti [6], called Train-Ecomuseum in Figure 1. The platform used consists of some microserver and sensors, distributed on the area to support mobile users moving in smart scenarios with the aim to combine context aware information and high quality geo marketing services. Our App works on the same web infrastructure enhanced with sensor and it is composed by two front-ends. The first one for interfacing the train, and showing the various stops of the route by highlighting that to which we are closer. The other one serves to locate on the map georeferenced the touristic points of interest (t-PoIs). To this purpose, a platform is used, which is able to manage the set of train stops and the urban surroundings which are geo tagged and linked to a mobile cultural info-system able to notify passengers and citizen in Rome while walking close to train stops. Generally speaking, Info Urban Mobility systems are well known systems, often implemented through Internet connected geo-referenced apps. Unfortunately, it also happens that these applications are not well designed and synchronized with peripheral areas where there is a great amount of cultural elements distributed at different levels and that are hard to explain without being close to them. Moreover, there are technical problems to keep the user connected while using the train due historical problems and consequently connecting technology must be adapted to be used through IoT (Internet of Things) paradigm in which it occurs to sense mobile users in proximity and trying to push as much as possible the information close to them without using an external Internet provider. These reasons motivate the use of STREET WEB as an ad hoc mobile system designed for such cultural train museum. We adopt a paradigm defined in accord to Digital Niches Models in which each train stop is represented as a set of points included in a Digital Niche and managed by a devoted Web-gis (Microserver Niche).

A. STREET WEB and Digital Niches

STREET (*S*ensor network "on *T*he *R*oad " for *E*nhanc*E*d Internet of *T*ouristic things) Web, as described in [1] is a conceptual framework, useful to support mobile users moving in smart scenarios with the aim to combine context aware information and high quality geo marketing services in the same Web infrastructure enhanced with sensors. STREET Web makes possible to implement smart services in an easy way by integrating microservers, distributed in the scenario (servers on the road), called smart boxes, working as a geo based Cloud system in an autonomous way, as a Distributed Local Storage system, without remote Internet access, working as a geo based Distributed Local Storage system. The physical architecture of the system is based on a network of microservers (called Smart Box -SB), each representing a complete working station linked with a node sensor station composed of a localization device BLE (Bluetooth Low Energy) Beacon, eventually enriched with QR (Quick Response) code or NFC (Ner Field Communication) tag to improve locality visibility and based on the Mobile First paradigm. Each microserver is devoted to three main tasks:

1) to allow mobile users to access stored data;
2) to listen to data sent by the connected sensor;
3) to store data in database MySQL or NoSQL(InfluxDB);

The proposed microserver is realized by Raspberry Pi 2 - Model B. Raspberry Pi is a fully-functional single-board computer with a Broadcom processor. It has programmable I/O pins where you can attach physical devices and sensors.

Main Features:

- RAM:1GB LPDDR2 SDRAM
- CPU: 900 MHz quad-core ARM Cortex-A7;
- Raspberry Pi 2 can run as Operating System the full range of ARM GNU/Linux distributions.

Through STREET Web platform, the users fit together all necessary activities concerning communications, mobility, environment, energetic efficiency, shopping (digital business) and social networking. The icon depicted in Figure 2 shows the logical architecture of STREET Web model, based on a generic mobile device, equipped with a Mobile-First application front-end working in accord to three types of interactions: event-alerting, local content interaction, dynamic map navigation. The logical architecture of Street Web assumes that a Wi-Fi zone is offering local service without connection to a global Internet provider.

If we consider that a Wi-Fi zone is defined as a logical zone useful to be considered equivalent to a niche of tourism or set of touristic Point of Interests (t-PoIs), we can merge different niches contiguous or close to each other in a cloud of niches (Figure 3).

B. Microservers and APP Definition

As mentioned before, thanks to the microservers platform, it is possible to acquire information about cultural points of interest that are the one for which the user interested to reach from the selected stop without the need to connect to remote servers. To furnish the access to this cultural content to all visitors walking in such place, we consider two app layers:

- APP on TRAIN (TRAIN APP)
- APP niche (STOP APP e other t-PoIs APPs)

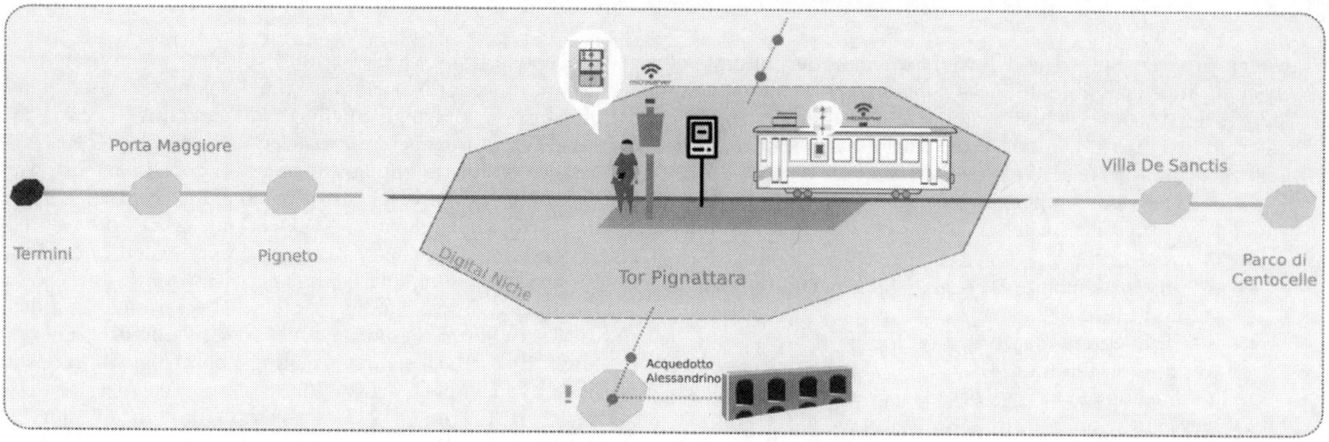

Fig. 1: TRAIN-ECOMUSEO Working Scenario

Fig. 2: The STREET WEB Model for Web 4.0

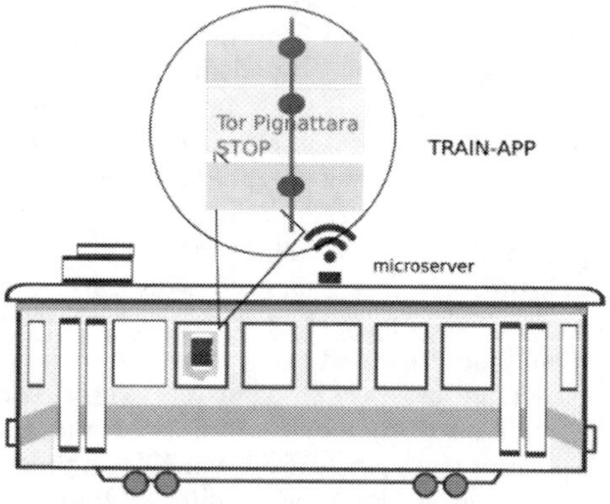

Fig. 4: Screen Train APP -Microserver

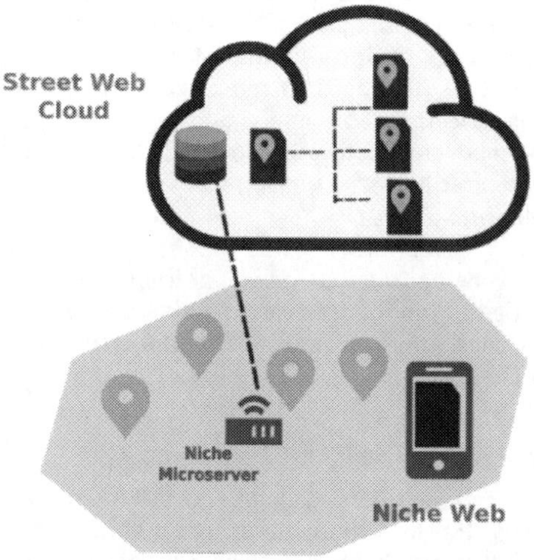

Fig. 3: The Application Architecture of Digital Niches.

The former one (TRAIN Mobile APP) at each train stop shows the name of the train-stop place. Then, once a passenger gets off the train area, he can adopt the STOP APP front-end to see what's interesting in the neighbourhood. Figure 4 shows the front end of the STOP APP that is useful to display the digital niches on the map.

When being near a niche, the user can access digital content using 2 buttons: the button that indicates the global access makes use of the Web Internet. The button that refers to the t-PoIs is coupled to the local Cloud (represented by Street Web microserver). It is linked through the Wi-Fi address. If the user clicks the t-PoIs button, he goes to the microserver home where the local content can be found. The working scenario depicted in Figure 1 shows the pathway executed by a generic mobile visitor, equipped with a Mobile-First application front end. Through a localization/alerting system (based on BLE Beacon) the user, while walking, is notified of all application steps. These steps are organized in accord to three types of interaction: event-alerting, local content interaction, dynamic map navigation. Figure 3 describes the type of application used

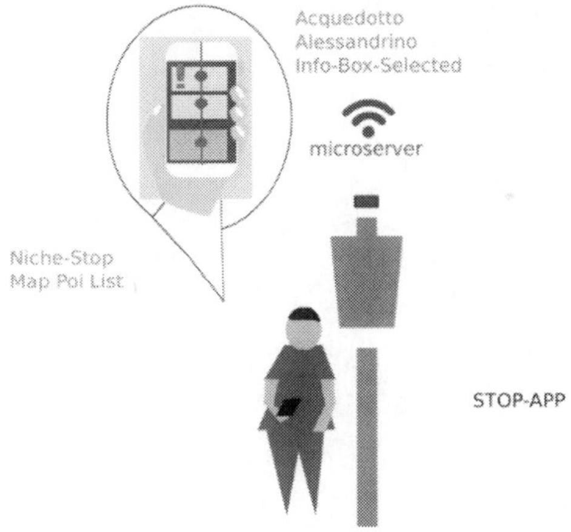

Fig. 5: Screen STOP APP –Microserver

Fig. 6: Home Screen of the APP–Microserver

in the TRAIN while moving and before arriving to the next stop. In this case the user is notified of the next stop and could be alerted for any message related to that niche before to leave the train. After niche-stop notification from the microserver, the user automatically is guided to selected an area in which further details on the selected monuments will be provide by the corresponding microserver of the niche (5).

In every case, the user is alerted without any external beacon or another means but just through well known alerting system prompting a pop up window for selecting current wifi network address (see Figure 6).

Fig. 7: Wireless Audio systems scenario

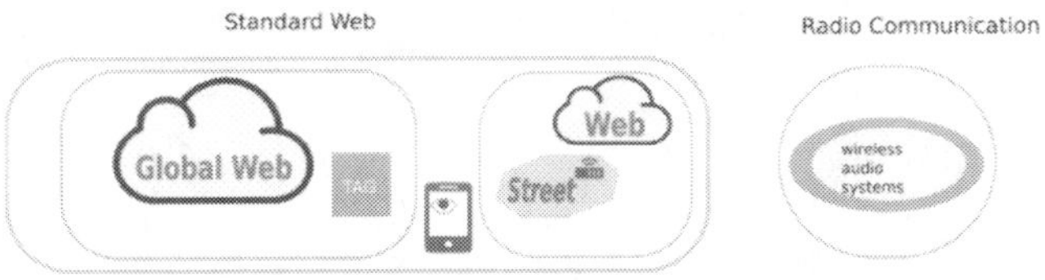

Fig. 8: TRAIN-ECOMUSEUM by STREET WEB comparison with global Web and local audio wireless systems

IV. Discussion and Conclusion

The Microserver based TRAIN – Mobile System (Figure 1) allows an effective way to mobile users for obtaining information related to touristic Points of Interest on land. To our knowledge this might be considered a first Web 4.0 solution in the sense that the host provider is no long external to the current niche but it is implemented inside the niche through a complete local Wi-Fi. The only comparable solutions come from a different technological point of view, that is wireless audio system. For instance, Quietvox [8] is a wireless audio communication system. As shown in Figure 7, the system is related to wireless audio communication designed primarily for museum with a large nuber of people. In the case of TRAIN ECOMUSEUM, however, the problem is due to the fact that such systems are not adequate. On the contrary, Digital Niches and Street Web Model gives the access through a generic smartphone (hence alwais connected system principle) following a mobile first interface paradigm.

Our solution hence goes a step further with respect to voice systems thus providing a true and effective mobile system without any non standard device and by following Web application paradigms (see Figure 8).

References

[1] M. Angelaccio and B. Buttarazzi, *Street Web A Framework for -Web on the Road - Smart Services*, Proceedings of the 12th International Conference on Web Information Systems and Technologies, WEBIST 2016, Volume 1, SciTePress 2016, ISBN 978-989-758-186-1, Rome, Italy, April 23-25, 2016.

[2] M. Angelaccio, A. Basili, B. Buttarazzi, and W. Liguori, *Smart and Mobile Access to Cultural Heritage Resources: a Case Study on Ancient Italian Renaissance Villas*– IEEE Wetice Copech 2012, Toulouse, (France),June 25-27 2012.

[3] J. Kim and J. Y. Lee, *Development of Local Cultural Resources Based on the Concept of Ecomuseum -Focusing on Cheorwon, Gangwon Province*, International Journal of Multimedia and Ubiquitous Engineering, pp.297-302,Vol.8, No.5 (2013).

[4] N. Viswanadham, S. Kameshwaran, *Ecosystem Aware Global Supply Chain Management*, World Scientific 2013

[5] Dr.P.D. SireeshaKumari, Mosalikanti.Subha Lakshmi, *Internet of Things (IoT) gateway to smart villages*, International Journal of Innovative Research in Advanced Engineering (IJIRAE) ISSN: 2349-2763, Issue 12, Volume 3 December 2016

[6] Ecomuseo Casilino, http://www.tramroma.com/tramroma/rete_ext/sfv/storia/sfvsto02_1.

[7] Internet of Things: Converging Technology for Smart Environments and Integrated Ecosystems (River Publishers series in Information Science and Technology), June 2013, Editors OvidiuVermesan and Peter Fries

[8] Wireless Audio System QuietVox Report, http://www.quietvox.com/

[9] M. Angelaccio, B. Buttarazzi, *A "Mobile first" perspective for Future Internet*– ICIW 2017 IARIA Conference, Venice (italy), June 25-29 2017.

Smart Interfaces at ESTIA, zer da hori?

Jean Esterle

ESTIA
Bidart, F-64210
Email: j.esterle@estia.fr

***Abstract*—Smart Interfaces at ESTIA, what is that (zer da hori in the local basque language) ? Smart Interfaces for Engineering is one of the topics of the iaria conference at Venice. This notion emerged as a unifying research theme at the engineering school ESTIA at the end of the year 2014, after several years of common work between researchers in Sciences and Technology and researchers in Management Sciences. There is a good flow of papers on various aspects of smart interfaces, but it is not easy to find in the literature a global approach to this notion. The purpose of this paper is to contribute tio fill this gap. In section 2 we give some historical background, going back to the Macy Conferences and the Palo Alto group, to Levins equation and Action Research, and to Edgar Morins approach to complexity. In section 3 we analyze several recent thesis at ESTIA and show how the notion of smart interfaces for engineering appears on topics as different as, for example, flight critical systems, isolated rural microgrids and the Lean approaches in corporate management. We hope that this survey will contribute to the stucturation of Smart Interfaces for Engineering as a branch of modern research.**

***Index Terms*—smart interfaces for engineering, complex systems, microgrids**

I. Introduction

ESTIA-Recherche started as a research team in 2008, when GRAPHOS (Groupe de Recherches Appliquées Pluridisciplinaire sur l'Hôpital et les Organisations de Santé) and LIPSI (Laboratoire en Ingénierie des Processus et des Services Industriels) decided to merge in order to work together to develop research activities in both Management Sciences and Sciences and Technology, and at the crossroads of these domains.

Research at ESTIA is aimed at:

Giving ESTIA engineering students an opportunity to work with established researchers who belong to both national and international scientific networks.

Developing a synergy between research works and evolution of academic programs.

Proposing innovative answers to technological, economic and societal questions.

Raising awareness among students and companies about the practice of research.

Contributing to the influence of ESTIA and to the attractivity of the territory.

The research project concerns engineering and technology; hence complex systems, open and self-organizing, in which there are also (and mainly) human beings, users, managers, etc. The dynamics of ESTIA-Recherche follows from the action of constraints, goals and objectives which may appear as contradictory: there is a need to obtain applications while producing theoretical contributions, and to contribute to transfert of technology while insuring academic valorization of research results through publications in internationnally recognized journals; also the researchers at ESTIA need to develop scientific links with Bordeaux University, but they are employed by ESTIA, a private entity linked to the Chamber of Commerce and Industry of Bayonne-Pays Basque and their research is partially supported from answers to calls for projects. They have to combinate in investigations about corporate management individual initiative and top-down approach, and to provide a continuous flow of electricity from intermittent sources, etc.

Generally speaking, scientific activity at ESTIA consists in studying interactions inside systems which are often complex.

Hence, researchers at ESTIA try to address simultaneously the need for academic recognition and the need for concrete benefits for firms. This double need lies at the heart of the research strategy of ESTIA. This explains why part of the research, especially the part which involves Creativity, Innovation and Management Sciences is performed through Action-Research, as explained below.

ESTIA-Recherche relies on an interdisciplinary team of researchers working on scientific, technological and societal topics in order to adress transversal projects. Innovation requires common work between specialists in sciences and technologies, but also between specialists in sciences and technologies and researchers in human sciences. Hybridation of ideas, concepts, methods and scientific domains is there a powerful fertilizer.

The prospective discussions within ESTIA-Recherche to prepare the external evaluation performed in January 2015 by ANR (Agence Nationale de la Recherche) led to the elaboration of the concept of Smart Interfaces for Engineering. Before illustrating this concept through examples we will go through a little amount of historical background.

II. Some historical background

A. *Interaction: Macy Conferences and the Palo Alto group*

The objective of Macy Conferences, organised from 1942 to 1953 (at Hotel Beekman, 575, Park Avenue, New-York, except for the last one, organized at auberge Nassau, Princeton, New-Jersey), was nothing less than building a general science of the way thinking works. These conferences were organized by a pluridisciplinary group of mathematicians, logicians, anthropologists, psychologists and economists. A description of these ten conferences can be found on Wikipedia [30]. There were two main participating groups, the first wished to establish an interaction between mathematics, physics and well-established psychological sciences, and the second, a group of "cyberneticians", including the famous mathematician Norbert Wiener, that wanted to fight well-established psychological sciences on behalf of mathematical and physical sciences. The group also included John Von Neumann, another prominent mathematician who played an important role at the beginning of computer science. This cycle of conferences played a seminal role in the emergence of Information Theory, Cybernetics and Cognitive Science, and led one of the participants, the anthropologist Gregory Bateson, to form a group, known as the Palo Alto group. The object of this group was to study the "paradox of abstraction in communication". We refer to [35] for more information about this group, whose work led to a deep change in the diagnostic of mental illness. Analyzing a "personnality" is impossible without taking into account the complex network of interpersonal relationships. Schizophrenia can be understood as a way for the patient to adapt to the pathological structure of his relations with his family [9]. They also thought that the best moment for a therapist to intervene was during a crisis, when the patient would be ready to do something to find a new equilibrium, unlike the traditional method of waiting for the patient to "cool down". Of course ESTIA Recherche does not intend to perform mental therapy, but the idea of taking into consideration the interactions of a person or a system with external environment plays an important role in the scientific approach developed at ESTIA.

B. $B = f(P, E)$, *Lewin's equation and Action-Research*

Action-Research did not arise all of a sudden from nowhere. In the XIX-th century, Karl Marx encouraged workers in industry to think about their living conditions by answering questionnaires (used as militant tools). This tradition of "inquiries" about peasant and/or worker situations and movements was followed more recently by Robert Linhart in his study of the struggle of workers in northeastern sugar areas of Brasil [24]. Of course ESTIA, which was created by the Chamber of Commerce and Industry of Bayonne-Pays Basque, does not have any revolutionnary goal in its research objectives, but Lewin's equation $B = f(P, E)$[23], which states that the behavior B is a function f of the person P and her or his environment E, describes heuristically various aspects of Estia-Recherche investigations. Kurt Lewin was a professor at Berlin University, specialized in Gelstat psychology. At the beginning, he was mostly interested in child psychology, and after moving to the United States he played a crucial role in the development of Action-Research, a research method where the researcher intervenes during the research and in the research, in order to bring positive changes and also to produce knowledge and theory. (He became very influential, and the U.S. government asked him during World War 2 to help dealing with food scarcity by helping customers to learn how to use and cook cheap cuts of cattle, like heart, tongue, tripe and kidneys). These ideas had been introduced by the "Chicago group," which asked sociologists to rely on leaders of communities under consideration (population of poor neighborhoods, ethnic minorities, professional groups) in order to elaborate knowledge which comes from the bottom and goes back to the bottom. Thus, the academic researcher and community leaders become "co-researchers" who produce new knowledge and act together in various domains. We refer to [8] and [19] for modern developments of Action-Research. This approach, which sometimes relies on a thorough investigation of a single case, inspired a lot of the research performed at ESTIA on innovation and on change in corporate management and organization.

C. *Complex systems and the principle of dialogy*

The dialogy principle is a concept introduced by Edgar Morin to understand complex systems. "The dialogy principle means that two or several different "logics" are linked in a single entity, in a complex way (complementary, concurrently and antagonistically) without the duality getting lost in unity. Hence the unity of european culture is not a judeo-christian-greek-roman synthesis, it is the game not only complementary, but also concurrent and antagonistic, between these cultures which have their own logic: this is their dialogy" [28], p. 28. " "The number and depth of interactions increase when one goes to the level of interactions, not only between particles, but between organized systems, atoms, stars, molecules, and over all living being, societies . . . , and the diversity and complexity of effects and transformations produced by these interactions increases as well. Once the organisations that are the atoms and the stars are in place, the rules of the game of interactions may appear as Laws of Nature. Hence interaction is a hub between disorder, order and organization. This means in turn that order, disorder and organization are now tied, via interactions, in a single interdependent loop, where none of them can be conceived without refereeing to the others, and there they have complex (dialogic) relations, that is to say complementary, concurrent and antagonistic [27].

We refer, for example, to [3] for a survey of Edgar Morin's contributions to complexity theory. It is not necessary to perform research at ESTIA to have read the six volumes of La Méthode, or to understand deeply the filiation between the principle of dialogy and the idea of dialectics (Heraclite, de Cruse, Hegel, Marx), but the fact that ESTIA Recherche arose from the union of research groups from Engineering Sciences and Management Sciences which have been working together since 2008 allows all these researchers to have a systemic approach in their various research directions, and one could say that the concept of Smart Interfaces for Industry comes from a sucessful dialogy between these two groups.

The module "Transformées" for second year students, which is taught at ESTIA by the author of the present paper, culminates with the celebrated Shannon sampling theorem, which reconstructs all the values of a square integrable function having a compactly supported Fourier transform from the values it takes on the integers, [22] (théorème 9.5.1 p. 131). Claude Shannon was working as an engineer for Bell Telephone company, and attended the 7th, 8th and 10th Macy Conference, where he presented his Information Theory in which signification was deliberately not taken into account. Reading Edgar Morin during the preparation of this paper, I realized that the approach to noise which was presented during some conferences on signal that I attended rather recently were based on Shannon's approach - where noise is a form of disorder which should be eliminated from the signal, while other appoaches could rely on finding some order in the disorder related to the dialogy order/disorder. Of course experts in signal theory are aware of this.

III. Working on Smart Interfaces for Engineering

We now briefly describe the eight theses completed at ESTIA during the years 2015 and 2016. At first glance the topics look different:

Augmented Reality applied to conception, gestion and maintenance of urban structures and furnitures; use of model reduction algorithms to optimize placement of robotized fibers, reduced model of scavenging to optimize cylinder for a 2-stroke diesel engine; design of an architecture for measurement and diagnosis of physical parameters in critical airborne systems, algorithms and architectures for control and diagnosis of flight critical systems; study of a hybrid fuel cell/turbine system in the context of an isolated rural microgrid; visualization for an informed decision to design space exploration by shopping, accompanying maturation of concepts in eco-innovation, taking in account human factors to overcome the limitations of the Lean approaches.

But, in all situations the researchers dealt with complex systems, for which a smart approach is proposed:

Combining a monocular georeferenced tactile device with a topography laser in order to diminish the edition and interpretation errors of cartography of urban structures;

Using model reduction algorithms to reduce the number of parameters in optimization of placement of robotized fibers, and introducing a cognitive dimension in reduced and separated meta-models of the scavenging by ports in 2-stroke Diesel engines;

Relaxing tolerance to the defects of the processing chain of signal obtained from the captor by improving the mathematical model of the processing chain and introducing dynamical models in measurement, diagnosis and control of flight critical systems;

Combining a fuel cell of type SOFC and a microturbine to reach the best electrical performance with a low environment impact for isolated rural microgrids;

Finding efficient graphs for information visualization in design space exploration according to the paradigm design by shopping, supporting the maturation of eco-innovative concepts to overcome the so-called collective fixations during the development of eco-innovations, defining a performance model supporting an actor vision of man at work to overcome the limitations of the Lean approaches.

From these eight theses, which we now describe briefly, we see why the notion of Smart Interfaces for Engineering emerged at ESTIA.

Environment of Augmented Reality for conception, gestion and maintenance of urban structures and furnitures is the topic of the University of Bordeaux thesis of Emeric Baldisser in computer science, prepared at ESTIA (2013-2016) under a CIFRE contract [18] with SIG-IMAGE, a company located at Technopole Izarbel at Bidart [7]. This work points out the relevance of Augmented Reality in order to diminish the edition and interpretation errors in cartography of structures. A prototype is proposed, evaluated and discussed. It combines a monocular georeferenced tactile device with a topography laser. It allows to draw and consult technical plans on a 2D representation of the site in real-time. The validity of this approach with respect to french reglementation remains limited. Another approach is proposed, which consists in fitting/matching the clouds of dense points obtained from topography scanners with the orthoscopic 2D representation of the site. The interactions in the augmented environment of the site then depend on its cloud of points. They are geolocalized and follow the paradgim of Picking-Outlining-Annotating. These interactions are described in [6].

Development of model reduction algorithms to optimize the PFR process is the topic of the UTC (Université Technologique de Compiègne) thesis of Nicolas Bur, prepared at ESTIA (2012-2015) [15]. The realization by robotized processes of composites parts intends to improve productivity. Nevertheless the "Placement de Fibres Robotisées" (PFR) is still at a stage of maturation and requires numerous developments, in particular in the case of composites with thermoplastic matrix or with dry fibers. The thesis proposes different tools in order to determine in advance the best heating power to implement these composites. The difficulty arises from the fact that this power depends on many parameters, arising not only from the components (density, etc.) but also from the process itself (moving speed, number and orientation of the folds). The technique called Proper Generalized Decomposition (PGD) has been used to construct a reduced multi-parametric model and thus overcome the complexity of the system. The results were compared to those obtained by more conventional methods and also to experimental data, [14].

Reduced and separated meta-models of the scavenging by ports in 2-stroke Diesel engines to use evolutionary algorithms in search space is the topic of the thesis prepared at ESTIA by Stéphanie Cagin [16], [17]. The use of numerical methods to design a product became more and more common over the past 30 years. However, numerical models are still specialized and they do not run fast which makes their use problematic. So, some reduced models of scavenging have been developed. These models are analytical and generic; they run quickly and avoid the numerical treatment problems. They are also efficient tools in the search of design solutions. The work carried out has led to a new methodology based on a behavioral meta-model called neuro-separated including a neuronal model of state, a pseudo-dynamic neuronal model and a model with separated variables. Then, exploiting the models previously developed, a process of decision with evolutionary algorithms (genetic algorithms) is used to determine optimal designs and the fast behavioral simulation of the optimal designs solutions is done, thanks to the kriging approach. This design approach is multi-viewpoints, multi-criteria and multi-physics. It also includes a cognitive dimension: both free and controlled evolutionary explorations of solution spaces have been done. To validate the method, some qualification criteria have been evaluated for each model. They allow to understand and to assume the gap between the reduced models and the initial CFD base (where the model are coming from). This approach has led to the development of a tool of model and decision aids using Python and Matlab software programs

Study of an hybrid system fuel cell/turbine in the context of an isolated rural microgrid is the topic of the Bordeaux University thesis of Sylvain Baudouin (2012-2015) [11]. Rural areas, often located far away from the main electrical network, are particularly suitable for deploying microgrids (MG), which allow to use efficiently a large number of renewable energy sources. Biogaz, obtained from methanation of agricultural waste, is a renewable energy source available in rural areas which is esay to store in large quantities, and more reliable and less dependent from random phenomena than solar or wind turbine energy.

A study of the state of the art leads to the conclusion that an hybrid system combining a fuel cell of type SOFC and a microturbine (MT) allows to reach the best electrical performance with a low environmenral impact. A unique multilevel converter of type SLNPC has been used to integrate the microgrid to the main electrical network. The first objective of the command strategy applied to the SLNPC converter was to regulate the power of the SOFC fuel cell to its nominal value, and the second objective was to fix the tension and the frequency of the microgrid when it is disconnected from the main electrical network. This system has been tested and validated through simulation and then experimentally on the EnerGea platform [21] of ESTIA.

Design of an architecture for measurement and diagnosis of physical parameters in critical airborne systems is the topic of the University of Bordeaux thesis of Romain Martin (2012-2015) [26]. The objective of this work was to propose a new architecture for measurement of physical parameters as temperature, pression and speed in airborne systems in critical situations. The goal for this architecture is to improve the integrity of the measured data while keeping their level of disponibility and fiability in highly critical airborne systems. The solution consits in relaxing tolerance to the defects of the processing chain of signal obtained from the captor. In order to do this more functions are introduced, including the mathematical model of the processing chain, to make the system smarter. The thesis was supported by a CIFRE contract [18] with the Thales company [34].

Algorithms and architectures for control and diagnosis of flight critical system is the topic of the Bordeaux thesis prepared at the same time by Alexandre Bobrinskoy [12],[13]. Flight-Critical Systems such as Electromechanical Actuators driven by Engine Control Units (ECU) or Flight Control Units (FCU) are designed and developed regarding drastic safety requirements. In this study, an actuator control and monitoring ECU architecture based on analytic redundancy is proposed. In case of fault occurrences, material redundancies in avionic equipment allow certain critical systems to reconfigure or to switch into a safe mode. However, material redundancies increase aircraft equipment size, weight and power (SWaP). Monitoring based on dynamical models is an interesting way to further enhance safetyand availability without increasing the number of redundant items. Model-base default detection and isolation such as observers and parity space are recalled in this study. The properties of differential flatness for nonlinear systems and endogenous feedback linearisation are used with nonlinear diagnosis models. Linear and nonlinear observers are then compared with an application on hybrid stepper motor (HSM). A testing bench was specially designed to observe in real-time the behaviour of the diagnosis models when faults occur on the stator windings of a HSM. The thesis was also supported by a CIFRE contract with the Thales company.

Information Vizualization for an informed decision to design space exploration by shopping is the topic of the Centrale-Supelec thesis prepared by Audrey Abi Akle at ESTIA (2012-2015) [2]. In Design space exploration, the resulting data, from simulation of large amount of new design alternatives, can lead to information overload when one good design solution must be chosen. The design space exploration relates to a multi-criteria optimization method in design but in manual mode, for which appropriate tools to support multi-dimensional data visualization are employed. For the designer, a three-phase process - discovery, optimization, selection - is followed according to a paradigm called Design by Shopping. Exploring the design space helps to gain insight into both feasible and infeasible solutions subspaces, and into solutions presenting good trade-offs. Designers learn during these graphical data manipulations and the selection of an optimal solution is based on a so-called informed decision. The objective of this research is the performance of graphs for design space exploration according to the three phases of the Design by Shopping process.

The results reveal three efficient graphs for the design space exploration: the Scatter Plot Matrix for the discovery phase and for informed decision-making, the Simple Scatter Plot for the optimization phase and the Parallel Coordinate Plot for the selection phase in a multi-attribute as well as multi-objective situation. In consequence, five graphs, identified as potentially efficient, are tested through two experiments. In the first, thirty participants tested three graphs, in three design scenarios where one car must be chosen out of a total of forty, for the selection phase in a multi-attribute situation where preferences are enounced. A response quality index is proposed to compute the choice quality for each of the three given scenarios, the optimal solutions being compared to the ones resulting from the graphical manipulations. In the second experiment, forty-two novice designers solved two design problems with three graphs. In this case, the performance of graphs is tested for informed decision-making and for the three phases of the process in a multi-objective situation. Part of this work was presented in [1].

How to support the maturation of eco-innovative concepts?: proposition of the method MIRAS to overcome collective lock-ins and explore stakeholder networks is the topic of the thesis prepared at ESTIA by Marion Real [31], [32], using a Research-Action approach inside the support group APESA. During the development of eco-innovations, companies are looking to implement a new activity that can create ruptures with its existing practices and cause many changes in their business model. In such complex situations, the stakeholders of emerging projects have some difficulties to consciously deviate from existing cognitive frameworks to explore alternatives in line with the initial goals of the project. Thus, they take trajectories that may lead to a dilution of the environmental and social values or cause the abandonment of projects. The work presented in the thesis focuses on the maturation of eco-innovative concepts and seeks to develop tools and methods to avoid and overcome such situations called collective fixations. The methodological approach is structured in two steps:- The analysis of three case-studies of eco-innovative projects allowed to characterize supporting practices and deepen the knowledge on the collective fixation present during the maturation of concepts. This first study has fueled the design process of the MIRAS method, the main contribution of this research. The MIRAS method offers a toolkit designed for eco-innovation intermediaries in order to help them to structure their intervention during the stage of concept maturation. Specifically the tools help to improve the sustainability potential of concepts, to analyze project group behaviors during sessions and to revisit stakeholder networks so as to anticipate future mutations and news ways of incubation.

Taking into account the human factor to overcome the limitations of the Lean approaches: proposal for a performance model and an accompanying methodology is the topic of the thesis prepared by Patrick Badets at ESTIA [4], [5]. Lean is an approach aiming at eliminating non-value added operations, used by companies to improve the performance of their production activities. Companies applying this approach are observing rapid gains in operational terms but gradually some observe a fall in operating results or a degradation of the health of work force. The objective of the thesis was to overcome these limits and improve the ability of those of the company to anticipate and to take corrective actions. The performance model and the decision adopted by corporate actors to deploy Lean was questioned. It is proposed that corporate actors evaluate the efficiency of production, processed by the Lean approaches, taking into account not only the operational level of performance, but also the human dimension integrating realwork activity. A performance model that supports a kind of actor vision of man at work is defined. To help corporate actors to change their existing model of Lean performance, a support methodology based on a reengineering approach integrating coaching aimed at changing there presentations of the actors by a sociocognitive learning is offered. This methodology is based on modeling tools to represent the impact of this new performance model on the decision and on the sustainability of the lean benefits.

IV. Conclusion

We hope that this survey will help the researchers in the field of Smart Interfaces to Industry to have a more global vision of scientific activities in this direction and understand how science and technology and management sciences can help each other. We also hope that this paper will help other scientists to discover this emerging subject, and, more generally, to get interested in a systemic approach to complex systems.

Acknowledgment

The author, who has been the Research Director of ESTIA from november 2007 to July 2015 and is still present at ESTIA, would like to thank all the members of ESTIA-Recherche for the warm and creative pluridisciplinary environment he has been enjoying there during all these years. He also wishes to thank Jean-Roch Guiresse, who was director of ESTIA until March 2016, and the new director Patxi Elissalde, as well as the ESTIA corporate fund for their constant support to research activities. The intervention of Patxi Elissalde at the symposium on Smart Interfaces held at ESTIA on November 18, 2016 gave an interesting synthesis about complex systems and the societal, environnemental and economic, technological and conceptual challenges that need to be adressed by researchers at ESTIA working on Smart Interfaces for Engineering in the following years [20]. The author also benefited from many conferences given at ESTIA, in particular from the conference given before the opening of the 2012 edition of "24h de l'Innovation" by Jeremy Rifkin, an internationnally recognized expert in scientific and economic prospective [33], who presented in October 2012 at ESTIA his convictions concerning the challenges of globalisation, the emergency of climate change and the impact of energy revolutions which change the economic paradigm.

References

[1] Audrey Abi Akle, Stéphanie Minel, and Bernard Yannou, *Information visualization for selection in Design by Shopping*, Research in Engineering Design **28** 1 (2017), 99-117.

[2] Audrey Abi Akle, Visualisation d'information pour une décision informée en exploration d'espace de conception par shopping, thèse, Ecole Centrale Paris, 2015.

[3] Ali Aït Abdelmalek, *Edgar Morin, sociologue et théoricien de la complexité*, Sociétés **86** 4 (2004), 99-117.

[4] Patrick Badets, Véronique Pilnière, and Christophe Merlo, *Kaizen en contexte Lean : La santé des opérateurs mise à mal*, Projectics/ Proyctica / Projectique, **13** 1 (2015) 11-22.

[5] Patrick Badets, Prise en compte du facteur humain pour pallier les limites d'une démarche Lean: proposition d'un modèle de performance et d'une méthode d'accompagnement, thèse, Université de Bordeaux, 2016.

[6] Emeric Baldisser, Jean-Marc Cieutat, and Pascal Guitton, *Apports de la Réalité Augmentée à la Gestion de Réseaux et de Mobiliers Urbains*, 8èmes journées de l'Association Française de Réalité Virtuelle, Augmentée, Mixte et d'Interaction 3D, Oct 2013, Laval, France.

[7] Emeric Baldisser, Environnement de réalité augmentée pour la conception, la gestion et la maintenance d'ouvrages et de mobiliers urbains, thèse, Université de Bordeaux, 2016.

[8] René Barbier, La Recherche-Action, collection Anthropos, 1996.

[9] Gregory Bateson, Don D. Jackson, Jay Haley and John Weakland, *Toward a theory of schizophrenia*, Behavioral Science **1** 4 (1956), 251-254.

[10] Sylvain Baudoin, Ionel Vechiu, Haritza Camblong-Ruiz, Jean- Michel Vinassa, and Linda Barelli, *Sizing and control of a Solid Oxide Fuel Cell/Gas microTurbine hybrid power system using a unique inverter for rural microgrid integration*, Applied Energy **176** (2016), 272-281.

[11] Sylvain Baudoin, Etude d'un système hybride pile à combustible/microturbine dans un contexte microréseau rural isolé, thèse, Université de Bordeaux, 2015.

[12] Alexandre Bobrinskoy, Franck Cazaurang, Michel Gatti, Olivier Guérineau, and Benoît Bluteau, *Model-based fault detection and isolation design for flight-critical actuators in a harsh environment*, 31st Digital Avionics Systems Conference (2012), Williamsburg, États-Unis.

[13] Alexandre Bobrinskoy, Algorithms and architectures for control and diagnosis of flight critical systems, thèse, Université de Bordeaux, 2015.

[14] Nicolas Bur, Pierre Joyot, Chady Ghnatios, Pierre Villon, Elas Cueto, and Francisco Chinesta, *On the use of model order reduction for simulating automated fibre placement processes*, Advanced Modeling and Simulation in Engineering Sciences, **3** 1 (2016), 1-18.

[15] Nicolas Bur, Développement d'algorithmes de réduction de modèles pour l'optimisation du procédé de Placement de Fibres Robotisé, Thèse, Université de Technologie de Compiègne, 2015.

[16] Stéphanie Cagin, Xavier Fischer, Eric Delacourt, Nachida Bourabaa, Céline Morin, Daniel Coutellier, Bernard Carre, and Sylvain Loumé, *A new reduced model of scavenging to optimize cylinder design*, Simulation Transactions of the Society for Modeling Design, **92** 3 (2016), 507-520.

[17] Stéphanie Cagin, Méta-modèles réduits et séparés du comportement de balayage d'un moteur Diesel 2-temps pour l'exploration évolutionnaire des espaces de solutions, thèse, Université de Bordeaux, 2015.

[18] Conventions CIFRE cifre.anrt.asso.fr

[19] Linda Dickens, and Karen Watkins, *Action research: rethinking Lewin*, Management Learning, **30** 2 (1999), 127-140.

[20] Patxi Elissalde, oral communication, Workshop on Smart Interfaces, 11 november 2016, ESTIA, Bidart (France), in Rapport d'Activit Scientifique 2015-2016 de l'ESTIA, chap. 3, ESTIA, 2017.

[21] Plateforme Technologique EnerGea energea.estia.fr

[22] Jean Esterle, Transformées, cours ESTIA, 2017.

[23] Kurt Lewin, Principles of Topological Psychology, translated by Fritz and Grace Heider, McGraw-Hill, New-York, 1936.

[24] Robert Linhart, Le Sucre et la Faim, Enquête dans les régions sucrières du Nord-Est brésilien, Editions de Minuit, 1981. (ISBN 978-2-7013-0306-6)

[25] Romain Martin, Guillaume Terrasson, Renaud Briand, Michel Gatti, and Olivier Guérineau, *Process for Diagnosis Method Selection of Flight Critical Systems*, Proceedings of the Digital Avionics Systems Conference- 31st DASC (2012), Williamsburg, États-Unis.

[26] Romain Martin, Design of an architecture for measurement and diagnosis of physical parameters in critical airborne systems, thèse, Université de Bordeaux, 2015.

[27] Edgar Morin, La Méthode: la Nature de la nature, Editions du Seuil, Paris, 1977

[28] Edgar Morin, Penser l'Europe, Gallimard, Paris, 1987.

[29] Edgar Morin, Introduction à la pensée complexe, Editions du Seuil, Paris,1990.

[30] Wikipedia, *Conférences Macy*, 2017.

[31] Marion Real, Iban Lizarralde, Jérémy Legardeur, Benjamin Tyl, and Dominique Millet, *A cognitive approach to complement support practices for the maturation of eco-innovations*, Projectics / Proyctica Projectique, **14** 1(2015), 23-39.

[32] Marion Real, Accompagner la maturation des concepts au sein de l'eco-innovation: proposition de la méthode MIRAS, pour aider à surmonter les fixations collectives et explorer les réseaux de parties prenantes, thèse, Université de Bordeaux, 2015.

[33] Jeremy Rifkin, The third Industrial Revolution, Palgrave MacMillan, 2011, ISBN 978-0230341975

[34] Groupe Thales www.thalesgroup.com/fr

[35] Jean-Jacques Wittezaele, and Teresa Garcia, *A la recherche de l'Ecole de Palo-Alto*, Seuil, Paris, 1992. (ISBN 2020136260)

Precision Livestock Farming: A Multidisciplinary Paradigm

Guillaume Terrasson, Eric Villeneuve, Véronique Pilnière, Alvaro Llaria
ESTIA, F-64210 Bidart, France
e-mail: {g.terrasson, e.villeneuve, v.pilniere, a.llaria}@estia.fr

Abstract—**Since several years, Precision Livestock Farming (PLF) has experienced a significant progress mainly due to the electronics and embedded systems miniaturization, along with the Internet of Things expansion. Geolocation and animal behavior identification are common research subjects in PLF, and several solutions have been proposed in this frame. Nevertheless, the development and generalization of this kind of tools must still face up several technical and societal challenges and, in order to overcome these difficulties, a multidisciplinary work is necessary. In this context, this paper presents the e-Pasto experimental platform, which employs different smart interfaces, as a case-study to analyze the main issues related to the implementation of PLF solutions. Along with this analysis, some relevant aspects of current systems are studied and discussed from different points of view, from technological to human ones, with the aim of offering a new vision, which tries to take into account, as far as possible, the final user needs.**

Keywords-Smart Interfaces for Engineering; Data Processing; Decision-making; Systemic Approach; Precision Livestock Farming.

I. INTRODUCTION

The evolution of electronic devices, the improvement of wireless communication networks and the Internet access availability during the last years are the main reasons of the Internet of Things (IoT) expansion. Nowadays, IoT based solutions are considered a promising way to collect data that can be processed and analyzed by final users in order, for example, to supervise a manufacturing process or to monitor the health of home-based patient.

In this frame, solutions based on aggregation of technologies, such as interconnected ubiquitous objects, represent an interesting option to offer new tools that may improve livestock productivity and product quality, reducing at the same time the work hardness. Moreover, other information about animals and the whole cattle, such as physiological conditions combined with environmental data, is necessary to correctly monitor the livestock: survey of animal activity and location in large pastures and small areas, diseases prediction or detection, improvement of livestock nutrition effectiveness, productivity and quality optimization, ensuring at the same time the animal well-being. However, nowadays, the development of this kind of tools stays in a research phase because of a number of challenges that must be still faced up, from both technical and societal points of view without forgetting final user needs. In this context, the aim of this paper is to identify and analyze, using the e-Pasto platform as case-study, the different difficulties to be overcome. The need for a multidisciplinary approach to provide useful smart interfaces that allows the interaction among livestock, farmers and also the environment, based on suitable technical solutions, is also proved.

This document is structured as follows. In Section II, after a brief review of the existing research work concerning Precision Livestock Farming (PLF), the e-Pasto platform is presented together with the obtained results. Section III illustrates, considering the e-Pasto case-study, that a multidisciplinary approach, covering from technical knowledge to human sciences, is needed to face up the different found problematics. Finally, Section V concludes this paper.

II. CASE-STUDY: THE E-PASTO PLATFORM

A. *State of the Art of Precision Livestock Farming*

PLF consists essentially in acquisition, collection and analysis of data from each animal and its environment employing, as illustrated by Figure 1, different Information and Communications Technologies (ICTs) such as sensors, communication networks, decision-making algorithms and human-to-machine interfaces (HMIs) [1]. PLF allows farmers to access new services such as individual feeding, health monitoring, animal localization and, consequently, to conduct in a more effective way their livestock ensuring at the same time productivity, animal well-being and economic benefits.

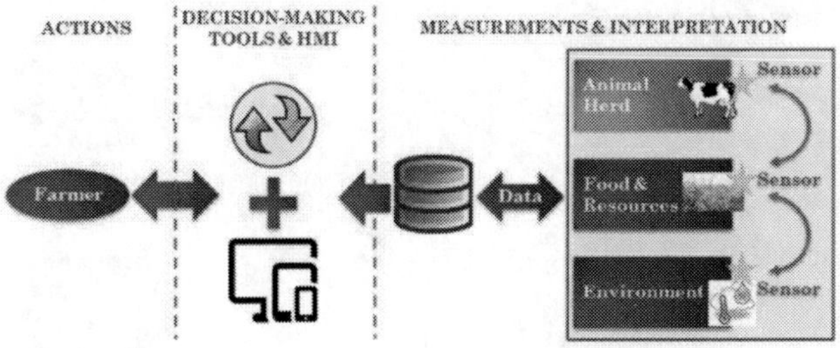

Figure 1. General architecture of a PLF solution [1].

There is a number of research works and solutions concerning PLF that can be found in the scientific literature [2]. A frequently employed solution is Radio Frequency Identification Technology (RFID), which is used to identify animals. From a regulatory point of view, RFID animal identification guarantees the traceability through the feed-animal-food chain. However, some current works and commercial solutions use also this technology in order to manage and automatize animal feeding regime or to allow the heat detection [1].

Moreover, ICT for domotics applications can be also applied to monitor the animal and to control cattle environment [3]. In barns, this kind of technology is useful to guarantee the animal well-being and health by regulating temperature, humidity and concentration of ammonia, among others. In the case of extensive farming exploitations, meteorological sensors help to predict the displacement of the cattle and, consequently, to improve their management.

In addition, accelerometer and other sensors (temperature, geolocation) are commonly used for animal's health and behavior monitoring. In the scientific literature, accelerometers and dataloggers have been largely applied to identify the animal behavior and principal activities [4]: grazing, resting, walking. This information, provided by accelerometers and coupled with a decision-making software, allows farmers to determine the welfare and health of their animals, optimizing the veterinary intervention.

Virtual fencing technologies are also a classical example of PLF solutions [5]. In extensive farming, virtual fencing combining Global Positioning System (GPS) and Geographic Information System (GIS) contributes to understand the cattle's displacements and also to enhance herd and grazing resources management. This capacity of remote monitoring allows farmers to optimize the time needed to accomplish their daily tasks, resulting in a better productivity, with a positive impact on the environment too.

B. e-Pasto Platform: Description and Main Results

In order to better illustrate what a PLF solution is, the e-Pasto platform [6] will be thereafter presented as a case-study. This solution, developed in the context of a European research project and dedicated to cattle supervision in extensive farming environments, is composed of four main parts: the motion devices, a communication infrastructure, an information system and a human-machine interface, as it can be seen in Figure 2.

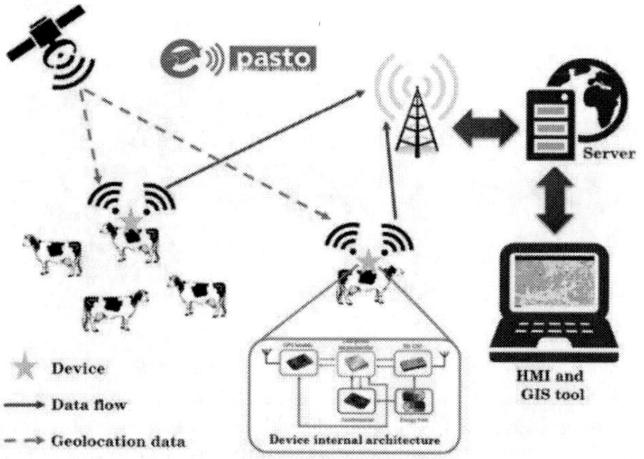

Figure 2. Global architecture of the e-Pasto platform.

The motion devices, which are directly embedded onto the animal collar, include a GPS and an accelerometer, and collect position and behavior data from animals. These data are transmitted to a remote server through the wireless communication network provided by SIGFOX©. The aggregated data can be remotely exploited by the farmer in two different ways:

- To locate animals in mountain pastures during the summer period, allowing at the same time a better management of the cattle and the grazing resources using a virtual fencing solution.
- To measure and supervise animal behavior with the aim to warn the farmer in case of eventual disease or predation activity against their cattle.

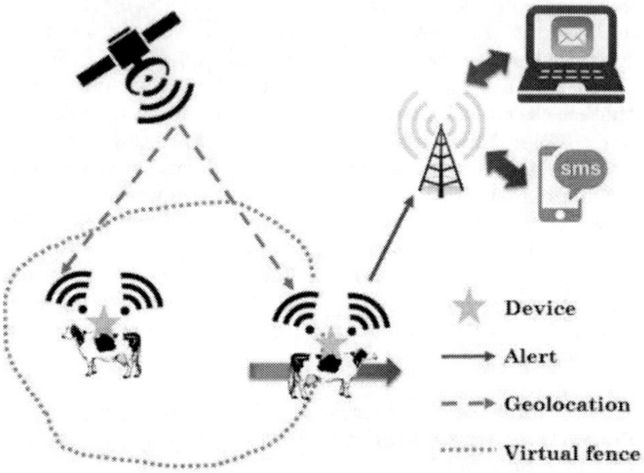

Figure 3. e-Pasto virtual fencing principle.

Real field tests were conducted in two experimental zones, one located in Ariège (France) and the other one located in Gipuzkoa (Spain), to validate the architecture of the platform and their global performances. During these field tests, the correct performance of the motion devices in terms of size, weight and autonomy was validated. More precisely, the motion devices employed in the e-Pasto platform offered a size and weight adapted to different animal species such as bovines, ovine and horses, along with an autonomy in energy generally equal or higher to 7 months, which was assured taking one location position per hour. These position data were sent afterwards through the long-range low-power consumption network developed by SIGFOX©.

As it has been said before, motion devices include an accelerometer. It has been proved that the data issued from the accelerometer can be processed in order to detect several behavior patterns (resting, walking and running), functionality which ameliorates the animal geolocation precision [7]. By the moment, this behavior identification has been only tested on humans.

To conclude, it is important to highlight that one of the most remarkable results of the e-Pasto platform was the validation of an innovative virtual fencing solution, whose principle of operation is depicted in Figure 3. This solution allows the farmer to draw and define the size and shape of their virtual fences, using the point-in-polygon geometric computation principle, by means of the HMI developed for the platform. If an animal equipped with the motion device goes out of the limits of its authorized virtual fence, an alert message is generated at the server level and transmitted to the farmer by SMS or e-mail. Consequently, contrary to other solutions proposed in the scientific literature [5], the e-Pasto virtual fencing solution is not based on a remotely application of negative cues (vibration, electrical stimulation) to induce a movement when the animal is detected out of the limits of a virtual fence. Instead, once the farmer is warned, he has the liberty to take a decision about how to solve the problem with the concerned animal.

III. Discussion of Main Issues

As it has been seen in previous sections, the application of PLF solutions based on ICTs seems to be an attractive way to motivate people to work in agriculture and livestock domains, by offering tools that improve productivity and product quality, reducing at the same time the work hardness and ensuring the animal well-being. In addition, the current changing context about intensive farming methods, implying a constant evolution of legislation, ethical issues and economic challenges, together with global warming, makes PLF solutions an interesting support to assist farmers in their decision-making process.

This section, always with the e-Pasto platform case-study, the state of the art and the current context in perspective, will highlight the main challenges and issues that PLF solution providers have to face up to generalize these solutions, applying a multidisciplinary approach.

A. *Technical Challenges*

From a technical point of view, several issues at different levels of a PLF solution can be identified.

1) Data collection and transmission

As illustrated by Figure 1, PLF solutions are based on the automation of data aggregation and transmission, not only at the animal level but also at the environment level [1] [3]. This way, technologies involving embedded electronics and sensors are very often used to capture the information needed for PLF applications.

First of all, accuracy and reliability of the collected data are major issues that directly impact the design of embedded electronics devices. In the frame of the e-Pasto platform, where animals have to be located in an outdoor wide area of 2000 hectares, it can be acceptable for end users a precision around 10 meter using GPS technology. On the other hand, when animals are located in an indoor environment such as barns, the employ of GPS is not reliable and, in addition, the technology to be used for animal geolocation should assure a more accurate position measurement, in the order of centimeters. Consequently, as shown by these simple examples, the election of the location measurement technology depends on several parameters like the environment, the sort of animal or even the application.

Data transmission in outdoor or indoor real environments is also a complex task due to eventual multipath propagation, shadowing, or signal attenuation [2]. Therefore, the choice among current communication technologies, such as Wifi, cellular telephony or ZigBee, in example, must take into account many aspects like data range, quantity of data to be transmitted, indoor or outdoor environment, always with the goal of minimizing any loss of data, which could perturb the overall reliability of the PLF solution.

Finally, it must be pointed up that the main challenge concerning data collection and transmission is to achieve an optimal trade-off among different aspects: accuracy, reliability of data collection and transmission, together with acceptable size and weight of embedded devices carried by animals in harsh environments, offering at the same time enough energetic autonomy to assure the correct operation during long periods of time [6].

2) Processing and exploitation of the data

The processing and the exploitation of the collected data within the framework of the e-Pasto platform are intended to help breeders in their decision-making process in order to improve their management of livestock placed in mountain pastures.

In addition to data issued from sensors placed on animals (geolocation, accelerometer, physiology, etc.) and mapping of the pastures area, the decision support mechanisms can use numerous additional data such as:

- Topographic data to qualify areas suitable for feeding livestock but also risky areas (cliffs, rocks, etc.).
- Data derived from the expert knowledge (breeders, scientists, mountain guides, etc.) to identify hazardous or accident-proning areas, protected areas for environmental reasons, as well as information about predators (attack locations, predator identification...). It is also possible to integrate collaborative aspects into the e-Pasto platform to allow an exchange of information between breeders and thus have expert knowledge updated more regularly and about wider areas.

Consequently, the data capitalized by this kind of PLF platform are diverse and can represent a large volume of information. The heterogeneity and the amount of data collected highlight several challenges that will need to be addressed to develop a powerful decision support tool.

Firstly, the diversity of capitalized data and their potentially random reliability [3] (failure of sensors, human errors, etc.) implies to choose a formalism adapted to the modeling of uncertain and heterogeneous knowledge. There are many tools relevant to this problem. For example, Case-Based Reasoning (CBR) [8], Constraint Satisfaction Problems (CSP) [9] or Bayesian networks [10] allow to cover part of the needs. Many methodologies linking several of these approaches to address the problem in its entirety are available in the literature [11].

Secondly, capitalized data can be used in several ways. The first possibility is to visualize the raw information on the map, such as the location of the last predator attacks, the protected areas or the current position of the livestock. These data alone help the user to decide. For example, when positioning a virtual fence, it may be useful to know if there has been a predator attack in the area. Another use may be to pre-process the data to obtain additional information [3]. For example, it would be possible, with time-based geolocation data, to identify overexploited areas to allow the farmer to act accordingly. A last way of using this data could be a virtual assistant, which, depending on the choices made by the breeder when using the platform, would offer additional information enabling him to refine his decision. For example, if the user defines a virtual fence too close to a risk area, the software would suggest an alternative positioning.

Finally, a major issue in decision-making is the level of autonomy of the tool. It is possible to propose a solution which, based on the capitalized data, calculates and decides alone the procedure to be followed (for example, define automatically virtual fences). An alternative to this kind of tool lies in the suggestion by the tool of possible choices for the user (based on the capitalized data) but leaving him the final decision. This major design choice is a very important criterion for the acceptance and therefore the use of the tool by the breeders [12].

B. Challenges for Users

If a closer look at the challenges induced by technological innovations in the agricultural sector is token, the e-Pasto platform finds its place. Indeed, looking at the evolution of the agricultural sector since the 1950s, there is little in common with practices applied today. The agricultural sector is constantly evolving (decrease of agricultural occupation for 50 years, evolution of agricultural policy, etc.). Being a breeder 50 years ago is no longer the same thing today. The evolution of farmers' practices is accompanied by a change in their needs. This aspect refers to a broader issue: what are the users' needs? Identifying the needs of users is inherent to technological developments. One of the reasons for this importance is that if the system does not satisfy a need, it will not be used by the user [2].

In addition, behind all these elements, for the farmer the question is: what is the impact of the technology on his daily tasks? In order to define the daily tasks, researchers and designers must precisely list different work situations of farmer and see with the farmer which of them are easy or difficult to do. Researchers must also understand what the work of the farmer is. A farmer cannot be forced to use a system that involves more constraints in his work than facilities. It is the system that must be adapted to the user, not the opposite.

Furthermore, many other important aspects should be considered: to be farmer in a country A is not the same thing that be farmer in a country B, and the needs of young farmers are different from those of very experienced ones. In addition, the farmer is not the only one user: animals must be also taken into account. For example, behaviors of cows in a cattle are different from one animal to another. All these aspects lead to define plenty of different work situations [13] [14]. Once these work situations defined, researchers and farmers will be able to dialogue and find solutions adapted both to the farmer and the animal. The found solutions must be always a trade-off between possibilities, constraints of daily work and technology.

Finally, it should not be forgotten that the agricultural sector is in continuous evolution. Thus, it is necessary to think about changes and the technological system could take into account these changes, creating a virtuous circle. To make a change, it is crucial to identify users in the earliest phases of the project and also integrate them into the development process.

IV. Conclusions and Perspectives

The work presented in this paper has presented some basic characteristics of PLF systems, showing at the same time the main contributions of the e-Pasto platform to these area, but not only: this article tries to initiate an exhaustive reflection concerning smart interfaces and their empowerment capacity, described in Figure 4.

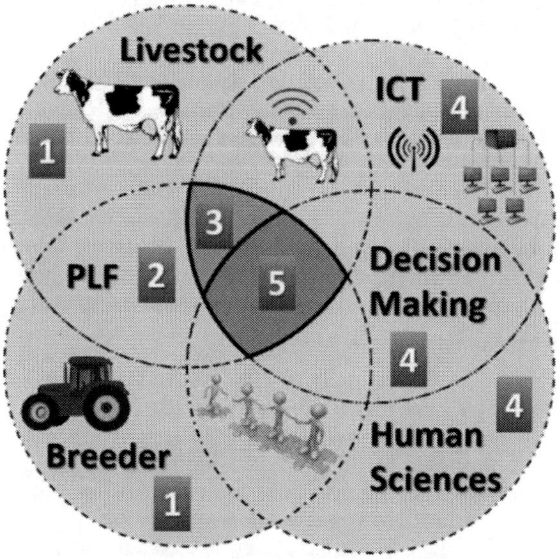

Figure 4. Smart Interfaces in a transdisciplinary project.

Contrary to classical thinking and as it has been said before, users (Label 1 in Figure 4) must be integrated the earliest as possible in the innovation project (Label 2 in Figure 4). This is the starting point.

Smart interfaces can be defined from two complementary and inseparable points of view. Firstly, the interface considered as the main contribution of the project: technological product or system (Label 3 in the Figure 4). Secondly, the interface considered as the transdisciplinary innovating process (Labels 4 and 5 in the Figure 4) [15]. In other words, to overcome the different issues analyzed in this paper, it is necessary that researchers and designers work together along with an integration of users in their reflections. Working together is not easy for people who are specialists in a precise field because everyone has his own logic. To work together, a decompartmentalization of scientific disciplines is mandatory, as well as an open-mindedness of researchers and the respect for different thinking. Consequently, it is imperative to exchange throughout the project to better understand each other. The result of this work is a trade-off between the expectations of the different stakeholders [16].

ACKNOWLEDGMENT

The work presented in this paper has been developed in the frame of the e-Pasto project (pilot project of AGRIPIR), which has been financially supported by the European Commission in the frame of the Spain-France-Andorra Territorial Cooperation Operational Program (POCTEFA 2007-2013) and the FEDER funds.

REFERENCES

[1] F. Bocquier et al., "Elevage de précision en systèmes d'élevage peu intensifiés [Precision farming in extensive livestock systems]," INRA Productions Animales, pp. 101-112, vol. 27, 2014.

[2] T-M. Banhazi et al., "Precision Livestock Farming: an international review of scientific and commercial aspects," International Journal of Agricultural and Biological Engineering (IJABE), pp. 1-7, vol. 5, no. 3, 2012.

[3] L. Ruiz-Garcia, L. Lunadei, P. Barreiro, and J-I. Robla, "A Review of Wireless Sensor Technologies and Applications in Agriculture and Food Industry: State of the Art and Current Trends," Sensors, pp. 4728-4750, vol. 9, 2009.

[4] D-D. Brown, R. Kays, M. Wikelski, R. Wilson, and A-P. Klimley, "Observing the unwatchable through acceleration logging of animal behavior," Animal Biotelemetry, pp. 1-20, 2013.

[5] D. M. Anderson, "Virtual fencing-past, present and future," The Rangeland Journal, pp. 65-78, vol. 26, 2007.

[6] A. Llaria, G. Terrasson, H. Arregui, and A. Hacala, "Geolocation and monitoring platform for extensive farming in mountain pastures," Proc. IEEE International Conference on Industrial Technology (ICIT 15), March 2015, pp. 2420-2425.

[7] G. Terrasson, A. Llaria, A. Marra, and S. Voaden, "Accelerometer based solution for precision livestock farming: geolocation enhancement and animal activity identification," IOP Conference Series: Materials Science and Engineering, pp. 1-5, vol. 138, no. 1, 2016.

[8] A. Aamodt and E. Plaza, "Case-based reasoning: foundational issues, methodological variations, and system approaches," Artificial Intelligence Communications, IOS Press, pp. 39-59, vol. 7, no. 1, 1994.

[9] R. Dechter, "Constraint processing," Morgan Kaufmann Publishers, Inc., 2003, ISBN 1-55860-890-7.

[10] F. Jensen and T. Nielsen, "Bayesian Networks and Decision Graphs," Information Science and Statistics, Springer, 2007.

[11] E. Villeneuve, C. Béler, F. Pérès, L. Geneste, and E. Reubrez, "Decision-Support Methodology to Assess Risk in End-of-Life Management of Complex Systems,". (In Press: 2016) IEEE Systems Journal, pp. 1-10, ISSN: 1932-8184.

[12] D.J. Panell, "Social and economic challenges in the development of complex farming systems," Agroforestry Systems, pp. 393-409, vol. 45, 1999.

[13] V. Pilnière and C. Merlo, "Une approche transdisciplinaire et systémique pour favoriser le changement dans l'entreprise [A transdisciplinary and systemic approach to promote changes in the enterprises]," International Journal of Projectics, pp. 63-73, vol. 7, no. 1, 2011, ISSN: 2031-9703, ISBN: 9782804165222.

[14] C. Merlo and V. Pilnière, "Analyse des situations de travail dans une démarche de prévention des risques professionnels: proposition d'une méthodologie d'apprentissage à destination des acteurs [Analysis of work situations for the prevention of occupational risks: proposal of a learning methodology oriented to the involved actors]," 84th ACFAS Conference, May 2016.

[15] E. Morin, "Quelle Université pour demain ? Vers une évolution transdisciplinaire de l'Université [What University for tomorow? Towards a transdisciplinary evolution of the University]," Motivation, no. 24, 1997.

[16] C. Merlo and V. Pilnière, "Intervention conjointe SPI-SHS au service de la performance d'une organisation de soins à domicile [Combined application of Engineering Sciences and Social and Human Sciences for the performance of a home care organization]," ProjecticSanté, Oct. 2015.

Restructuring Unstructured Documents

On the use of smart and semi-automatic interfaces to structure unstructured data

Jacques Péré-Laperne[1, 2]
[1]A3I
F-64210 Bidart, France
email : j.perelaperne@gmail.com

Nadine Couture[2]
[2]ESTIA, Univ Bordeaux, LaBRI, UMR 5800
F-64210 Bidart, France
email: nadine.couture@u-bordeaux.fr

***Abstract*— Every day, the volume of the world's digital data increases considerably. Over 75% of these data are non-structured. This paper is about restructuring graphic information contained in Portable Document Format (PDF) files and/or vector files. These documents are generally held by "Smart Factory" services: design offices, methods departments, new work departments and company maintenance services. To restructure these data, we propose using Knowledge Discovery in Databases (KDD) methods. Although, theoretically, the user is present during the KDD, in practice, this is not the case. This was observed by Fayard in 2003 at the KDD conference. Generally, the user is only present during the validation phase. We show why, in data restructuring, the user must be at the heart of the process and present at all stages. We can talk about (A)KDD for the Anthropocentric Knowledge Discovery in Databases .The first stage of this restructuring consists of extracting graphic and text objects contained in Portable Document Format (PDF) files to put them in a pivot data format. The second stage consists of coding this information in the form of an alphabet. The third stage consists of recreating the graphic and text components which are repeated in these files (which we shall refer to as graphemes). And the fourth stage consists either (1) of automatically identifying these graphemes based on knowledge or (2) presenting them so the user identifies and introduces them into the knowledge base. It is this entire restructuring process, which we will describe in this paper. As we highlighted, in this incremental process it is people who play the main role, assisted by computers and not the opposite.**

Keywords- Data Minning; Computer Human Interface (CHI); Portable Document Format (PDF); Knowledge Discovery in Databases (KDD); Graphic reconstruction; Pattern recognition .

I. Introduction

A. *Context*

Currently, almost all information which is generated and circulates worldwide is digital. In 2001, Nigay [1] stated in "Modality of interaction & multi-modality", a University of Berkeley project estimated, that the quantity of data generated annually in the world was an exaoctet (1 million terabytes = 10^{18} bytes). 99.997% of these data are available in digital form''.

The International Data Corporation (IDC) predicted that these data would between now and 2020 increase to 40 zettabytes (ZB), = 10^{21} octets), i.e., 50 times more than in 2010 and 40 000 times more than in 2001[24].

Digital data are increasing considerably. These digital data are mostly non-structured or more exactly destructured. Destructured because, today, they are produced by software, but stored in very "poor" data format files. Computer World states that non-structured information could represent over 70% - 80% of all world data, and, 95 % of the "Big Data" [25]. These data contain a priceless wealth for the companies which own them, provided they are restructured.

B. *Real industrial need*

The data present in destructured files are visible, transmissible and archivable, but they cannot be used, modified, and more generally they are inoperable. Any mechanism which enables these data to be restructured and used represents an extraordinary benefit for their owners. This explains the explosion of research in the field of KDD.

Restructuring does not need to be total. Often partial reconstruction is sufficient and it is the user who will decide on the level of reconstruction.

We can take, for example, the case of an aircraft manufacturer, which has aircraft wiring diagrams. If it needs to know the whys and wherefores of equipotentials for part of the aircraft, the user will not need to restructure all the information. Knowing only several pages of connectors and equipotentials, as well as several components, is enough.

In 2003, the LORIA team from Nancy made the following observation [2]: "Grassroot users, as well as large companies, have a huge amount of information at their disposal, but this information is available in very "poor" formats: paper documents, or low-level, poorly structured digital formats such as Postscript, PDF or DXF. The challenge is, therefore, to convert this poorly structured information into enriched information which can be used within an information system".

C. *Case study and application*

All these digital data, which we are interested in and want to restructure, include graphic and vectorial digital data. These data come from computer-assisted drawing, computer-aided design and desktop publishing or "technical" software. The main feature of these data is the mixture of text and drawings, with the particularity that there are generally more drawings than text.

These graphic and vectorial data are present in technical files, plans, notices, machining sequences, etc. These data are held by design offices, methods or production departments of "Smart factory" industrial concerns.

For example, in the precise field of diagrams Process & Instrumentation Diagrams (PID), the total amount of graphic data held by Small & Medium-sized Enterprises (SME) is very small compared to the total world volume of destructured data which we mentioned above. We can talk about "Small Data" for SMEs and perhaps "Medium Data" for large companies. This is a far cry from "Big Data", which is often behind KDD.

D. Our vision

"Deep learning" algorithms or convolution neural networks [3] cannot be used in our case for 2 main reasons: the small amount of information available in the smart factory and the difficulty of creating learning data.

Our approach differs from current work. It is more graphic and places the user at the heart of the extraction process. We do, of course, use all the text present in files, but we also use all the graphic objects which materialise title blocks, connecting elements, components, functions, etc.

As we have just said, the user is present in all the restructuring phases. It is much less expensive and more efficient to get the user to intervene throughout the process (and especially at the beginning) rather than at the end to validate or correct errors. Getting the user to take decisions (which only takes a few seconds according to the Man Machine Interface implemented) considerably reduces and even cancels the error rate for all the tasks.

In the restructuring process, there are around twenty tasks to be carried out. If each task is fully automated and produces an error rate of between 2 and 3 % (which is very low, 97% to 98% exact recognition rate), we can observe that at the end of the validation chain the user will have to take decisions about information with between 40% and 60 % errors. Errors in the first tasks lead to errors in subsequent tasks.

It is the error rate which can lead the user to reject the system. In the validation phase, the user must modify, reclass or cancel over 40 % of results. If the destructured datum contains 10 000 pieces of basic information, over 4000 pieces of information will have to be modified. These correction tasks will take a considerable amount of time, which is unacceptable in the world of industry.

Our aim is to restructure "Smart factory" user-anthropocentirc technical data. This allows us to offer the user a more ergonomic interface, which we can qualify as "Smart Interface" in the "Smart factory".

In section 2, we make the state of the art, then, in section 3 we explain why the user must be at the center of the process. In section 4 we describe the principle of restructuring, and in section 5 we decompose this principle into phases, stages, tasks and sub-tasks. The issue of visualization of a great deal of information is discussed in section 6. We conclude and we precise the future work in section 7.

II. STATE OF THE ART

Since the 2000s, many teams have dealt with restructuring these destructured data.

(i) Restructuring the pages of newspapers or magazines contained in PDF files [4] [5]: Major work was carried out on extending "PDFBox" functionalities to restructure text information, and separating it from graphic information using "best-first clustering". Information is dealt with as a whole.

(ii) Analysing PDF files and extracting mainly text data in XML format by Dejean and Meunier in 2006 [6]: The aim is to recreate words, associate letters, then lines, paragraphs and articles, and then separate text from images or vector areas. Images and vector areas are also, in this case, considered as a whole.

(iii) Extracting tables from PDFs [7]: They developed several heuristics to recognise, extract and store information in tables in XML files. These heuristics are based on the absolute position of elements.

(iiii) Extracting tables and forms from PDF [8] : After having defined the notions of tables and forms, they present a set of solutions for extracting data mainly based on the proximity of elements in a 2D space (X, Y) and finish by quoting university and commercial tools.

(iiiii) Extracting knowledge from scientific papers in PDF [9]: Developed using Python, the interactive tool, enables paper headers, quotations, figures, tables and algorithms to be extracted. Images are extracted without interpretation.

(iiiiii) Extracting and identifying graphs and images from PDF files [10]: They define 16 graphemes for identifying 36 types of graphs (curves, bar graphs, etc.), from a base of 14,000 BioMed Central (BMC) papers. They use "machine learning" algorithms to identify 16 types of graph (Weka 3 and LogitBoost).

Finally, we observed that not much research has been carried out into extracting knowledge from documents with a high graphic component. The Bordeaux INRIA Mnémosyne team dealt with this issue in the paper[11] ''Implicit knowledge extraction and structuring in electrical diagrams''. Ikram Chraibi Kaadoud extracted all the text from PDF files, then used methods inspired by KDD to obtain the information required to structure knowledge. This knowledge was modelled with dendrograms.

III. THE ESSENTIAL ROLE OF THE USER IN THE RESTRUCTURING PROCESS

In the abstract, we described the main stages of this restructuring. These stages are the same as (KDD) described by Fayard in ''From Data Mining to Knowledge Discovery in Databases. Advances in Knowledge Discovery and Data Mining''[12].

In 1996 Fayyad insisted on the fact that knowledge should be extracted with the user's help. At the 2003 KDD conference, he observed that a great deal of KDD work is carried out without the user. The user only intervenes in the final phase [13].

The same observation was made by Chevrin et al. [14]. They insisted on the user's role and this was one of the first times the term ''Anthropocentric'' could be seen to take on such importance in KDD.

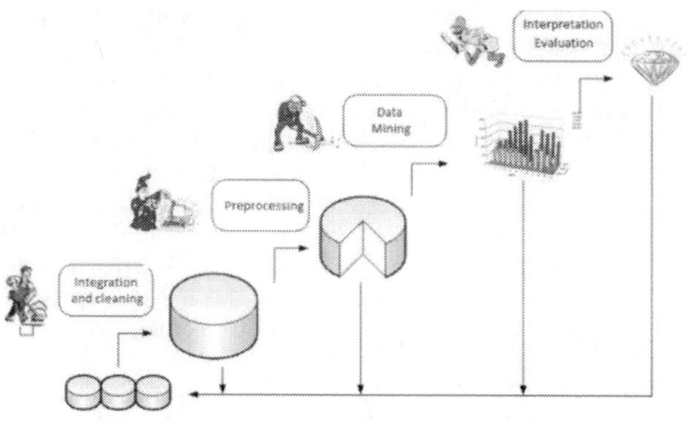

Figure 1. The KDD view by Chevrin [14]

We also made this observation: in most of the work we have quoted with regard to restructuring destructured documents, the user is present (sometimes very little). However, this work is not "Anthropocentric", based on the user.

This observation can still be seen today in a large number of works on knowledge extraction. Most of the time, the aim of research is to automate this extraction as far as possible. This is certainly possible when there are a lot of data to be processed, but in our case it is impossible. The user wishing to restructure these data does not have enough data available to fully and reliably automate the restructuring process.

Generally, in the ''Smart Factory'' it is the user who pilots restructuring with the help of the computer due to cost and efficiency, and to avoid rejection of the system.

IV. THE RESTRUCTURING PRINCIPLE

The general restructuring principle is quite simple. We search for "Graphemes" (as described by Jacques Bertin [15]) which are repeated in the same types of documents. According to how often they appear, the user analyses whether these graphemes correspond or not to notions which the user is used to handling. Once analysed by the user, these elements are integrated and parameterised in "the Knowledge Base" (true and false). In reality, "The" knowledge base is made up of a whole range of knowledge bases, each of which corresponds to a type of document or document sub-type.

After the analysis by the user of a grapheme or set of graphemes, the search for graphemes is restarted, taking into account the knowledge acquired in the previous phase. The user is presented with new proposals. The 3 "I's" are the **I**terative, **I**nteractive and **I**ntegration aspect of KDD defined in [12].

In this case, this principle for reconstruction is Incremental (KDD's 4th ''I''). Once basic graphemes have been recognised, "Supers Graphemes" are searched for. These are the associations of graphemes and basic graphic objects. They are, in turn, presented to the user and integrated in the knowledge base. This process is recursive until any knowledge to be searched for in the destructured documents is obtained.

The restructuring of documents is highly prioritised. It is described by an ontology which is created, or adapted, by the user based on general ontologies or parts of ontologies which act as a model.

The ontology is created throughout the KDD process.

If, for example, we take the case of a factory and its technical documents, we will find: methods documents, production documents, maintenance documents, etc. -- For maintenance documents: building plans, plans of industrial processes, fluid circulation plans, etc. -- For fluid circulation plans: hydraulic plans , pneumatic plans, electric plans, etc. -- For electric plans: building electric plans, electromechanical plans and plans of machine automatons, etc. -- For automaton plans: those created with 'AutoCad' software, those created with'Elec'View' software, those created with 'See Expert' software.

By making the knowledge base as close as possible to the document subtype, we obtain better restructuring rates. The information presented to the user is more reliable. If the basic symbols to be restructured are the same for AutoCad, Elec'view or See Expert (all these software are CAD software), this is not the same for title blocks, automaton input and output cards, variators, specific cards, etc. These graphic data differ from one software program to another.

Likewise, objects to be restructured in architectural plans are very different from those of automation diagrams or pneumatic diagrams. Ontologies differ greatly according to the field.

V. THE STAGES OF RESTRUCTURING DESTRUCTURED DOCUMENTS

Each of the phases of (A)KDD is divided into tasks and sub-tasks so that the user can intervene and make choices. The word "User" is a general term which concerns all types of users intervening in restructuring, from experts to simple users.

"One of the key words in Interface Human Machine (IHM) is user centered. User-centred design by Norman & Draper [16] is a paradigm defining 12 key principles which place the user at the heart of development processes". This is the paradigm stated by Dupuy-Chessa [17] which we use for user and system tasks. For reasons of clarity, we will only describe the main tasks of each of the phases in this paper.

For each of the stages and tasks we state how this task can be implemented in a real industrial data structuring process. We highlight the tasks for which, as far as we are aware, there are no efficient implementable solutions. It is for these tasks that we will show that a main system interaction loop appears to us to be the only efficient one.

A. *Phase 1 of (A)KDD: cleaning and integration*

To integrate data, the user must define the arborescence of data. This is this phase's first task. This arborescence will be created in an ontology. To create the ontology we use Stanford University's *Protégé* software. *Protégé* is the most popular software for creating ontologies and knowledge [18], based on figures from Jorge Cardoso's 2007 study. *Protégé* is very user-friendly and simple, and works well for the needs of restructuring.

The second task is a system task. It consists of inputting different types of highly destructured file formats and extracting the following graphic information from them:

- Segments, of polylines
- Text from 1 to n characters
- Pens, brushes and fonts.

When more complex graphic objects are present, like circles, circular arcs, ellipses, squares, rectangles, triangles, etc., these objects are transformed into polylines.
This graphic information is put into a pivot format. We chose the Autocad format (DXF/DWG). This format is readable by the main computer-aided design, drawing and desktop publishing software. Input file formats include: Portable Document Format (PDF), PostScript (PS), Enhanced MetaFile (EMF), Metafile (WMF), Computer Graphics Metafile (CGM), Scalable Vector Graphics (SVG, SVGZ), AutoCad formats (DXF, DWG), Hewlett-Packard formats (HPGL, HPGL2, PCL), Initial Graphics Exchange Specification(IGES), Standard for the Exchange of Product model data(STEP), Stereolithography file format (SLT), etc.

This system task is more or less complex according to the type of input files. It is essential for data restructuring. It is a pure engineering task.

The third task is for the user to select the files or parts of files to be processed. A tree based on the ontology model and a highly interactive file viewer are used to help the user choose.

B. Phase 2 of (A)KDD: Pre-processing

When we analyse PDF files and vectorial files from the same software, we can see that graphic objects are always drawn in the same chronological order. This is true for basic graphic objects, squares, rectangles, etc., and also more complex graphic objects, such as title blocks, automaton cards, etc. Generally, this chronological information is adjacent. For some software, this is not the case. We first of all find segment type graphic objects, then a little further in the file letter type graphic objects.

Most solutions, to restructure information, use the X and Y positions of objects, and their closeness. This is a solution which we use, but we give priority to the chronological nature of data. To achieve this, we code all the basic graphic objects (like for an alphabet). We can therefore handle "character" (code) chains instead of 2D graphic objects. Search times are reduced considerably.

We use 2 types of coding. Firstly, coding which takes into account the length, position and orientation of objects in a point of reference X,Y which originates at the bottom left of the page. Secondly, coding which codes an object according to the previous object; this way our coding is not sensitive to translation, rotation or a change of scale. A very simple example of coding could, for long segments, be 'V' for Verticals, 'H' for Horizontals, 'O' for Obliques, and 'h', 'v', 'o' for short segments. This is the principle we chose with greater distinction for lengths and angles.

The first system task consists of determining the density with which segments are distributed according to their lengths and orientations.

The second task presents the results to the user via a very visual and ergonomic interface to make a choice. The coding thus implemented will be more or less extensive.

C. Phase 3 of the (A)KDD: Data mining

Data mining for restructuring can be broken down into several stages, which the Incremental part of (A)KDD:

<u>Stage 1:</u> Restructuring dotted and dash lines: This involves defining the types of lines and identifying them based on their composition (length of features and spaces).

<u>Stage 2:</u> Restructuring letters: (some software directly draws the letters of words, especially for tracer files). This involves defining the font, size, style, orientation and letters which associate one or several scripts, eg. "e", "é", "ë", a type of font (Arial, Courrier, ISO, etc).

<u>Stage 3:</u> Restructuring words: This involves grouping together identified letters to form words, then text (sets of words). For assembly notices we have to identify phases and paragraphs.

<u>Stage 4:</u> Restructuring basic symbols: This involves defining these symbols and associating basic graphic elements and text.

<u>Stage 5:</u> Restructuring complex symbols: This involves defining these symbols and associating graphic elements from identified text and symbols. This stage is recursive.

<u>Stage 6:</u> Restructuring functions: This involves associating simple and complex symbols and basic graphic elements which make up a function. This stage is also recursive, a function is made up of sub-functions, itself made up of sub-functions, etc.

<u>Stage 7:</u> Restructuring the file: This involves defining the major fields and sub-fields in which we group together functions. It is also recursive.

Each of the stages can be broken down into 2 main tasks.

The first task defines the present notions. It is the user who introduces them into the knowledge base's ontology or duplicates them from close knowledge base ontologies.

The second task is a system task. It consists of identifying graphic patterns which are repeated the most in files. This identification is based on "Stringology" methods which we apply to the 2 codifications of the graphic elements described above and which we validate with positions X and Y. Throughout restructuring these codifications evolve and the recognised graphemes are automatically replaced by a new code associated with this new grapheme.

The main techniques of stringology that we use are as follows: Creating "chain tables"; Searching for one or several chains among a set of chains; Regular expressions.

D. Phase 4 of (A)KDD : Evaluation & presentation

For each stage of the previous phase 3 it is the user who evaluates and validates the information presented. This phase 4 can be broken down into 3 main tasks. Firstly, a system/user task which presents all the information from a system task for the stage in question, enabling the user to interact. Secondly, a user task which selects and introduces information into the knowledge base. Thirdly, a system task which recalculates all the information taking into account the identified "object", and loops back on the first task. It is the first task which is the core issue that will develop in the next section.

VI. How to visualise a large amount of information

Restructuring is a long and complex operation. It must be 100% exact, which is why it is user "Anthropocentric". However, the user tasks described above must be ergonomic, implicit, simple and efficient, especially those which visualise a lot of data, which are the core issue.

The problem is simple:

How to visualise as much information as possible on a station which will be used by the "Smart factory's" technical work services over the next 10 years?

How to navigate through this large amount of information? We have between 100 and 200 pattern to recognize in a document, and for each pattern we have between 1 and 10 proposals.

How to identify the information that we want to restructure because everything is not to restructure?

How to choose which of the information displayed and grouped by pattern similarity corresponds exactly to the element to be restructured?

How to introduce it into the knowledge base?

If the problem is simple, the solution is more complex. It can be seen that each of these questions involves system and user sub-tasks that interact with one another. The task T1 is thus divided into several sub-tasks in which the user is at the center of the action.

The issue is simple: How to visualise as much information as possible on a station which will be used by the "Smart factory's" technical work services over the next 10 years? The solution is more complex.

This is why we have focused our research on the "Overview first, zoom and filter, then details-on-demand" concept described in Shneiderman's "information seeking mantra" [20], respecting TTT taxonomy (Shneiderman 96) and its seven tasks: "overview, zoom, filter, details-ondemand, relate, history and extract" which Kleim in 2004 [1] covers in the definition of the "Visual Exploration Paradigm".

"Focus + Context" techniques, such as "FishEyesView" are very promising in certain fields, like that of rules of association [14]. However, they are not suited to our issue because the possibility for enlargement is small (4 to 5 times the original size). An in-depth study by Mikkel Rønne Jakobsen and Kasper Hornbæk shows that, on small screens (640x267) or medium screens (1920x800), "Overview + Detail" methods perform better than "Zooming + Panning", which itself performs better than "Focus + Context", even for very large screens (5760x2400).

We made the same observation, which led us to develop a combintaion of both methods: "Overview+Detail" and "Zooming+Panning". In this combination, the methods and uses can be divided into three groups, those fixed by the system, those chosen by the system and those chosen by the user.

VII. Conclusion and future work

This work is part of integrating visualisation techniques with disciplines, such as knowledge extraction, learning, handling and exploring high volumes of data.

The final aim is to contribute the power of IHM in each computer in "Smart factory" design offices to enable data to be explored better, more quickly and more intuitively. The final objective is to improve the economic performance of these companies.

What we wanted to show is that in a complex process like the restructuring of the graphic documents it is the user who must be at the heart of the system. Without the user or with a late intervention in the process, the system is not viable. Like Fayyad, we decompose the process into 4 main phases. Each phase breaks down into stages. And each step, as advocated by Dupuy-Chessa, is broken down into tasks and sub-tasks either system or user. This is how we can put the user at the heart of stage step.

Our observation is that the user must be present from the beginning to reduce errors. This forces us to design a user-friendly HMI this throughout the restructuring process.

The "anthropocentric" character of this approach is opposed to the automatic work that is to be found in many of the work around KDD. This leads us to develop this method (A) KDD with the sole objective of obtaining better results and, above all, a better efficiency, two notions necessary in the industrial world.

Our next work will aim to demonstrate that the systematic application of (A)KDD gives better results than automatic methods for complex problems.

References

[1] L. Nigay, "Modality of interaction & multi modality," In Thése habilitation diriger des recherches. préparé au Laboratoire de Communication Langagire et Interaction Personne-Systme (IMAG), Université Joseph Fourier, pp. 1-74, 2001.

[2] K. Tombre and B. Lamiroy, "Graphics Recognition – from Re-engineering to Retrieval," 7th International Conference on Document Analysis and Recognition, Aug 2003, Edinburgh, Scotland. UK, IEEE Computer Society Press, pp. 148-155, 2003.

[3] Y. Bengio and Y. LeCun, "Scaling learning algorithms towards AI," in Large Scale Kernel Machines, (L. Bottou, O. Chapelle, D. DeCoste, and J. Weston, eds.), MIT Press, 2007.

[4] T. Hassan and R. Baumgartner, "Table recognition and understanding from PDF files," in Proc. 9th Int. Conf. on Document Analysis and Recognition, Parana, pp. 1143-1147, 2007.

[5] T. Hassan, "User-guided wrapping of pdf documents using graph matching techniques," In 10th International Conference on Document Analysis and Recognition. IEEE Computer Society, Los Alamitos, CA, USA, pp. 631–635, 2009.

[6] H. Déjean and J.-L. Meunier, "A system for converting PDF documents into structured XML format," in DAS 2006: Proceedings of the International Workshop on Document Analysis Systems, pp. 129-140, 2006.

[7] B. Yildiz, K. Kaiser, and S. Miksch, "Automatic Table Recognition and Extraction from Heterogeneous Documents," in Journal of Computer and Communications 03(12), pp. 100-110, January 2015.

[8] B. Coüasnon and A. Lemaitre, "Recognition of Tables and Forms," in Doermann, D., Tombre, K. (eds.) Handbook of Document Image Processing and Recognition, pp. 647–677. Springer London, 2014.

[9] J.Wu and al., "Pdfmef: A multi-entity knowledge extraction framework for scholarly documents and semantic search," in K-Cap, 2015.

[10] M. Shao and R.P. Futrelle, "Recognition and Classification of Figures in PDF Documents," in W. Liu and J. Llados (Eds.): GREC 2005, LNCS 3926, pp. 231–242. Springer-Verlag Berlin Heidelberg, 2006.

[11] I. Chraibi Kaadoud, N. Rougier and F. Alexandre, "Implicit knowledge extraction and structuration from electrical diagrams," at IEA/AIE, 2017.

[12] U. M. Fayyad, G. Piatetsky-Shapiro, and P. Smyth, "From Data Mining to Knowledge Discovery in Databases Advances in Knowledge Discovery and Data Mining," in AAI Press / The MIT Press, pp. 1-43, 1996.

[13] U. M. Fayyad, G. Piatetsky-Shapiro and R. Uthurusamy, "Summary from the kdd-03 panel: data mining: the next 10 years," in SIGKDD Explor. Newsl., ISSN 1931- 0145, vol.5, no.2, pp.191-196, 2003.

[14] V. Chevrin, O. Couturier, E. Mephu Nguifo and J. Rouillard, "User-driven association rules mining to decisions supports systems," in revue IHM (RIHM) ISSN 1289-296, Vol.8, pp 201- 220, 2007.

[15] J. Bertin, "Sémiologie graphique, Les diagrammes – Les réseaux – Les cartes," (Graphical Semiology, Diagrams - Networks – Map), in Paris, Editions de l'EHESS, 4e éditions, (1ère édition: Paris, Editions Gauthier-Villar, 1967), 2005

[16] R. D. Pea, "User Centered System Design: New Perspectives on Human-Computer Interaction," in Journal educational computing research, pp. 129-134, 1987.

[17] S. Dupuy-Chessa, "Modeling in Human- Machine Interaction and Information Systems: At the Crossroads," Interface homme-machine [cs.HC]. Université de Grenoble, 2011.

[18] N. Malviya, N. Mishra and S. Sahu , "Developing University Ontology using protégé OWL Tool," in International Journal of Scientific & Engineering Research Vol.2, Issue 9, September 2011.

[19] J. Cardoso, "the Semantic Web Vision: Where are We?" in IEEE Intelligent Systems, pp.22-26, September/October 2007.

[20] B. Shneiderman, "The eyes have it: A task by data-type taxonomy for information visualizations," in Proceedings of Visual Languages'96, IEEE Computer Science Press Publ., pp. 336-343, 1996.

[21] D. A. Keim, "Information Visualization and Visual Data Mining B., The eyes have it: A task by data-type taxonomy for information visualizations," in IEEE Transaction on Vizualizationn and computer graphics, vol. 7, no. 1, January-March 2002.

[22] G. Bothorel, M.Serrurier and C. Hurter, "Using visual data minning tools to explore a set of association rules," in RIHM Art. N° 12, 2011.

[23] M. Rønne Jakobsen and K. Hornbæk, "Sizing Up Visualizations: Effects of Display Size in Focus+Context, Overview+Detail, and Zooming Interfaces," in Proceedings of the SIGCHI Conference on Human Factors in Computing Systems, ACM, New York, NY, USA, pp. 1451–1460, 2011.

[24] D. Cuny, "The Great Information: The New Revolution", from a study IDC-EMC, "Extracting the Value of Chaos" by EMC Gartner, Tribune No. 42, pp. 4, March 29 to April 4 2013

[25] A. GANDOMI and M. HAIDER, "Beyond the hype: Big data concepts, methods, and analytics". International Journal of Information Management, 2015, vol. 35, no 2, pp. 137-144.

Building Pathways for Empowering User Toward Prosumer Behaviour

The Design for Experience with the Prosumer Empowerment Concentric Model

Marion Real, Quentin Tabart, Audrey Abi Akle
ESTIA
F-64210 Bidart, France
e-mails: m.real@estia.fr, q.tabart@estia.fr, a.abiakle@estia.fr

Abstract— **Acting as prosumers can help the transition toward low carbon and circular economies. This paper discusses what can be defined as "prosumer behaviours" and proposes an innovative approach that fosters users in adopting daily virtuous experiences about energy production and consumption. Such experiences are based on smart interfaces as they emerge from complex socio-technical systems that combined ICT devices, smart grids and user-centred tools created to empower users and facilitate the emergence of a positive intelligence. The Prosumer Empowerment Concentric (PEC) Model is presented here as an integrative vision to support the emergence of prosumer behaviours and perspectives are outlined via an interregional project that proposes to experiment the PEC model in households and citizen energy cooperatives.**

Keywords - smart interface; smart grid; energy consumption; user-centred approach.

I. *INTRODUCTION*

At individual and community level, low carbon economies rely on decreasing the energy consumption of households and improving the local production of renewable energy. Empowering consumers and encouraging them to act and become prosumers remains a key challenge to provoke effective impacts on sustainability. The term "prosumer" has different meanings in academic works [1] [2] and recent reports from European Parliament [3] [4]. It is used here in line with Greenpeace [5] definition of active customer: "*a customer who performs any of the functions of generation, storage and/or supply of energy from renewable sources, or energy efficiency/demand-side management, either individually or through a community energy*". Acting as a prosumer is adopting virtuous behaviours that create energy savings, reinforce the good understanding of energy bills and participate, in a direct or indirect way, in the production of local and renewable energy.

For designers, new systems, environments, experiences, products or/and solutions need to be imagined and developed so as to facilitate the adoption of prosumer behaviours.

In a technological viewpoint, different types of solutions are developed:

- Information and communication technology (ICT) solutions are the most widespread, mainly composed by sensors and connected objects. Visualization interfaces and serious games are also created for improving the awareness on energy bills and encouraging energy savings.
- Small renewable energy like solar and wind turbines and home energy storage can be interfaced to the main grid through a local scale grid. The microgrid concept allows a local grid to operate independently from the national grid and thus enable a decentralized and cooperative energy distribution system.

Recent works underline new business models who involve changes in the relation between consumers and energy Service Company and communities [6]. In this line, citizen energy cooperatives are emerging models that participate to the production of renewable energy in territories through the involvement of consumers/citizens by financing new installations and diffusing awareness. Besides, small renewable producers and energy storage holders along with consumers can be aggregated using the Virtual Power Plants (VPP) framework [7]. It allows local producer/consumers to exchange their production (renewable energy, heat, etc.) locally and buy/sell from other VPPs. The European FENIX project [8] currently investigates the practical implementation of such concept.

However, there are some barriers and limits in the adoption of such solutions that prevent behavioural changes. Indeed, currently there are solutions that do not have long-term benefits. It is pointed out in [9] that the gamified solutions offer only a gain of 0.2% of long-term energy saving. Moreover, a key determinant of energy performance is the behaviour of occupants. Occupants use energy to perform various activities of daily life and most of the complex processes that occur in dwellings energy consumption result from human behaviour. The activities they undertake are stochastic in nature and difficult to predict [10].

We think that the new solutions have to be in line with the needs and habits of consumers while proposing feedbacks and stimulations that help them to pursue their paths toward the adoption of new eco-efficient and sufficient behaviours.

This is why in our work, we propose a holistic human-centred approach that goes beyond classic product/service design, and give a particular focus on designing experiences for consumers, users and prosumers. User experience (UX) design consist in (i) exploring the real personal motivations, needs and representations of consumers [11], (ii) involving them in all stages of the design of future systems [12], (iii) monitoring the evolution of their environment through responsive interfaces [13] [14]. In our approach, UX tools and methodologies will be integrated in a systemic view combining both social, technical and user aspects.

Theoretical background on change and transition management is also investigated in this work to reach the design of coherent and adaptive experiences. Ethically, behavioural changes could not be managed externally without the consent and the intent of users. It exists a challenge for designers, and intermediary organisations, in persuading consumers through interfaces with the objective to inspire emergence of prosumers behaviours while reducing the diffusion of constraint feelings. Supports need to integrate the evolution of consumers and to guarantee solutions which will gradually influence the adoption of prosumer behaviours.

This paper proposes to describe a Prosumer Empowerment Concentric (PEC) model that fits the necessity to build pathways toward prosumer behaviours (presented in Section 2) and explain how it will be used, integrated and experimented in households through a further European projects (see Section 3).

II. *PROSUMER EMPOWERMENT CONCENTRIC MODEL*

The model represents a set of user-experiences containing socio-technological solutions to move from standard consumer toward prosumer behaviour. Each individual can build his/her own paths to become a prosumer by releasing different actions which includes different types of solutions. Structures and institutions like cooperatives or change managers can also use the model as an interface to fit consumers' needs with solutions providers and stimulating changes.

A. *Structures of the PEC model*

The model is built through concentric layers representing levels of empowerment toward prosumer behaviours. Based on Carvallo and Cooper's work [15], four layers have been identified. They represent different levels in which consumers can move: from "standard consumer", "consumer awareness", "active consumer" to "prosumer" (see Figure 1).

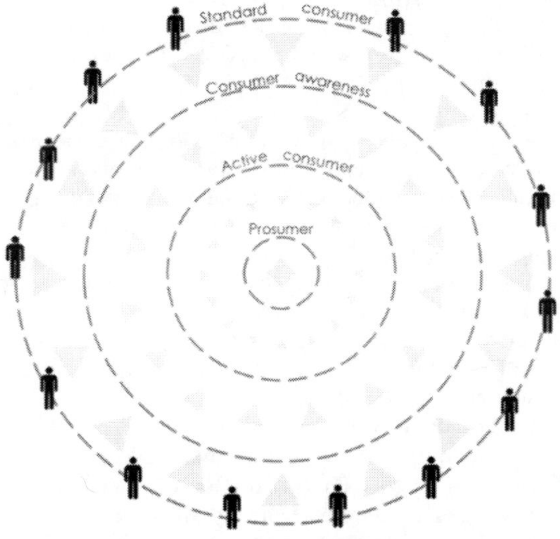

Figure 1. Concentric layers: going deeper in the engagement.

On each circle/layer of the model, we position "states" and in connection with these states we relate existing solutions (see Figure 2).

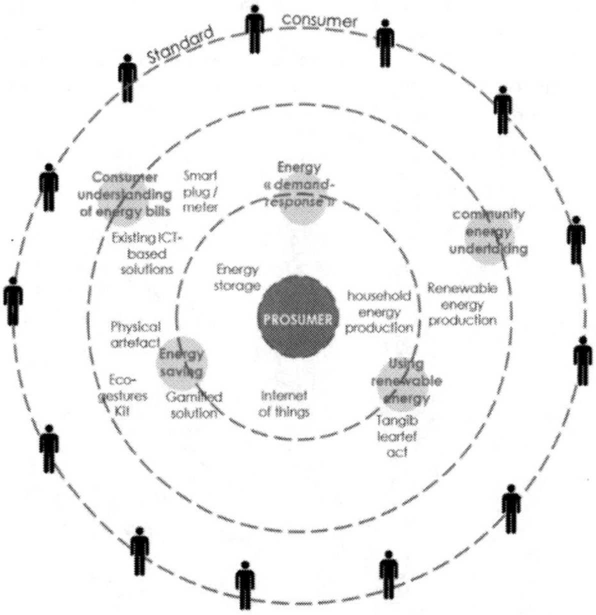

Figure 2. Model with statutes connected to existing solutions.

On the first circle so called "consumer awareness" there are two statutes possible: (i) "Consumer understanding of energy bills" where the objective is to facilitate understanding of energy bills and encourage the identification of equipment in the household that consumes a lot and possible energy losses within the home and (ii) "Community energy undertaking" which correspond to the involvement of consumers in citizen organisations, like cooperative. They can participate in financing parts of renewable infrastructures.

On the second circle "active consumer", three states are possible: (i) "Energy saving", people will be encouraged to reduce their energy consumption within their homes; (ii) "Energy demand-response" where the objective is to encourage consumers to consume differently i.e. change / move consumption behaviours to avoid periods of significant demand in energy. One of the first actions (for example) is to inform consumers about energy cost and efficiency; and (iii) "Using renewable energy", here, we have the ambition to motivate people (according to their location) to consume only when their region / territory produces renewable energy. This state is close to the previous one but it is much more stochastic in the behaviour because directly related to the production of "green" energy.

On the third circle, only "prosumer" status is possible, this is the last status available in this model. It consists in the production of energy directly produced by the consumer. It is encouraged on the one hand by all other states but also supported by existing solutions.

B. Pathways and evolution in the PEC Model

The model is built in order to adapt the path toward the consumer profile. Indeed, with this approach, the consumer chooses his/her own path towards "Prosumer" typology. In this way, the consumer chooses the «gateway» according to his/her profile (and his/her motivation) and defines step by step the objectives. In order to illustrate this adaptive pathway, the Figure 1, 2 and 3 present scenarios of various possible paths towards the status "prosumer".

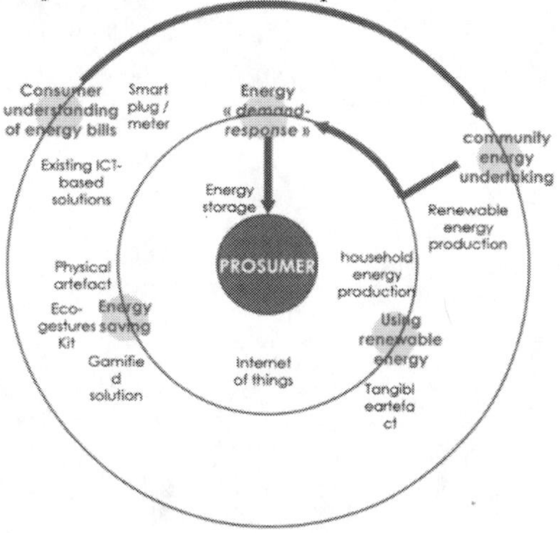

Figure 3. Example of path 1.

In the first scenario (Figure 3), the consumer initiates consciously his/her path toward prosumer typology by improving the awareness of his/her energy consumption. To do so, s/he starts to use an appropriate smart-meter and a visualisation tool to read its own energy bill and after one month choose to become a member of an energy cooperative. After an important reduction of consumption, s/he decides to test new ICT devices which help him/her to better know when s/he has to consume (e.g.,when to use a washing machine) to be in line with the energy production peaks. Finally, s/he decides to adopt renewable energy systems at home so as to gain in autonomy and participate in local electricity production. The scenario 2, depicted in Figure 4, insists on the role of energy communities as catalysers that motivate and advise consumers in adopting new habits and eco-efficient devices while the scenario 3 illustrates, in Figure 5, the case where people have already environmental awareness and start by actions that have a higher level of engagement (situated in both active consumer and prosumer).

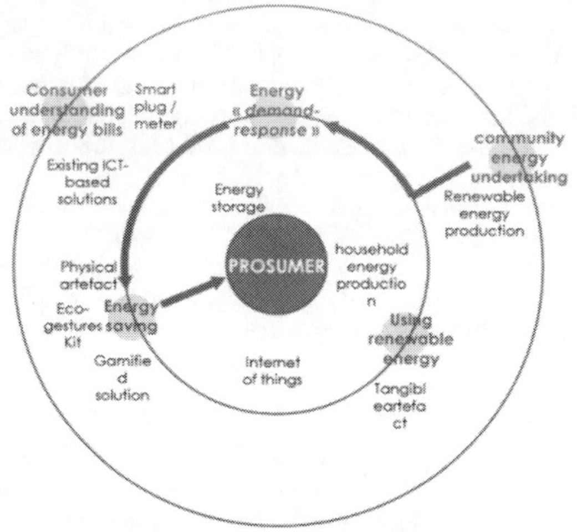

Figure 4. Example of path 2.

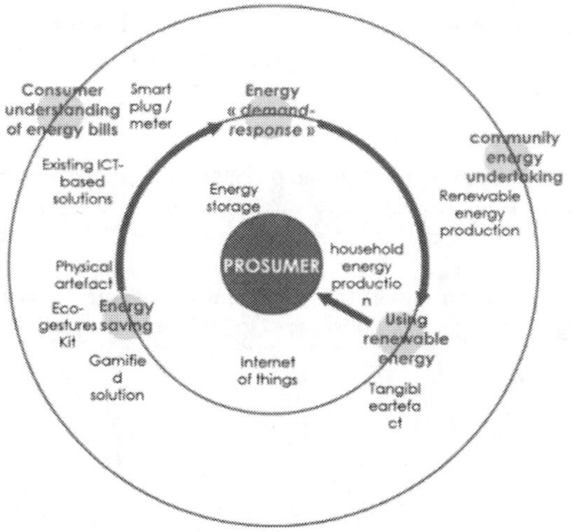

Figure 5. Example of path 3.

C. *The PEC Model integrated in Smart Interface*

"Smart and empowering interfaces" is coined as "the design and implementation of human-human interaction, human-system and system-system that may foster the emergence of a positive intelligence for users". For several reasons, we are convinced that the PEC model is part of this area. First, it includes the study of behavioral changes and the interaction between solution kits and consumers in order to identify the potentials of deconsumption within each status (human-system interface). Then, it proposes the study of the interactions between the consumers within cooperatives to extract vectors of motivations towards a more virtuous behavior (human-human interface). Moreover, this work focuses on the exchange of energy between the VPPs (system-system interface). These interactions are also embedded in a systemic conceptual interface that connects different layers of environmental awareness within society.

III. *CONCLUSION AND FUTURE WORK*

The PEC model has already gained the confidence of two cooperatives (from Spain and France) and will be implemented and tested through a future European project, in three different regions of France, Spain and Portugal. In each region, cooperatives, energy service providers, intermediary organisations and households will be involved. The project will pursue the state-of-art of existing solutions helping in completing the PEC model. Then, the project will consist in defining the experiences offered to consumers whatever their profiles are. Each experience will be materialized by solution kits composed by a mix of ICT, renewable energy products, energy storage devices and pedagogical or gamified solutions. The first kit will be the installation box (i.e., the smart meters) and the other kits will be boxes sent monthly. The content of these boxes will obviously be adapted to the profiles and desires of consumers. A recruitment phase will select a panel of two types of consumers: members of cooperatives and aleatory households. A pre-analysis of consumers' needs and motivations will be realized. Once the solution kits and consumers will ready, the experimentation will begin. It will consist in four series of solution kits implemented in each household. The 4 phases of planned tests correspond to 3 states (on the "awareness" and "active consumer" layers) and a final test phase for the status "prosumer". For each series, different tasks will be reached: installation, learning stage, use phase with stimulations, feedbacks, behaviour changes and energy saving and production assessments. An approach to analyse human behaviour, behaviour change and their barriers will be deployed. The objective is to understand on the one hand the transition from one layer to the other (of the model) and on the other hand the transition from one status to another. Testing these experiences in real households will lead us to have direct feedbacks, to define new strategies of business models, especially for cooperatives and to draw conclusions for consumer empowerment. The experimentation will end by a capitalization and realization of a deep analysis on effective behavioural changes. Actions will also be engaged to transform citizen cooperatives in an interface organization for energy behavioural changes supported by the PEC model: a practical tool will be developed to help them in supporting the involvement and engagement of their members toward pro-active behaviours.

ACKNOWLEDGMENT

We would like to thank the INTERREG EUROPE RETRACE [16] the French national FUI project INSULGRID and the GreenPlay [17] project that has received funding from the European Union's Horizon 2020 research and innovation program under grant agreement No. 649621 for supporting this work.

REFERENCES

[1] P. Kotler, "Prosumers-A New Type of Consumer". Futurist, 20(5), 24-25. 1986,

[2] A. Toffler and T. Alvin, The third wave, New York: Bantam books, pp. 32-33, 1981,

[3] N. Sajn, "Electricity 'Prosumers", In Briefing November 2016.European Parliamentary Research Service. PE 593.518,

[4] Practical Law Competition, "CEER Position paper on well-functioning retail energy markets", In Legal update archive from European Union Jurisdiction. C15-SC-36-03, 14 October 2015,

[5] J. Roberts, "Prosumer Rights: Options for a legal framework post-2020". Greenpeace European Unit (TR 9832909575-41), May 2016,

[6] M. Hamwi, I. Lizarralde and J. Legardeur, "Energy Product Service Systems as core element of energy transition in the household sector: The Greenplay project". Conference Paper · May 2016. ISDRS, Lisbonne. (RG.2.2.30854.37448),

[7] C. Kieny, B. Berseneff, N. Hadjsaid, Y. Besanger, and J. Maire, "On the concept and the interest of virtual power plant: Some results from the European project Fenix," IEEE Power Energy Soc. Gen. Meet., pp. 1–6, Jul. 2009,

[8] http://www.fenix-project.org/ [accesses June 2017]

[9] A. Abi Akle and I. Lizarralde, "Helping inhabitants in energy saving and getting inputs from usage for eco-design: cooking case study". In DS Proceedings of the 21th International Conference on Engineering Design (ICED 17). August 2017, Vancouver, Canada, in press,

[10] T. Zaraket, "Stochastic activity-based approach of occupant-related energy consumption in residential buildings". Doctoral dissertation, Châtenay-Malabry, Ecole centrale de Paris, 2014,

[11] A. Retegi, Inclusive experience design: una metodología de diseño de experiencias basada en las capacidades de las personas. Tesis Doctoral de Mondragon Unibertsitatea. Arrasate-Mondragón, España. 2016,

[12] S. Sharma and K. Patil, "Past, Present and Future of Collaborative Design: From User Centric to User Driven Design". In: Chakrabarti A., Chakrabarti D., Research into Design for Communities, Volume 1. ICoRD 2017. Smart Innovation, Systems and Technologies, vol. 65, Singapore, pp. 1025-1036, Springer 2017,

[13] B.J. Fogg, "Persuasive technology: using computers to change what we think and do. Ubiquity, 2002 (December), 5, 2002, 10.1145/764008.763957,

[14] M. Daniel, G. Rivière, N. Couture and S. Kreckelbergh, "Une Analyse des Systèmes Interactifs et Persuasifs pour la Maîtrise de l'Énergie". In Actes de la 28ième conférence francophone sur l'Interaction Homme-Machine, pp. 197-210, 2016,

[15] A. Carvallo and J. Cooper, "The advanced smart grid: Edge power driving sustainability", Artech House, 2015.

[16] www.interregeurope.eu/retrace/, [accesses June 2017]

[17] http://www.greenplay-project.eu/, [accesses June 2017]

IdeaBulb: A Smart and Tangible User Interface for Monitoring Ideation During Creative Sessions

Julien Ambrosino
ESTIA, Technopôle Izaberl
F-64210 Bidart
IMS, UMR 5218, Bât.A31,
351 Cours de la Libération, F-33400 Talence
Aerospace Valley, Chez ENSAM ParisTech
F-33405 Talence Cedex
ambrosino@aerospace-valley.com

Dimitri Masson
ESTIA, Technopôle Izaberl
F-64210 Bidart
d.masson@estia.fr

Maxime Daniel
ESTIA, Technopôle Izaberl
F-64210 Bidart
LaBRI, UMR 5800,
351 Cours de la Libération, F-33400 Talence
m.daniel@estia.fr

Jérémy Legardeur
ESTIA, Technopôle Izaberl
F-64210 Bidart
IMS, UMR 5218, Bât.A31,
351 Cours de la Libération, F-33400 Talence
j.legardeur@estia.fr

Abstract—**In this paper, we propose a tangible user interface for the monitoring of new ideas generations (ideation phase) during creative sessions. Based on the analysis of different brainstorming, we highlight the dynamic of ideas production by different groups during ideation phase using electronic devices. We claim that this tangible user interface is designed in order to give live feedback concerning these dynamic of ideas production to the participants and the facilitator. Our work is the result of the interaction between two scientific approaches: the analysis of creative sessions and the design of tangible user interface. The result of our experiments show a creative cliff and propose a design concept for monitoring ideation phase.**

Keywords—creativity; ideation; tangible interface; idea generation.

I. Introduction

The use of creative processes is a factor increasingly recognized as essential in the emergence of new ideas or business opportunities [1]–[3]. These processes can be declined in a punctual way by involving groups of participants in a creative session, or a brainstorm session [4].

Open-Innovation oriented creative sessions gather participants from different backgrounds – services, companies - from clusters are more likely to be competitive domestically and globally when their business is competitive and collaborative at the same time [5]. These ambivalent aptitudes create a context of coopetition [6].

Creative sessions are day events led sometimes by a facilitator (internal or external) to help the generation and the evaluation of new ideas, also they follow a process characterized by a succession of convergent and divergent main phases according to the facilitation model proposed by Ambrosino et al. [7].

The generation of ideas called the ideation phase is a critical part of the innovation process [8] where participants are asked to produce as many ideas as possible in an allotted time. Time-constrained is thus important, because when deadline is fixed, it add an emotional power in the form of fear, lest participants may fall down [9].

In this article, we propose first to analyze the ideation phase of creative sessions in order to highlight the dynamic of ideas production within the group.

Second, we propose a tangible user interface for the monitoring of ideation phase in order to improve creative sessions by giving to the participants and the facilitator a live feedback concerning these dynamic of ideas production.

II. Brainstorming Technique and Support Tools

Classic brainstorming usually causes blocking and slows down the generation of ideas in groups [10]. Galuppe et al. [11] show electronic brainstorming systems can improve creative sessions by acting on three classes of explanatory mechanisms which can cause productivity loss in brainstorming groups:

- Procedural mechanisms like production blocking [12], when just only a person can speak at a time.
- Social psychology mechanisms like drive-arousal [13] and self-attention [14], which is due to the presence of the other people and individual membership in the group.
- Economic mechanisms like social loafing [15] and free-riding [16], which correspond to an intentional withdrawal.

IdeaValuation [17] is a structured electronic brainstorming tool. It supports the ideation and evaluation through a discovering matrix [18]. The matrix is composed of needs (rows) and means (columns). As advised by [10], the facilitator using *IdeaValuation* invites participants first to generate their ideas in individually in the relevant cells of the matrix.

Then, these ideas are discussed and evaluated in a group session, following the instruction of the facilitator to evaluate each idea in turns. For each idea, the evaluation is done along four criteria and is followed by a short discussion between participants.

III. CHARACTERIZING THE IDEAS PRODUCTION

A. *Experimental setup and process*

Simultaneously, two creative sessions were performed in an event dedicated to Innovation in France. Groups are composed of participants who are members of the regional Agency of Development and Innovation in Nouvelle-Aquitaine (ADI-NA). There are located in two different rooms and the rooms do not interact together.

First participants are introduced to *IdeaValuation* tool and in particular the discovering matrix used for this event. Then, participants are then invited to generate as many ideas as possible, following one of the 4 fundamental rules of brainstorming [19]. They use a Samsung Galaxy Tab A tablet connected by WIFI.

Some characteristics of these ideation phases, which last 20 minutes, are described in the matrix, in TABLE I.

TABLE I. CHARACTERISTIC SETTINGS OF TWO WORKSHOPS

Information according phase concerned			**Workshop 1**	**Workshop 2**
Registrering		*Thematics adressed*	Marine Renewable Energies	Biomimicry for Sustainable Housing
		Number of participants registred	42	26
	Initial motivation	*"Expand my network"*	10	6
		"Generate ideas for collaborative innovation projects"	25	14
		"Other"	7	12
Discovering matrix		*Type of entries*	Needs vs Means	Needs vs Means
		Size	4 x 5	5 x 5
Results of ideation phase		***Number of participants who generate ideas***	**23**	**26**
		Total amount of ideas	**79**	**79**

While there were more participants registered to the workshop 1, only 23 of them submitted ideas through *IdeaValuation*, resulting in two groups of 23 and 26 idea producers.

B. *Observations and analyses*

The use of an electronic brainstorming tool such as *IdeaValuation* allows to monitor the production of ideas during the ideation phase. During 20 minutes of ideation phase, we compute every 2 min two metrics: the amount of ideas generated and the flow.

1) Evolution of amount of ideas generated

Figure 1 indicates the evolution of the amount of ideas generated during the ideation phase for both workshops.

Participants slowly start to produce ideas. Then, 10 minutes after the beginning, the group reaches a peak followed by a sharp drop: we observe it in the amount of ideas proposed after 12 minutes for group 1 and after 16 minutes for group 2. In the case of group 2, no idea was proposed during the last three minutes. This part of the curve can be called the creative cliff.

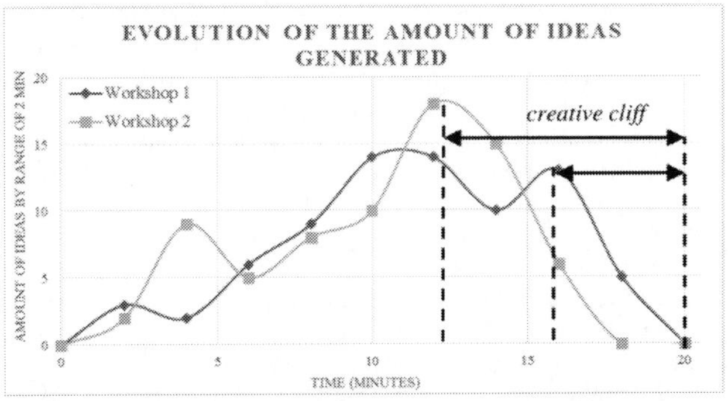

Figure 1. Highlighting the creative cliff

An ideal ideation phase could see all participants produce regularly until the end of the session. Without any external solicitation, the participants seem to be more limited by their ability to generate ideas than by time.

2) Evolution of ideation flow

Figure 2 indicates the evolution of ideation flow acceleration during ideation phase.

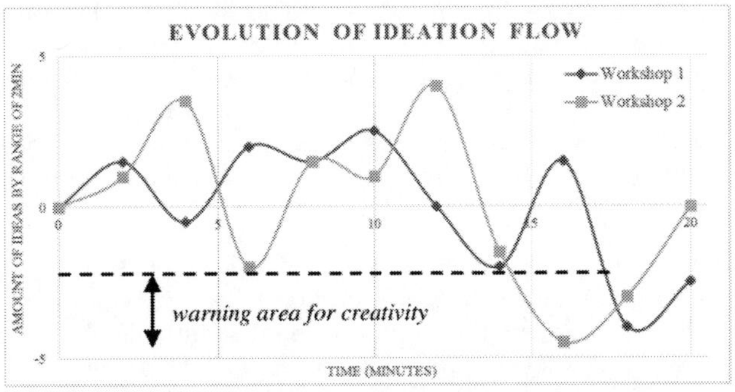

Figure 2. Highlighting of the warning area of creativity

There are some positive and negative variations of values which reflect the acceleration or deceleration flow of amount of ideas proposed. It seems to be a boundary beyond which the production of ideas tends to a zero value. When the curves tend to intersect this boundary, ideation flow is alarming. This part of the curve can be called the "*warning area for creativity*".

C. *Opportunities for a tangible support tool*

1) Lack of efficiency: boost productivy

As we have seen the time allocated to ideation phase is not fully used by all participant, the idea production cliff in the last quarter of the ideation phase. Individual generation lets them express and formulate ideas as they want, but the absence of external action, for example by giving to participants a live feedback about their progress may be a lever to increase their productivity.

In workshop 1, many participants do not generate any idea. Although, the absence of propositions by 19 participants in this workshop is notable, it is difficult to identify clearly the causes, but the use of a full digital solution may be at stake.

2) Lack of competition and collaboration

Despite the fact that competition benefits between intergroup are clearly highlighted as described in Introduction, participants need to have a live feedback of their progress. The only element which may be perceived as a competition one is the visualization of the other participants keyboarding during ideation phase. Currently, participants do not have any information about the real progress of the other participants.

Collaboration benefits are implied since participants accept to involve themselves in an open-innovation oriented creative session. However, they individually generate ideas and they cannot read the ideas of the others. So, collaboration may be perceived as limited during ideation phase.

In order to investigate these opportunities, we consider tangible user interfaces as a mean to give back control to participants on the productivity.

IV. IDEABULB: A TANGIBLE USER INTERFACE DESIGNED FOR IMPROVING CREATIVE SESSIONS

Tangible User Interfaces (TUIs) use physical objects to represent and/or manipulate digital information [20]. With the use of electronic brainstorming systems, we think TUIs to be adequate for enhancing collaboration and ideation in creative sessions thanks to a live feedback represented by a physical object, in order to make the ideation more tangible. They are known to support social interaction (e.g., collaboration) and to support thinking process (e.g., problem solving) through bodily actions, physical manipulation, and tangible representations [21].

A. *Peripheral Interaction and Ambient Interfaces*

Because ideation phase during a creative session is a cognitive process that requires central attention and a lot of mental resources, we wish to design an ambient TUI working with peripheral attention and requiring little mental resources to interact with.

Ambient awareness makes human beings aware of surrounding information [22]. Weiser and Brown [23] defined *calm technologies* as technologies able to move from the peripheral attention to the central attention of users, and backwards. They affirmed that calm technologies enhance ambient awareness by bringing more details into the periphery: it makes users aware of what is happening around them, what is going to happen, and what has just happened. In line with calm technologies, Ambient Interfaces use perceptible artefacts (e.g., shape, motion, sound, color, light, smell, air) to represent unobtrusively digital information. Bakker et al. [24] peripheral noted that recent studies have been conducted under the term *peripheral interaction*, aiming to broaden the scope of calm technology by designing not only for the *perceptual periphery* but also enabling users to physically interact with the digital world in their periphery.

B. *Design concept: IdeaBulb*

We think that giving live feedback to participants on their performance can mitigate ideation off-peaks. Therefore, we propose to design a smart interface to inform participants on the amount of idea they generated and their flow of ideation. Because we do not want to interrupt participants during their ideation process, we wish to design an ambient interface to subtly inform participant without being intrusive.

1) General design: metaphorical items

For designing *IdeaBulb*, we choose the metaphor of a bulb held by a hand, in Figure 3. Light bulb shape is part of the clichés to symbolize the ideation of an individual [25], while the hand holding it represents the group.

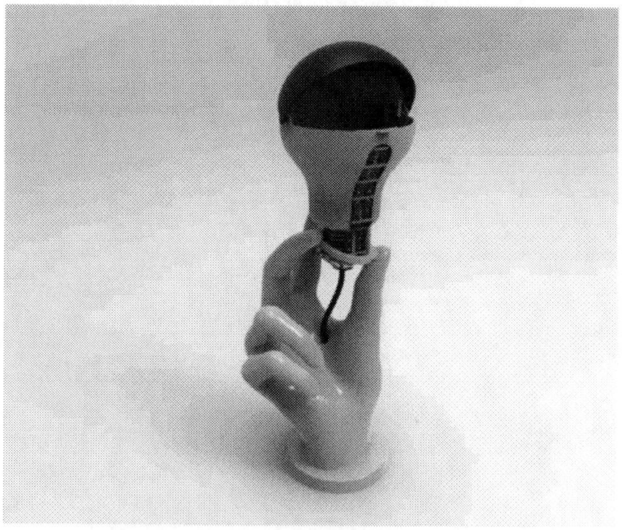

Figure 3. IdeaBulb's metaphorical design

2) Feedbacks

The smart interface *IdeaBulb* will give in real-time two types of feedback during ideation phase.

a) Cumulative feedback on the amount of ideas submitted

Using a led strip, *IdeaBulb* lights on its "belly" according to the amount of ideas submitted. For instance, *IdeaBulb* informs participants that there is a total of 3 ideas submitted by turning on 1 led over 30 leds maximum, as shown in Figure 4 (a).

b) Immediate feedback on the flow and the submission of ideas

Using a servomotor, *IdeaBulb* opens its "mouth" according to the flow of ideation. For instance, a flow of 0 ideas by minute is represented by a mechanical dome widely opened meaning that *IdeaBulb* is "hungry" for ideas. In contrary, a flow of 4 ideas by minute is represented by a "mechanical dome" completely closed meaning that *IdeaBulb* is "satisfied", in Figure 4 (b).

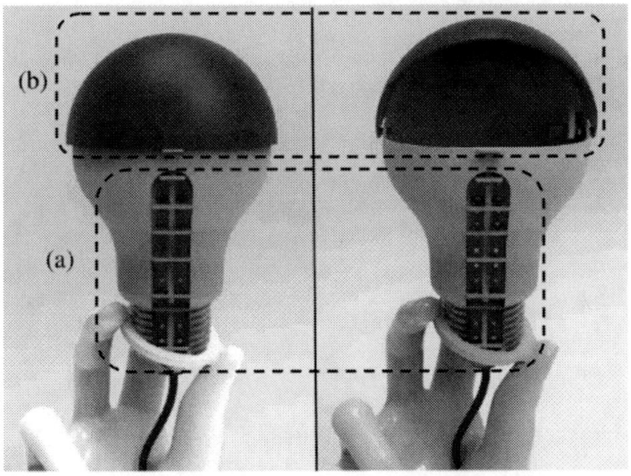

Figure 4. Opening mechanism (b) and lighting of leds (a)

Each time an idea is submitted, *IdeaBulb* quickly opens and closes its mechanical "mouth" meaning that an idea was eaten. Moreover, when *IdeaBulb* "eats" an idea, the led strip is animated informing participants that the idea is going down in the "belly" of *IdeaBulb*.

V. Conclusion and Perspectives

Our work presented here is the result of the interface between two main scientific fields: analysis of live facilitation during creative sessions and the design approach for a tangible user interface in a context of competition and collaboration. Based on the analysis of our many experimental results, including the two workshops presented here, the monitoring of ideation phase highlights a *creative cliff* and a *warning area for creativity*, when generation of ideas becomes low. Then, we present a smart and tangible user interface, *IdeaBulb*, which could counteract the off-peaks observed.

The prototyping and testing during creative sessions could validate our assertions. The total amount of ideas, ideation flow and participant experience should be monitored. The context of competition and so creative performance could be increased by dividing the group into many sub-groups in order to enhance group creativity [26]. An *IdeaBulb* could be assigned for each sub-group. The implementation of a physical interaction or rewarding in a non-game context, can also be a process to foster participant's performance, as gamification invite to in [27].

Acknowledgment

The authors would especially like to thank the NEPTUNE project, coordinated by the Aerospace Valley competitiveness cluster and the New-Aquitaine Development and Innovation Agency, which support the work presented here.

The NEPTUNE project received funding from the European Union's Horizon 2020 Research and Innovation Program under Grant Agreement No. 691554.

References

[1] W. A. Long and W. E. McMullan, *Mapping the New Venture Opportunity Identification Process*. University of Calgary, Faculty of Management, 1984.

[2] G. E. Hills, R. C. Shrader, and G. T. Lumpkin, "Opportunity recognition as a creative process," *Front. Entrep. Res.*, pp. 216–227, 1999.

[3] D. R. DeTienne and G. N. Chandler, "Opportunity Identification and Its Role in the Entrepreneurial Classroom: A Pedagogical Approach and Empirical Test," *Acad. Manag. Learn. Educ.*, vol. 3, no. 3, pp. 242–257, 2004.

[4] A. Osborn, *Applied imagination principles and procedures of creative problem solving*. Oxford, England, 1953.

[5] P. Christensen, N. Mcintyre, and L. Pikholz, "Bridging community and economic development-A strategy for using industry clusters to link neighbourhoods to the regional economy.," 2002.

[6] M. E. Porter, "Clusters and the New Economics of Competition," *Harv. Bus. Rev.*, 1998.

[7] J. Ambrosino, D. H. Masson, and J. Legardeur, "STAR : An animation methodology to facilitate the emergence of interclustering projects," in *AIP Primeca : Concevoir et produire dans les industries du futur*, 2017.

[8] N. W. Kohn, P. B. Paulus, and Y. Choi, "Building on the ideas of others: An examination of the idea combination process," *J. Exp. Soc. Psychol.*, vol. 47, no. 3, pp. 554–561, May 2011.

[9] C. C. Clark, *Brainstorming*. Paris: Dunod, 1962.

[10] M. Diehl and W. Stroebe, "Productivity loss in brainstorming groups: Toward the solution of a riddle.," *J. Pers. Soc. Psychol.*, vol. 53, no. 3, pp. 497–509, 1987.

[11] R. B. Gallupe, L. M. Bastianutti, and W. H. Cooper, "Unblocking brainstorms," *J. Appl. Psychol.*, vol. 76, no. 1, pp. 137–142, 1991.

[12] H. Lamm and G. Trommsdorff, "Group versus individual performance on tasks requiring ideational proficiency (brainstorming): A review," *Eur. J. Soc. Psychol.*, vol. 3, no. 4, pp. 361–388, 1973.

[13] R. G. Geen and B. J. Bushman, "Theories of Group Behavior," in *Time*, vol. 37, no. July, B. Mullen and G. R. Goethals, Eds. Springer, 1979.

[14] B. Mullen and R. F. Baumeister, "Group effects on self-attention and performance: Social loafing, social facilitation, and social impairment," 1987.

[15] B. Latané, K. Williams, and S. Harkins, "Many hands make light the work: The causes and consequences of social loafing.," *J. Pers. Soc. Psychol.*, vol. 37, no. 6, pp. 822–832, 1979.

[16] N. L. Kerr and S. E. Bruun, "Dispensability of member effort and group motivation losses: Free-rider effects," *J. Pers. Soc. Psychol.*, vol. 44, no. 1, pp. 78–94, 1983.

[17] J. Ambrosino, D. H. Masson, J. Legardeur, and G. Tastet, "IdeaValuation : Favoriser les échanges lors d'un atelier de créativité

par le vote qualitatif des idées à l'aide d'un outil numérique," in *Proceedings of ERGO'IA 2016*, 2016.
[18] A. Moles, *The scientific creation*, Kister. Genève, 1954.
[19] A. Osborn, *Your Creative Power*. 2008.
[20] H. Ishii and B. Ullmer, "Tangible bits: towards seamless interfaces between people, bits, and atoms," *Proc. 8th Int. Conf. Intell. user interfaces*, no. March, pp. 3–3, 1997.
[21] O. Shaer and E. Hornecker, "Tangible User Interfaces: Past, Present, and Future Directions," *Found. Trends® Human–Computer Interact.*, vol. 3, no. 1–2, pp. 1–137, 2009.
[22] C. Wisneski *et al.*, "Ambient displays: Turning architectural space into an interface between people and digital information," *Lect. Notes Comput. Sci.*, vol. 1370, pp. 22–32, 1998.
[23] M. Weiser and J. S. Brown, "The coming age of calm technology," *Xerox PARC*, pp. 1–8, 1996.
[24] S. Bakker, E. van den Hoven, and B. Eggen, "Peripheral interaction: characteristics and considerations," *Pers. Ubiquitous Comput.*, vol. 19, no. 1, pp. 239–254, 2015.
[25] J. M. Kennedy, "Metaphor in pictures," *Perception*, vol. 11, no. 5, pp. 589–605, 1982.
[26] M. Baer, A. K. Vadera, R. T. A. J. Leenders, and G. R. Oldham, "Intergroup Competition as a Double-Edged Sword: How Sex Composition Regulates the Effects of Competition on Group Creativity," *Organ. Sci.*, vol. 25, no. 3, pp. 892–908, 2014.
[27] S. Deterding, K. O'Hara, M. Sicart, D. Dixon, and L. Nacke, "Gamification: Using game design elements in non-game contexts," *Proc. 2011 Annu. Conf. Hum. Factors Comput. Syst. (CHI 2011)*, pp. 1–4, 2011.

Management Approach for Microgrid Operation Using Multi Agent System (MAS) Technique

Zina Boussaada
Ecole Nationale d'Ingénieurs de Tunis
Université de Tunis El Manar
Tunis, Tunisia
University of the Basque Country
San Sebastián-Spain
e-mail: zina.b.88@hotmail.fr

Ahmed Remaci
ESTIA, F-64210 Bidart, France
e-mail: a.remaci@estia.fr

Octavian Curea
ESTIA, F-64210 Bidart, France
e-mail: o.curea@estia.fr

Olfa Belkahla Driss
École Supérieure de commerce de Tunis
Université de la Manouba
Tunis, Tunisie
e-mail: Olfa.Belkahla@isg.rnu.tn

Haritza Camblong
University of the Basque Country
San Sebastián-Spain
ESTIA, F-64210 Bidart, France
e-mail: aritza.camblong@ehu.eus

Najiba Mrabet Bellaaj
Institut Supérieur d'Informatique
Université de Tunis El Manar
Ariana-Tunisia
e-mail: najiba_bm@yahoo.fr

Abstract— **The integration of renewable energies in the electrical grid and the shift to a distributed structure of the grid had made the control operation extremely complicated. This complexity has prompted researchers to take an interest in the conception of smart interfaces in order to manage the operation of microgrids. This paper proposes an approach of microgrid management using the Multi Agent System (MAS) technique. Based on the distributed nature of MAS and their ability to communicate heterogeneous entities with each other's, the studied approach consists in ensuring the adequate interactions between the concerned agents in order to perform two microgrid operation modes: the first one is the operation of the microgrid without connection with the main grid. In this case, the balance between supply and demand of energy must be achieved. The second operation mode consists on the sale and the purchase of electricity to/from the neighbors' microgrids and the main grid.**

Keywords-Smart Interface; management; Multi Agent System (MAS; microgrid; operation mode.

I. INTRODUCTION

Because of the increase of environmental conscience, renewable energy has invaded electrical grid. As a result the concept of smart grid was created. With the implantation of renewable generators in dispersed locations, the electrical production passed from centralized to a distributed structure. In fact, the grid has been converted into an array of "smaller" grids, which can work in a connected or islanded operation mode. It is the concept of microgrid. This concept increased the complexity of electricity management and control. In fact, when the microgrid works in connected mode, the direct connection with the main grid doesn't ensure the energy optimization for the system. When the microgrid works in islanded mode, the electric interface is not sufficient to stabilize the microgrid operation. Hence the requirement for a software smart management interfaces, which must ensure the microgrid operation in islanded and connected mode, as well as in the moment of switch between these two operation modes. In the literature, the management of the microgrid operation had been performed using different Energy management frameworks [1][2], but, artificial intelligence techniques have proven their performances in the management of complex systems particularly the systems with behaviors similar to those of microgrids (Network management, intelligent platform management interface, database management, etc.) [3]. Assuming that the microgrid consists of a set of heterogeneous entities, which interact with each other's in a distributed way, these characteristics match with the MAS working. In fact, the MAS is a software level based on a distributed operation. Therefore, it was used in several microgrid applications, such as spot market mechanism and economic dispatch [4], smart grid control [5], demand response [6], service restoration mechanism [7], and Virtual Power Plant (VPP) control [8].

The disadvantage of the most of previous researches is that, they considered the agent as all the element of the microgrid. Then, they turned the physical aspect of the microgrid into a purely software aspect, based on the communication between agents, in the same computer or in a different computers by a TCP-IP protocols [9]. However, it is not the case of real systems. Therefore, in our research, it is assumed that each agent is implemented in a computing system, associated to each microgrid element. The exchange of information between agents is ensured by a communication system. Besides this system, each agent exchanges information with its associated physical microgrid element. The aim of our research is to ensure the microgrid operation using the above described MAS. The proposed approach is to build a smart management system, which must ensure the balance between supply and demand of energy in the two operation modes (connected and islanded). In islanded mode, the MAS predicts the energy to be produced and that to be consumed in real time in order to supply all local loads. However, in connected mode the mission of MAS is to ensure two tasks: the sale and the purchase of electricity to/from the neighbors' microgrids and the main grid using an optimization algorithm.

The paper was organized as follows. In Section 2, the microgrid will be defined. In Section 3, the MAS will be presented by defining Agent and its classification. Then, Section 4 will present the reasons of the MAS choice. Section 5 will focus on the proposed approach and the description of the different scenarios. Finally, Section 6 will conclud the paper.

II. MICROGRIDS

A. *Definition and structure of microgrid*

With the integration of renewable energy sources in the electrical grid, the electricity production has become intermittent. This situation requires the integration of storage facilities and units of computing and control to supply the demand of consumers in energy. At this level, the electrical grid passed to a smart grid. In order to maintain the consumption – production balance in all circumstances, and to enable the final consumer to better control his demand, the production of electricity has become decentralized. For example, a consumer can instal his own Photovoltaic panel and wind turbine on the roof of his house. This is the concept of microgrid.

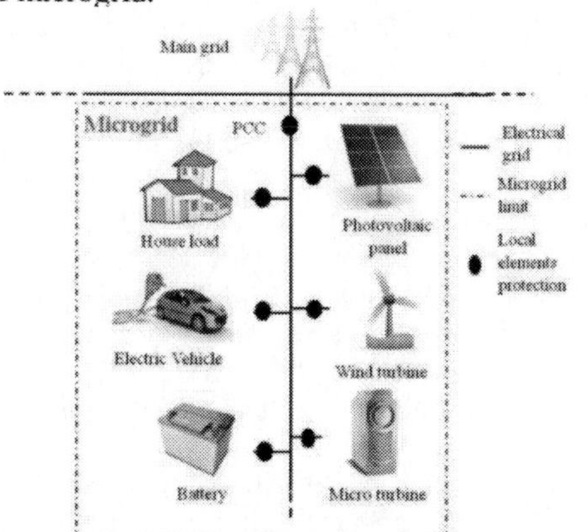

Figure 1. Example of Microgrid structure

The structure of microgid varies from one microgrid to another. But, as shown in Figure 1, three necessary elements must exist to obtain the microgrid: generators (photovoltaic panel, wind turbine, micro turbine), storage systems (battery, electric vehicle) and loads (house load, electric vehicle). The distributed generators are the producers of energy. The distributed storage systems are the components which store the energy and provide it depending on the situation of microgrid. However, the loads are the consumers of energy.

B. *Operation modes of microgrid*

Microgrids have two operations modes: the connected and the islanded mode. In connected mode, the microgrid is connected to the main grid, which is the superimposed grid. Therefore, in the connected mode the energy balance between supply and demand is ensured through the exchange of energy with the main grid or the microgrids neighbors, which are connected to the main grid. In islanded mode the microgrid is electrically isolated from the main grid. There are no energy exchange between grids. As a result, maintaining the energy balance in islanded mode becomes a challenging task.

III. MULTI AGENT SYSTEMS (MAS)

A Multi Agent System is a system consisting of several interacting agents with each other's and with the elements of their environment.

A. *Agent definition*

An agent is an autonomous entity (software or hardware), which acts on itself and on its environment. In the Multi Agent context, an agent is able to communicate with the other agents. Its behavior is the result of its observations, its knowledge, and its interactions with the other agents and the entities of its environment.

B. *Properties of Agents*

In MAS, agents are characterized by several properties, where the most importants are:

- Autonomy: An agent is able to act without the direct intervention of another entity (agent or human). It can also control its actions and its state.
- Reactivity: An agent perceives its environment and responds to the changes occurring there.
- Communication: An agent can communicate with another agents and entities (Software, Hardware or human).
- Sociability: An agent can interact with the other agents in a collaborative or a competitive way in order to achieve its objectives.
- Pro-activity: An agent is able, on its own initiative, to set goals to reach its objectives [10].

C. *Classification of Agents*

Based on the evocated properties, researchers proposed several classifications of agents. According to Grislin et al. [3], agents can be classified according to the degree of autonomy, of cooperation and adaptation. These properties are generally seen as main characteristics in distributed artificial intelligence [11]. Three types of agents were distinguished in the MAS [12]:

- Reactive agent: This agent has limited ability for communication, has little or not a model on itself, on other agents or on the environment. Its behavior is of type "stimulus-response", then it operates based on receiving messages.
- Cognitive agent: This agent has a more "thoughtful" behavior, resulting from a choice among a set of possible actions. This choice is a result of reasoning.
- Hybrid agent: The hybrid agent is neither reactive nor cognitive. In fact, it has some level of every agent property. Therefore hybrid agent behavior can be placed between reactive agent and cognitive agent.

IV. MAS IN MICROGRIDS

Based on their size, their heterogeneity and their evolving nature, microgrids are considered complex systems. The choice of MAS technique for the microgrid control is justified by several reasons. In fact, microgrids are characterized by their distributed nature and the interaction of heterogeneous elements between each other's and with their environment. Microgrid elements have only a local view of the grid and do not have access to the global behavior of the system. Only the operators of the grid have a global view of the system macroscopic behavior. In addition, the microgrid has a history; its size and its structure vary over time, so its past is at least partially responsible for its current situation. Besides, in connected mode, the microgrid accomplishes interactions based on the market mechanism, which is one of the basic tasks of MAS. In fact, to supply local load, the microgrid performs a negotiation phase with main grid and neighbors' microgrids to purchase energy. In the same way, to supply external load, the microgrid negotiates to sell its production of energy.

V. PROPOSED APPROACH

Several propositions were performed to control microgrids using MAS [3]-[10][13]. The main principle is to develop a representative agent for each element of the microgrid, and one additional agent, which controls and represents the microgrid in its external environment (Main grid and neighbors' microgrids). The proposed approach of this paper is based on the capacity of information exchange between each agent and its associated microgrid element. This exchange is bidirectional. In fact, the agent is able to perform two functions: it recovers measures (current, voltage, temperature, etc.) and it acts on the physical part of the microgrid, in order to perform different operations as connection/de-connection, and change of operation point. Thus, the MAS presents the smart interface of the microgrid, when each agent is embedded in a system set up with the associated microgrid element.

As described in Figure 2, our first microgrid prototype consists of photovoltaic (PV) panels, batteries, and loads. The main grid is represented by a "global supervisor agent" and the microgrid by a "local supervisor agent". Each element of the microgrid is represented by a local agent: load agent, battery agent and PV agent. "Interface agent" was added in order to detect the connection and disconnection of microgrid elements and to ensure the interaction with the user platform. The interaction between agents is presented in Figure 3.

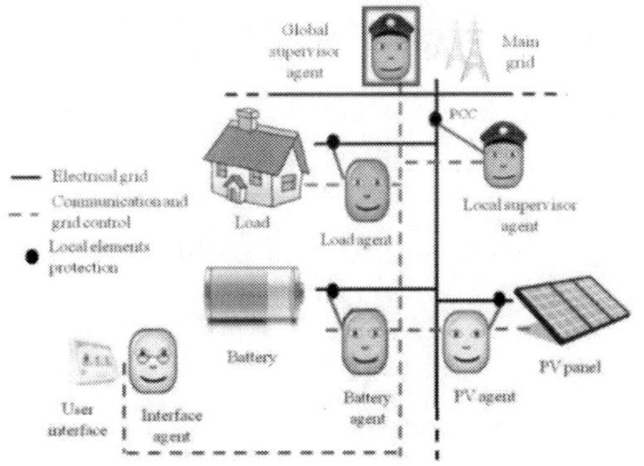

Figure 2. MAS for the proposed Microgrid management approach

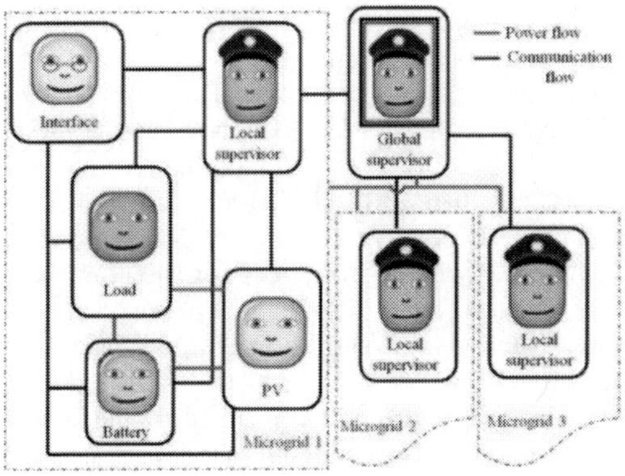

Figure 3. Interaction between agents in the proposed approach

The principle of the proposed management approach is based on sending and receiving of messages between agents in order to exchange information and to take decisions. Local agents communicate with their local supervisor agent and if the operation mode is connected, the local supervisor agent communicates with the global supervisor and the local supervisor agents of the neighbors' microgrids.

The proposed algorithm for the operation management is presented in Figure 4. It is important to note that drawn diagram describes both the progress of management program and the interaction between agents.

The used variables in the following paragraph and Figure 4 are as follows:

P_c: The power quantity to be consumed.
P_p: The power quantity to be produced.
P_{bat}: The available power of the battery.
SOC: The battery state of charge.

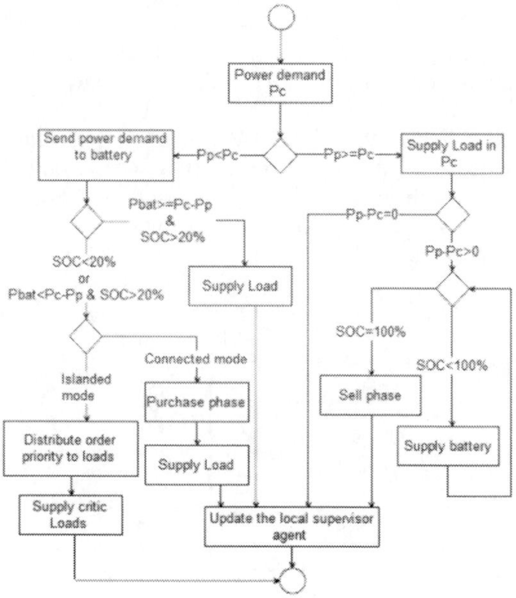

Figure 4. Proposed management algorithm for microgrid operation

It is supposed that in the starting state the demand and the supply are balanced. The MAS must be able to manage events, such as power demand in Figure 4. As a result of this event, three cases are possible:

1/ If the amount of produced power Pp is greater than or equal to the requested power Pc, loads are supplied and the local supervisor agent proposes to supply battery by Pp- Pc. If the SOC is less than 100% the battery is supplied. And after this, if there is an excess of power and the operation mode is connected, the local supervisor agent initiates a communication phase with the global supervisor agent and the neighbors' supervisor agents in order to perform a power sales phase.

2/ If the produced power summed with the available battery power is greater than or equal to the requested power Pc, loads are supplied by PV and battery.

3/ If the produced power summed with the available battery power is not enough to supply all loads, the management of this event depends on the operation mode. In connected mode, the local supervisor agent starts a power purchase phase with the global supervisor agent and the neighbors' supervisor agents, and it takes decisions based on an optimization algorithm identifying the minimal cost of the energy. Therefore, in islanded mode, the microgrid is no more able to supply all loads, so some loads can be disconnected. As a result, the local supervisor agent must distribute a priority order to all loads. The loads with the highest priority order are the critic loads. They must be supplied before other loads.

VI. Conclusion and Future Work

This paper proposed a management approach of microgrid using MAS technique. Based on the distributed nature of microgrid and the heterogeneity of its elements, the MAS presents an adequate smart management interface for the microgrid. This interface had the mission of ensuring energy balance between demand and supply in the connected and the islanded mode. The next step of this work is the implementation of agents in order to validate results.

References

[1] W. Shi et al., "Evaluating microgrid management and control with an implementable energy management system", the 5th IEEE International Conference on Smart Grid Communications, 3-6 Nov. 2014, Venice, Italy.

[2] A. Vaccaro, M. Popov, D. Villacci, and V. V. Terzija, "An integrated framework for smart microgrids modeling, monitoring, control, communication, and verification," Proc. IEEE, vol. 99, no. 1, pp. 119–132, 2011.

[3] E. Grislin, E. Adame, and C. Kolski, "Agents intelligents en interaction hommemachine dans les systèmes d'information", Environnements évolués et évaluation de l'IHM, pp. 207-248, 2011.

[4] H. F Wang, "Multi-agent co-ordination for the secondary voltage control in power system contingencis", In Proc. IEE Generation, Transmission and Distribution, vol. 148, pp. 61-66, Jan 2001.

[5] L. Phillips, M. Link, R. Smith, and L. Weiland, "Agent-based control of distributed infrastructure resources", Sandia National Laboratories, SAND 2005-7937, Jan 2006 [Online]. Available: www.sandia.gov/scada/documents/sand_2005_7937.pdf. (May 2017)

[6] I. Chung, W. Liu, D. Cartes, E. Collins, and S. Moon, "Control methods for multiple distributed generators in a microgrid system," IEEE Transactions on Industry Applications,vol. 46, no. 3, pp. 1078-1088, May/June 2010.

[7] S. D. J. McArthur, E. M. Davidson, J. A. Hossack, and R. McDonald, "Automating power system fault diagnosis through multi-agent system technology", the 37th Hawaii International Conference on System Sciences, Big Island, HI, USA, 2004.

[8] L. Cristaldi, A. Monti, R. Ottoboni, and F. Ponci, "Multiagent based power systems monitoring platform: a prototype", IEEE Power Tech Conference, Bologna, Italy, 23-26 June 2003.

[9] H. S. V. S. Kumar Nunna and D. Srinivasan, "An agent based energy market model for microgrids with distributed energy storage systems", IEEE International Conference on Power Electronics, Drives and Energy Systems (PEDES), Trivandrum, India, Dec 14-17, 2016.

[10] Z. Boussaada, O. Curea, H. Camblong, N. Mrabet Bellaj, and A. Hacala, "Multi-agent systems for the dependability and safety of microgrids", Int. J. Interact. Des. Manuf. (IJIDEM), 1-13, 2014.

[11] E. Adam, « Modèle d'organisation multi-agent pour l'aide au travail coopératif dans les processus d'entreprise : application aux systèmes administratifs complexes », Doctoral thesis, Université de Valenciennes et du Hainaut-Cambrésis, Sep. 2000.

[12] B. Chaib-draa, "Interaction between agents in routine, familiar and unfamiliar situations", *International Journal of Intelligent and Cooperative Information Systems*, vol. 1, n° 5, pp. 7-20, 1996.

[13] O. Curea, Z. Boussaada, N. Mrabet Bellaaj, A. Hacala-Perret, and H. Camblong, "Multi-Agent Systems for the Dependability of Microgrids", Virtual Concept Workshop 2014, Innovation in product design and manufacture, Medellin, Colombia, March26 - 28, 2014.

Toward Emotional Internet of Things for Smart Industry

David Antonio Gómez Jáuregui

ESTIA
F-64210 Bidart, France
Email: d.gomez@estia.fr

***Abstract*—In this paper, an approach to design and implement non-invasive and wearable emotion recognition technologies in smart industries is proposed. The proposed approach benefits from the interconnectivity of Internet of Things (IoT) to recognize and adapt to complex negative emotional states of employees (e.g., stress, frustration, etc.). Two types of connected objects are proposed: *emotional detectors* and *emotional actors*. The steps to design and implement these connected objects are described. The proposed approach is expected to ensure and maintain a healthy work environment in smart industries.**

Keywords–Emotion recognition; Internet of Things; Smart Industry.

I. Introduction

The proposed approach contributes to the development of new smart interfaces capable of adapting efficiently to users' emotions in the context of smart industries. Smart industry (also called Industry 4.0) is the current trend in which the industrial production, computing and communication technologies converge [1]. Smart industries are expected to increase operational effectiveness of employees as well as provide new services, new types of products, business models and reduction of pollution [2]. In order to work efficiently, smart industries must support interconnection of wireless devices, sensors, and people through the Internet of Things (IoT) [3]. Interconnected objects will provide new ways of collaboration between humans and machines in order to reach common goals in the manufacturing process. Studies have shown that the productiveness of employees are heavily influenced by their emotional states [4]. Negative emotions, such as stress, frustration and anxiety are strongly correlated with counter-productive work behavior [5]. Automatic emotion recognition could be an important requirement in smart industries in order to ensure and maintain the well-being of employees during the manufacturing process. However, despite recent advances in affective computing, emotion recognition in real-world conditions remains a challenging task. Existing sensors that can extract physiological signals associated to emotions (e.g., hearth rate (HR) [6], skin conductance [7], blood volume pressure [8], etc.) often require invasive technologies (e.g., electrodes), and hence may interfere with the users' production tasks. Smart interfaces could benefit from IoT devices in order to provide emotion recognition from employees using non-invasive and wearable devices (e.g., cameras, microphones, wearable hearth rate monitors, smartphones, etc.). These interconnected devices could be able to collect and exchange multi-modal signals associated with specific emotions of employees. Once a negative emotion is recognized, the interconnected objects can control actions to respond and adapt to this emotion in order to maintain a healthy working environment.

In this paper, a proposed approach to design and implement emotional IoT devices in smart industry is described. Section 2 reviews the state of the art regarding emotion recognition from non-invasive and wearable technologies. Section 3 describes the proposed approach. Conclusions and perspectives are discussed in Section 4.

II. Emotion Recognition from non-invasive and wearable technologies

A number of researchers in affective computing seek to recognize emotional states through the use of wearable and/or non-invasive technologies. Many of these technologies could be used in the context of industries or manufacturing tasks since they do not interfere with the user behavior. Recent advances in computer vision and speech recognition have led to the design of non-invasive systems capable of inferring user's emotions from voice [9], facial expressions [10], gestures [11], and body movements [12]. The advantage of these systems is that they do not require users to wear any sensors on their bodies since only cameras or microphones are needed. However, these techniques could not be precise under certain manufacturing tasks as they require users to face a camera (or a kinect) to recognize the emotion correctly. In addition, speech recognition systems require to isolate the user's voice from backgroung noise. The recent development of wearable computing devices has prompted a growing interest in using them for emotion recognition. Recent works [13] [14] have proposed intelligent wristbands including multiple sensors capable of acquiring physiological signals related to different emotions. Gao et al. [15] used wearable EEG headset technology to detect the brain's activity in response to different emotional states. Olsen et al. [16] showed that the accelerometer data recorded from a smartphone can be used to infer the user's emotional state. Despite many advances in emotion recogntion through wearable and/or non-invasive technologies, few works have been interested in detecting more complex emotional states such as stress, frustration, depression, pain etc. In addition, most of the proposed approaches do not beneffit of the interconnectivity of these devices to improve the recognition accuracy. Finally, using emotion recognition technologies in the context of industries or real-world manufacturing tasks is still unexplored.

III. Proposed Approach

The proposed approach consists in harnessing the interconnectivity of the Internet of Things to detect and respond to negative complex emotions of employees performing manufacturing tasks, thus ensuring a healthy working environment. In order to implement this approach, two types of connected objects are proposed: *emotional detectors* and *emotional actors*. *Emotional detectors* are wearable and/or non-invasive devices (e.g., cameras, microphones, wristbands, smartphones, etc.) capable of recognizing, in real-time, complex negative emotions (e.g., stress, frustration, anxiety, etc.) during the realization of several tasks involved in manufacturing processes. *Emotional actors* are smart systems or devices capable to respond properly to negative emotions of the employees. For example: adapting the difficulty of the task with respect to frustration levels of employees or activating stress management training systems installed in smartphones of employees. In order to design and implement *emotional detectors* and *emotional actors*, the following steps are proposed:

1) **Task identification:** manufacturing tasks inducing negative emotions will be identified. This identification can be achieved by applying psychological questionnaires to employees (e.g., anxiety scores [17]) before and after each task.
2) **Emotion induction protocols:** protocols capable of inducing identified negative emotions will be designed based on identified tasks. In these protocols, negative emotion-induction tasks will be similar to real-world manufacturing tasks.
3) **Multimodal data collection:** emotional induction protocols will be tested with a large population of employees. During these protocols, wearable and non-invasive devices will be used to collect multimodal data (e.g., physiological signals, video, audio, psychological questionnaires) from these employees.
4) **Analysis of emotional features:** multimodal data collected in the previous step will be processed and analyzed in order to find the most relevant features (e.g., facial expressions, body movements, hearth rate variability, etc.) associated with different negative emotions.
5) **Recognition of negative emotions:** the relevant features found in the previous step will be used to train machine learning models capable of reconizing negative emotions from different wearable and/or non-invasive devices.
6) **Emotional detectors:** wearable and non-invasive devices will be integrated into real-world manufacturing tasks. Wearable devices wil be used by employees while non-invasive devices will be located in specific positions where they will capture data from employees. Each device will integrate a computer system capable of extracting relevant features associated to negative emotions as well as providing syncrhonization (interconnectivity) with other devices. Each relevant feature extracted will be sent to a central computer system capable of recognizing negative emotional states using trained machine learning models.
7) **Emotional actors:** IoT systems capable of decreasing levels of negative emotions wil be designed and integrated into manufacturing tasks or wearable devices of employees (e.g., applications installed on smarthphones of employees).

IV. Conclusions and Perspectives

A novel approach to integrate emotion recognition IoT devices in smart industries is presented and described. The main objective of the proposed approach is to increase the productiveness of employees by maintaining a healthy work environment. Two types of IoT devices are proposed: *Emotional detectors* and *Emotional actors*. *Emotional detectors* will be used to recognize negative emotions from employees, while *emotional actors* will be used to decrease levels of negative emotions. Before implementing the proposed approach in real industries, a more detailed study of different IoT devices and manufacturing tasks will be required. In this study, several characteristics will be considered, such as perceived comfort of wearable devices, possibility of integration in different manufacturing tasks, etc. Finally, the social acceptability of using emotional IoT devices in industries must be considered.

References

[1] M. Hermann, T. Pentek, and B. Otto, "Design principles for industrie 4.0 scenarios," in 49th Hawaii International Conference on System Sciences (HICSS), 2016, pp. 3928–3937.

[2] H. Lasi, P. Fettke, H.-G. Kemper, T. Feld, and M. Hoffmann, "Industry 4.0," Business & Information Systems Engineering, vol. 6, no. 4, 2014, pp. 239–242.

[3] D. Giusto, A. Iera, G. Morabito, and L. Atzori, The Internet of Things. Springer, 2010.

[4] C. Fisher and N. Ashkanasy, "The emerging role of emotions in work life: An introduction," Journal of Organizational Behavior, vol. 21, no. 2, 2000, pp. 123–129.

[5] P. Spector, S. Fox, and T. Domagalski, "Emotions, violence and counterproductive work behavior," in Handbook of workplace violence, J. B. E.K. Kelloway and J. Hurrell, Eds. SAGE Publications, Inc, 2005, pp. 29–46.

[6] D. S. Quintana, A. J. Guastella, T. Outhred, I. B. Hickie, and A. H. Kemp, "Heart rate variability is associated with emotion recognition: Direct evidence for a relationship between the autonomic nervous system and social cognition," Int J Psychophysiol, vol. 86, no. 2, 2012, pp. 168–72.

[7] C. Holmgard, G. N. Yannakakis, H. P. Martinez, and K.-I. Karstoft, ""to rank or to classify? annotating stress for reliable ptsd profiling," in ACII 2015, 2015, pp. 719–725.

[8] M. Khezri, S. M. P. Firoozabadi, and A. Sharafat, "Reliable emotion recognition system based on dynamic adaptive fusion of forehead biopotentials and physiological signals," Computer Methods and Programs in Biomedicine, vol. 122, no. 2, 2015, pp. 149–164.

[9] C. Parlak and B. Diri, "Emotion recognition from the human voice," in 21st Signal Processing and Communications Applications Conference (SIU), 2013, pp. 1–4.

[10] D. McDuff, "Discovering facial expressions for states of amused, persuaded, informed, sentimental and inspired," in ICMI 2016, 2016, pp. 71–75.

[11] S. Piana, A. Staglianò, F. Odone, and A. Camurri, "Adaptive body gesture representation for automatic emotion recognition," ACM Transactions on Interactive Intelligent Systems, vol. 6, no. 1, 2016, pp. 1–31.

[12] G. Castellano, S. D. Villabla, and A. Camurri, "Recognising human emotions from body movement and gesture dynamics," in ACII 2007, 2007, pp. 71–82.

[13] A. M. Khan and M. Lawo, "Wearable recognition system for emotional states using physiological devices," in eTELEMED 2016, 2016, pp. 131–137.

[14] J. A. Rincon, A. Costa, P. Novais, V. Julian, and C. Carrascosal, "Using non-invasive wearables for detecting emotions with intelligent agents," in SOCO-CISIS-ICEUTE, 2016, pp. 73–84.

[15] Y. Gao, H. J. Lee, and R. M. Mehmood, "Deep learning of eeg signals for emotion recognition," in ICMEW, 2015, pp. 1–5.

[16] A. F. Olsen and J. Torresen, "Smartphone accelerometer data used for detecting human emotions," in ICSAI, 2016, pp. 410–415.

[17] C. Reynolds and B. Richmond, Revised Childrens Manifest Anxiety Scale (RCMAS) Manual. Los Angeles: Western Psychological Services, 1985.

AUTHOR INDEX